INSECURITY

Perils and Products of Theatres of the Real

Insecurity

Perils and Products of
Theatres of the Real

JENN STEPHENSON

UNIVERSITY OF TORONTO PRESS
Toronto Buffalo London

ISBN 978-1-4875-0185-3

Library and Archives Canada Cataloguing in Publication

Title: Insecurity : perils and products of theatres of the real /
    Jenn Stephenson.
Names: Stephenson, Jenn, 1971– author.
Description: Includes bibliographical references and index.
Identifiers: Canadiana 20189066423 | ISBN 9781487501853 (hardcover)
Subjects: LCSH: Theater – Canada. | LCSH: Theater and society – Canada. |
    LCSH: Theater – Psychological aspects. | LCSH: Theater – Philosophy. |
    LCSH: Theater audiences – Psychology. | LCSH: Reality in literature.
Classification: LCC PN2304.2 S74 2019 | DDC 792.0971—dc23

This book has been published with the help of a grant from the Federation
for the Humanities and Social Sciences, through the Awards to Scholarly
Publications Program, using funds provided by the Social Sciences and
Humanities Research Council of Canada.

University of Toronto Press acknowledges the financial assistance to its
publishing program of the Canada Council for the Arts and the Ontario
Arts Council, an agency of the Government of Ontario.

Canada Council   Conseil des Arts
for the Arts   du Canada

ONTARIO ARTS COUNCIL
CONSEIL DES ARTS DE L'ONTARIO

an Ontario government agency
un organisme du gouvernement de l'Ontario

Funded by the   Financé par le
Government   gouvernement
of Canada   du Canada

Contents

Acknowledgments

My profound thanks to the friends and colleagues who supported me through this work. Special thanks are due to Jill Scott, Lee Atkinson, Kim Solga, Marlis Schweitzer, Barry Freeman, Natalie Alvarez, Laura Levin, Grahame Renyk, Kelsey Jacobson, Ashley Williamson, and Ryan Claycomb. Olivia Choplin and Tanya Déry-Obin were my bilingual blind dates for *Polyglotte*, and later conference co-panelists. My mother, Gloria Brumer, was the first reader of every sentence. She was a sensitive non-expert, who corrected missing commas and challenged me to keep the argument clear and accessible. Thanks also go to my colleagues in the Dan School of Drama and Music at Queen's University, especially to director Craig Walker, who provided invaluable research support and approved mid-semester travel. As a visiting professor at the Centre for Drama, Theatre and Performance Studies at the University of Toronto in 2016–17, I was granted the opportunity to lead a graduate seminar based on the core ideas and concepts that underpin this research. Thanks are due to the students of that class, who ventured bravely and provided a valuable sounding board for this work. Over the years, I have been privileged to supervise thesis projects for students who later became colleagues and fellow travellers. My thanks to Kelsey Jacobson, Dylan On, Mariah Horner, Luke Brown, Morgan Anderson, and Signy Lynch for their bright and stimulating company. Tia Lunn, Madison Lymer, and Dana Sidebottom were indefatigable checkers of citations and chasers of permissions. Elaine Normandeau assisted with her insights into francophone-Quebecois culture.

Many portions of this book have been aired as conference papers at the annual meetings of the Canadian Association for Theatre Research. The Association has always been a welcoming environment for presenting work in progress and the work here is undoubtedly richer for this early exposure and feedback.

When writing about contemporary work, there is often little public documentation apart from the live performance itself. This research has also benefited from conversations – both in person over dinner and over coffee and remotely over email and Skype – with the artist-creators themselves. I am very appreciative of their time and their willingness to share insights and archival resources. Without their generous assistance, this work would have been impossible. My sincere thanks to: Marcus Youssef, Jamie Long, Maiko Yamamoto, Trevor Schwellnus, Kathryn MacKay, Judith Thompson, Olivier Choinière, Amiel Gladstone, Anne Wessels, Adrienne Wong, Dustin Harvey, Chris Abraham, Annabel Soutar, Ame Henderson, Frank Cox-O'Connell, Evan Webber, Timothy Carlson, Jeremy Waller, Aryo Khakpour, Joyce Rosario, Melanie Bennett, Michael Rubenfeld, Liam Karry, Alex Dault, Scott Dermody, Joanne Williams, Stephanie Vaillant, and Mary Fraser-Hamilton.

Chapter 2 first appeared in *Theatre Journal* as "Winning and/or Losing: The Perils and Products of Insecurity in Postdramatic Autobiographical Performance." Part of Chapter 3, titled "'Please Look at Yourself': Insecurity and the Failure of Ethical Encounter in Autobiographical Performance," appeared previously in *Theatre Research in Canada* in a special issue dedicated to Theatre and Disability. Part of Chapter 5 appeared in volume two of the New Essays in Canadian Theatre series, *New Canadian Realisms*: "After the Apple: Post-lapsarian Realism in *Garden//Suburbia* – An autobiographical site-specific work." I would like to acknowledge the work undertaken by the editors of those journals and collections – Ric Knowles, Joanne Tompkins, Kirsty Johnston, Kim Solga, and Roberta Barker – and the peer reviewers who offered such productive feedback. Thank you for granting permission to extend those pieces further here.

Thank you to the anonymous readers for University of Toronto Press for their comments and their constructive suggestions for improvement. Thank you too to University of Toronto Press editors Siobhan McMenemy, who encouraged this project in its early stages, and Mark Thompson, Frances Mundy, and Leah Connor, who saw it through to completion. Publication of this book was assisted by funding from the Aid to Scholarly Publishing Program of the Canadian Federation for the Social Sciences and Humanities.

Finally, my love and gratitude goes to my family – my husband John and children Jessica, Sarah, and Benjamin.

INSECURITY

Perils and Products of Theatres of the Real

1 Introduction

"To think with any seriousness is to doubt. Thought is indistinguishable from doubt.

To be alive is to be uncertain. I'll take doubt."

– Reality Hunger 139.

This is a book about theatre of the real in an age of post-reality. This is a book about theatrical performances in general that tap into an international documentary tradition – staging real people, real words, real places – to connect their audiences with that reality. This is also a book about specific examples of this phenomenon in Canada, being inescapably local, as all theatre always is. These are works that appeal to our contemporary yearning for authenticity, for unmediated contact, for truth, for the real. And yet, the same conditions that render our postmodern, post-national, poststructuralist sceptical lives profoundly insecure, the same conditions that underpin our desire for authenticity, thwart access to an impossible real. Each of the performances featured in the chapters that follow exhibits this promise of desire fulfilled and its inescapable disappointment. Intimate exposure through confessional autobiographical performance creates more distance and more unknowing. Encounters with non-actors, strangers to the stage, promise engaged rapprochement; but the lesson in the end is that strangers (should) remain strange. Verbatim testimonials invite doubt about the trust value that underpins witnessing both as a speaker and as a listener. In lieu of a grounded experience of a unique geography, site-specific performances refigure the audience lost as placeless ghosts. Hyperreal interactive performance environments offer full immersion in alternate realities, but ultimately audience experience turns inward, reversing the gaze so that the remaining real is the self-reflexive affect of my own emotions and visceral responses. Oscillating uncertainly between the actual and the fictional, these performances in the theatre of the real genre thematize that ontological indecidability, betraying our trust in the mechanisms of theatricality. The by-product of theatres of the real in the age of post-reality is insecurity.

It is an essential requirement for the full appreciation of successful parody that the receiving audience be well versed in the original cultural artefact targeted for acerbic mockery. That theatre performances which challenge the boundaries of reality and fiction to both thrill the audience while also rendering them profoundly uncomfortable are the targets of parody confirms for me that this phenomenon has reached its saturation point among a certain demographic. The same people who seek out the adrenaline highs of being immersed in Punchdrunk's *Sleep No More*[1] in New York or *You Me Bum Bum Train*[2] by Kate Bond and Morgan Lloyd and a cast of a hundred volunteers in London must also be social media followers of *McSweeney's Internet Tendency*. Articles on the daily humour website include: "Open Letters to People or Entities Who Are Unlikely to Respond," "How to Be a Better Teacher-Person through Apathy," "Tarzan's Guide to Elliptical Style for Effective Business Writing." I would characterize the attitude of the site as politically progressive, culturally attuned, NPR intellectual, and slacker-ironic. In this vein, Bryan Duff's faux theatre manifesto, "Our Fledgling Theatre Company's Only Goal Is to Constantly Betray Our Audience's Trust" fits right in, reflecting an extreme (and hilarious) reflection of this urban-cool, avant-garde, elite theatre trend. In typical *McSweeney's* style, the content of the article at first is disarmingly familiar, only gradually stretching the bounds of believability.

Redefining the frontiers of theatre, the goal of The Dien Bien Phu Experimental Theatre Company, as articulated here in their mission statement, is to "make our audiences feel as unsafe as possible; and thus we use every moment ... as an opportunity to betray our audience's trust." Among past performance techniques, the statement describes "stage combat that we never rehearse," and the use of mixed media incorporating actual surgery footage into their production of *Mary Poppins*. Actors are forbidden "to take the stage unless he/she is already crying. And of course dogs. Lots and lots of untrained dogs are always in our shows." According to the ideals of the company, the pinnacle of "Art" is most effectively achieved when "an audience is dragged into a parking lot, forced to lie down in each parking space, and doused with gasoline, so it Knows How It Feels To Be An American Automobile." The kicker to this manifesto of audience abuse in the face of "the real" is the plug at the end: "For booking corporate gigs, please see our 'Corporate' tab." Key elements of the genre are highlighted by the parody. Real things, which are normally excluded from performance as dangerous or unpredictable, invade the performance frame, proclaiming their "realness." And so this theatre of the real presents not a performance of crying but actual crying, not rehearsed and ostensibly safe stage combat but the risk of the spontaneous, and dogs. (More about dogs later.) The other key element is the immersion of the audience in the performance. Given things to eat and drink, tasks to perform, questions to answer – here they are soaked in gasoline – audiences are touched by the actors and physically dragged into the scene. Both of these features serve to reconfigure the audience experience, attempting to erase the usual gap between fiction and reality, between a constructed work of art made safe by the theatrical frame and the non-constructed realness of reality. The result is, as the title says, an audience whose trust is betrayed; an audience uncertain of what is real and therefore threatening versus what is fictional and therefore safe.

As David Shields notes in his manifesto *Reality Hunger*, "every artistic movement from the beginning of time is an attempt to figure out a way to smuggle more of what the artist thinks is reality into the work of art."[3] It is the job of the artist to reflect and comment on the real world and to use real-world materials to make that reflection as accurate as possible. Hamlet is perhaps the most famous proponent of this philosophy. As he expounds in his famous advice to the travelling actors who come to Elsinore from the city, "the purpose of playing, ... both at the first and now, was and is, to hold as 'twere the mirror up to nature: to show virtue her own feature, scorn her own image, and the very age and body of the time his form and pressure."[4] The task may be to hold the mirror up to nature, but the quality and shape of the mirror takes many forms. Nineteenth-century mimetic naturalism, exemplified by painter William Bliss Baker and playwright Émile Zola, sought to contextualize characters in their individual socioeconomic situations by replicating in great detail the clothes they wear, the rooms where they live and work, the colloquial way they speak. This is one strategy for increasing reality. But likewise Cubism is also an attempt to increase reality by showing us all sides of an object simultaneously. Picasso's portraits present both front view and side views, capturing multiple spatial perspectives in two dimensions. Marcel Duchamp's painting *Nude Descending a Staircase* unfolds time, increasing reality by suggesting the subject in elapsed motion. By the same token, Expressionism increases reality by communicating not merely surface appearances, but also the inner emotional reality. The viewer can know what something looks like but also what it feels like. In the early decades of the twenty-first century, artists in varying disciplines have responded to this perennial challenge of presenting reality by transporting larger and larger chunks of actual real stuff into their works.[5]

Theatre, however, constitutes a special case because any staging of real elements is complicated by the core operation of the theatrical frame, which is to take a real thing (an actor) and turn it into a fictional thing (Hamlet). In a work of literature, fictional worlds are created out of the real-world material of paper (or screen) and ink (or pixels). A literary apple in a poem or novel is made of black squiggles. Likewise, a still-life apple is made of paint applied to canvas. Fictional things are made from real-world things but they are not the same. Squiggles or paint become an apple. Theatre is the only art form where the real-world material used is (almost) the same as the fictional thing it performs. A human body becomes another human body. A chair becomes another chair. A light becomes another light. The transformation of everyday objects to fictional elements is the work of theatricality, effected by a change in their perceived ontology. Josette Féral describes theatricality as a process of "alterity," as emerging through "a cleft that divides space into the 'outside' and the 'inside' of theatricality."[6] This cleft is engendered cooperatively "first through a performer's reallocation of quotidian space that he occupies; second through a spectator's gaze framing a quotidian space that he does not occupy."[7] Significantly, the objects of performance themselves are not materially changed but their ontology has shifted as they are reframed by perception. It is the deployment of theatricalizing perception, imagined spatially as a frame or border, that separates fictional worlds from the mundane real world and brings fictional worlds of performance into being. It is perception alone that makes a prop chair into a throne, a theatre lighting instrument into the sun, and Sarah Bernhardt or Paapa Essiedu into Hamlet. How this perception operates (or fails to operate) to encourage the audience to comprehend something or someone as either "real" or "fictional" will be one of the key concerns of this book.

Even within the "special case" of theatrical mimesis, however, the interrelation between the actual and fictional is further complicated when these two poles approach near identity, as in calculus, like a curve approaching the limit of zero without ever actually arriving. When the body of the actor does not represent generically some other body but instead represents itself in autobiographical performance, the theatrical gap between actor-self and character-self is virtually nil. This same iconicity applies to site-specific performance where the site is the set and the set is the site. Or when language is not merely verisimilar to language in the vernacular world, but is a verbatim copy of the exact words, delivered to the stage as testimony. Or when the entire performance situation appears to eschew theatricality altogether, enacting (and inviting from the audience) behaviours that are indistinguishable from real life. In these cases, the real-world material employed in the creation of theatricality passes through fiction almost unaltered, like light through a window, to map precisely onto the real-world thing that it imputes to represent. All theatre makes use of real materials to depict the real world but by extending beyond a familiar naturalism to align these two aspects of realness in iconicity – the self-identical material with the thing it presents – these kinds of reality-engaged performances constitute a distinct genre.

"Documentary theatre, verbatim theatre, reality-based theatre, theatre-of-fact, theatre of witness, tribunal theatre, nonfiction theatre, restored village performances, war and battle reenactments, and autobiographical theatre,"[8] all these Carol Martin includes in her overview of theatre of the real. In *Theatre of the Real*, Martin prudently avoids offering strict defining parameters for this diverse genre. She does however note that performances in theatre of the real "claim specific relationships with events in the real world."[9] This criterion of specificity echoes the point made above that distinguishes the iconic relation of an autobiographical actor-self to her character-self from the more general relation of representation to the real world created by ordinary mimesis. The choice of the word "events" reflects Martin's particular interest in history and its representation in documentary performance forms. Given the centrality of iconicity in theatres of the real, I would add "objects" to "events." This modification opens the field slightly to also include examples of site-specific theatre, which may not necessarily be historically oriented, but which direct attention to the iconicity of space in the present. Likewise, actor bodies are iconic objects, potent in their immediacy. Also important to this definition is the active claiming of a relationship between the performance and its real-world counterpart – an explicit connection that is not merely coincidental to the context but that is a central part of how the performance situation is framed.

Martin identifies the wellspring of theatre of the real in today's "addiction to and questioning of the real."[10] As she writes, "today's theatre of the real both acknowledges a positivist faith in empirical reality and underscores an epistemological crisis in knowing truth."[11] It is a truism that we live in an age of uncertainty. These two poles in tension in theatres of the real – desire for realness and the recognition that reality is always a contingent construction – both arise out of and comment on this zeitgeist. It is not surprising then, following the work of reality-trend theatre makers Rimini Protokoll, that this genre in Germany is known as *Theater der Zeit*, literally "theatre of the time."[12] Some scholars link the origin of theatres of the real to a specific impelling event. The terror attacks of 9/11 and its instant global mediatization, and the subsequent War on Terror are commonly cited,[13] but alternately the fall of the Berlin Wall is marked as significant.[14] "Old orders, certainties and, it seemed, injustices were not just crumbling, but doing so with extraordinary rapidity."[15] Liz Tomlin describes the landscape of reality-based performance as impelled by: "the global events following 11 September 2001 that trapped us between the rock of pre-modernist fundamentalism and the hard place of advanced neo-liberalism, and the global economic meltdown which began in 2008."[16] In the last fifteen to twenty years, we have borne witness to unprecedented change in virtually all aspects of our lives, from changing social configurations to the redrawing of national borders, technological innovation, and the dismantling of traditional value systems. From global warfare on an unprecedented scale, the genocide of the Holocaust, and the advent of the capability for nuclear Armageddon to the profound reorganization of social structures by feminism and subsequent civil rights movements as well as by global flows of migration, the twentieth century certainly experienced its share of upheaval and change. Responses to that upheaval were captured in the art movements of Dada, surrealism, and absurdism. It would be disingenuous to argue that the new twenty-first century insecurity is entirely discontinuous from this previous history. And yet, its mood and intensity are different. In recent decades, it is not simply change over time that is unsettling but also the rapidity of that change. Whereas a nineteenth-century woman was born into more or less the same world as her eighteenth-century ancestor, a century later that stability of beliefs, of values, of the patterns of daily life no longer pertains across the generations. And then, layered on top of this extremity of change, the nature of the new paradigms seems to be different. Not only are the patterns changing, the notion of a pattern itself is dissolving. As these previously solid conventions and expectations evaporate, they are not being replaced by something equally solid. Zygmunt Bauman uses the term "liquid modernity" to capture this unmoored, floating feeling. What makes modernity liquid, to his thinking, is "its self-propelling, self-intensifying, compulsive and obsessive 'modernization' [where ...] none of the consecutive forms of social life is able to maintain its shape for long."[17] Bauman suggests that we are in a "post-paradigm" era.[18] How should we absorb and respond to this new liquid and highly insecure world? How does one live in an era characterized by social, political, and technological, but also epistemological, displacement, where not knowing or not being able to know is a basic condition? As Peggy Phelan writes,

> The condition of witnessing what one did not (and perhaps cannot) see is the condition of whatever age we are now entering. Whether we call this period "the post-postmodern age" or "the age of terrorism," it is characterized both by an intimate reawakening to the fragility of life and a more general sense of connection to one another that exceeds simple geophysical, ideological, or cultural proximity.[19]

Seeking realness, then, is an attempted anodyne to this desire for connection in the midst of fluid uncertainty as we try to grab on to someone or something solid. Twenty-first-century realness manifests primarily in a desire for things – commodities, experiences, ideas – that come to us unmediated, direct, and unadulterated from their source. Things that seem grounded. Things we can know. Thus the marketing appeal of catchwords like "grassroots," "organic," "local," "do-it-yourself," or "authentic." Detached cynicism and mass production are out. Homespun, homemade, and reclaimed vintage are in. Regarding this new earnestness, Andy Lavender writes, "The real had returned ... Culturally, the real could not be avoided, even where it was contested. And we developed a new taste for it."[20] Lavender connects this return of the real to what he terms "theatres of engagement," theatrical experiences and situations that offer moving, and often intimate, interpersonal encounter. Josephine Machon takes a similar tack as she traces one root of immersive theatre to a renewed desire for "conviviality and congregation,"[21] arising to counter increasingly secular atomized interactions. As a balm to "the alienation from real intimacy in our workaday lives, via such forums as Facebook, [theatre of the real/immersive practice] which demands bodily engagement, sensually stimulates the imagination, requires tactility," she notes.[22] Site-specific theatre and the historically grounded, testimonial theatre performances cited by Martin propose similar direct contact with real geographies and real personal narratives of the past to activate places and people that are usually silent to speak for themselves, as it were. Verbatim theatre, also known as "tribunal theatre," especially as it has evolved in the UK, enacts the same appeal to realness. So does autobiographical performance. Citing the same ideals as second wave feminism, declaring that the personal is political, these genres value the personal not only insofar as it is of the everyday, speaking to localized experience, but also in its closeness to the source as communication flows directly from person-to-person.

Regardless of the precise date chosen, the appeal to the real in the context of profound uncertainty, characterized by these varied forms of "new" documentary, is without doubt a millennial phenomenon, distinct from earlier waves of documentary in the 1930s – characterized by the Living Newspapers created by the US Federal Theatre Project (an agitprop style originating in Bolshevik Russia) and the didactic political theatre of Erwin Piscator; and the 1960s – featuring the collective creations of Peter Cheeseman and Joan Littlewood in the UK, The Wooster Group and The Living Theatre in the US, and Theatre Passe Muraille under the direction of Paul Thompson in Canada.[23] The work of Augusto Boal, manifesting in his designs for Forum theatre and legislative theatre, also draws on a similar impulse, using performance founded in current events and everyday situations as a rehearsal for real-world social change. The core distinction between millennial theatres of the real and their more traditional documentary predecessors lies in profound postmodern, poststructuralist doubt. It lies in an uneasy awareness that reality is a performative construction and therefore is always open to questioning, which renders it essentially unstable. The primary focus of contemporary theatres of the real then is self-reflexive, aimed at the necessarily imbricated relationship between the realness of the raw documents and materials of theatrical making and the cognitive theatricalizing apparatus that manages that realness. The locus of critical attention centres not simply on the reliability of newly mediated content but on the formal characteristics of that self-aware mediation.

Postdramatic theatre, as described by Hans-Thies Lehmann, offers one view of this contingent relationship of realness at the core of performance and how it is mediated in theatrical perception. The tenth item in Lehmann's listing of the "panorama" of postdramatic theatre is the "irruption of the real." Lehmann identifies this dialectical relationship between the actual and its fictional remediation residing at the core of theatricality as a key locus for the postdramatic. As he writes, the traditional idea of theatre is predicated on a "closed fictive cosmos,"[24] that is, conventional theatricality arises from the perceptual instigation of a fictional world that is self-contained, ontologically distinct from the surrounding actual world. The actions of fictional characters are clearly demarcated as separate, and allowed as provisionally real within those confines. Moreover, the mimetic processes of this creation and constitutive demarcation are hidden from view, giving the fictive world an illusion of autonomy. Under the operations of the "irruption of the real," however, this frame is made visible so as to draw attention to its existence and to the constructed nature of its contents, and sometimes more radically to suggest that the frame has been effaced entirely and that the contents of its presentation are not subject to fictionality. Although, as Lehmann recognizes, theatre has, at various times, admitted certain breaches of this boundary, both intentional and accidental, to acknowledge its underlying and surrounding realness, these have "been treated as an artistically and conceptually negligible aspect of theatre."[25] Lehmann claims that the postdramatic theatre is the first to turn the level of the real explicitly into a "co-player."[26]

Looking to older theories of realness and the operations of theatre, how audiences manage the relational interplay between the real and the constructed and bounded fictional cosmos is central to Samuel Taylor Coleridge's theory of the balanced audience belief stance, which he describes pithily as a "willing suspension of disbelief." For Coleridge, the achievement of the "transfer from our inward nature a human interest and a semblance of truth sufficient to procure for these shadows of imagination that willing suspension of disbelief for the moment, which constitutes poetic faith"[27] is "somewhat more assisted by the will."[28] Entry into the fictional world is a determined act. In addition to the purposeful adoption of this new perspective, Coleridge asserts that the audience always retains cognitive possession of their former perceptions as well. Both actual and fictional phenomena are held in balance through a kind of binocular vision. This situation is carefully described by Coleridge who avoids naming it as simple disbelief, but rather terms it a negative belief: "The suspension of the act of comparison [to reality ...] permits this sort of negative belief [...] The true stage-illusion in this and in all other things consists – not in the mind's judging it to be a forest, but, in its remission of judgment that it is not a forest."[29] The remission of judgment requires that the audience be acutely aware both of what is accepted and what is set aside. It is significant in the context of the real as co-player that in Coleridge's conception of the basic audiencing stance, the real does not vanish nor is it ignored; it is held in abeyance, actively and with conscious intent, remaining a potent part of the theatrical equation in that abeyance. It is only through perception of the real in its realness as not a forest, that the fictional forest comes into provisional existence.

Bert O. States (*Great Reckonings in Little Rooms*) also recognizes the real as a potent co-player in the work of theatrical creation, although his focus is on those exceptional cases when the real will not be easily set aside or quiescently held in abeyance. He collects instances when the usually concealed realness of things bubbles up to the surface, irruptions, similar to those of Lehmann, that he calls "upsurges of the real."[30] Ticking clocks that keep astronomical time rather than dramatic time, fire, fountains with running water, children, and animals all trigger this effect. States is somewhat pressed to identify precisely why these particular objects perform their realness so persistently. One proposed explanation notes that these objects retain a "certain primal strangeness" insofar as they are uncommonly unusual or fascinating in the context of the theatre and so this attentive interest does not easily yield to their aesthetic function within the fiction. Alternatively, States describes the objects as having an "abnormal durability" resisting theatrical transposition to being simply signs; these random objects have a "high degree of *en soi*."[31] Even without being able to pinpoint the exact mechanism behind the disruptive realness of these objects, it is easy to add to States's list. Celebrity actors are stubborn in this way, remaining themselves and resisting theatrical concealment in their fictional characters. Obdurate celebrities may be world-famous (back to Sarah Bernhardt as Hamlet) or simply famous locally to individual knowledge (performance by an intimate acquaintance).[32] Naked bodies also retain a disruptive realness. Indeed "remarkable" bodies (however one might define that) in general have a high degree of en soi. Actors who pretend to be corpses,[33] food (especially in quantity), alcohol, money, and babies are all objects that are routinely substituted for fakes (sometimes not very persuasive fakes) because of their stubborn actuality. It is often preferable to present a deliberately stylized likeness – faux food or a doll wrapped in a blanket – to release the audience from their preoccupation with the attractive and distracting realness of the original. Paradoxically, because the faux object assimilates easily into the fiction it poses less of a threat to the fictional world than the visually accurate original. As States says, "Theater is the medium, par excellence, that consumes the real in its realest forms ... Its permanent spectacle is a parade of objects and processes *in transit* from environment to imagery."[34]

Whereas for Coleridge the real is present but easily managed by suspension of disbelief, for States the real is more stubborn in asserting its presence in the theatrical equation as real. For both theorists, the explicit management of realness is central to the processes of theatricality. And for both, the distinct and subordinate ontological status of these real materials in relation to their fictional counterparts remains clear. For Lehmann, however, the situation is more ambiguous. A central characteristic of the irruption of the real in postdramatic theatre is a fundamental ontological insecurity that thematizes the experience of the real, often generating "an *aesthetics of undecidability* concerning the basic means of theatre."[35] Lehmann writes that "the main point is not the assertion of the real as such ... but the unsettling that occurs through the *indecidability* whether one is dealing with reality or fiction. The theatrical effect and the effect on consciousness both emanate from this ambiguity."[36] Whereas traditional manifestations of metatheatre are about managing the real in the continued support of drama, of the creation and maintenance of a fictive cosmos, postdramatic works tend to eschew drama altogether – thus the selection of the term postdrama. Postdrama attempts to subvert the power of the theatricalizing frame, setting aside drama and leaving only the real. The result is that Coleridge's double vision, which includes the deferred real in support of fiction, becomes resolutely singular. As Lehmann asserts, "It is in this sense that postdramatic theatre means: theatre of the real."[37]

Another aspect of the indecidability or precariousness of the management of the real and its constructions, manifesting as postdramatic irruptions of the real, is that the postmodern condition shaped by poststructuralist performativity has made reality itself a question. What is real and what is constructed illusion is not perfectly clear to us. The uncertain duality of theatricality has slipped out of the theatre and into the world. The notion of human behaviour as performed, promulgated by J.L. Austin, Erving Goffman, and Judith Butler, among others, leads to the view that what we take to be social reality is entirely constructed and that there is no independent reality. "It has become fashionable to see human beings as entirely culturally constructed ... What we can know is entirely culturally relative, what exists becomes reducible, either explicitly or implicitly, to what can be *said* to exist. In other words, epistemology subsumes or occludes ontology."[38] "With no territory to relate to, the map establishes its own landmarks."[39] The real – if indeed such a thing exists – is inaccessible, veiled by language, veiled by performance, veiled by the syncresis of all these things that we call culture. Metaphysical philosopher George Berkeley takes an idealist tack and declares that *"esse est percipi"* – to be is to be perceived; what cannot be known, that is, perceived by our senses, does not exist. Immanuel Kant says that what we know is not the same as what exists; there are things-in-themselves, distinct from that which can be perceived, which are forever inaccessible. David Hume is a sceptic who argues that reality in its entirety is empirically constituted. We can never be certain of the existence of an independent world; questions about independent reality are meaningless. Ultimately what these three agree on is that the real, if it does exist, necessarily lies beyond our ken, and so cannot (and should not) be our concern. And there is some naive comfort in this permission to avert our gaze from the abyss. Poststructuralism, however, does not look away; it does not deny that reality is limited by sense perception but it doesn't conflate what we can know exists with what actually exists. It leaves "open the possibility of a terrain of unmapped alterity which Jacques Lacan calls 'the real.' In contrast to the nonchalance of the culturalists ... poststructuralism holds on to a structural uncertainty which [Catherine Belsey calls] 'anxiety of the real.'"[40] It is this "awareness of the lost real" that plagues us.[41] Drawing on Lacan's articulation of the real which stands behind social reality, masked by the symbolic order of language, Belsey continues, "The signifier seems to evoke the existence of something on the other side of it, but refuses to tell us what this is ... [It] veils the unknown."[42] This anxious awareness of what is lost characterizes contemporary nostalgic desire for an impossible return to a state where we could distinguish with certainty between reality and constructed fictions – or at least a return to a prelapsarian state where our profound lack could be innocently ignored. For Lacan, the real resides not only in opposition to constructed realities but also in opposition to the symbolic, to the means of that construction. "One can only think of language as a network, a net over the entirety of things, over the totality of real. It inscribes on the plane of the real this other plane, which we here call the plane of the symbolic."[43] It is not possible to capture the real in the symbolic order. The real is that which remains outside representation. "[It] is what resists symbolisation absolutely."[44] It is only in truly harrowing situations, situations so alien, where articulation fails, that we encounter the real. In these traumatic gaps, rents in the symbolic, generated by experiences that are so incomprehensible, words fail. This is what is meant in German by *betroffenheit*. "The real is what our knowledge, individually or collectively, both must and cannot accommodate."[45]

Rather than remain paralysed by this failure of comprehension, caught in contemplation of our own impossible relation to the real, performance scholars Ulrike Garde and Meg Mumford engage the ontological indecidability enacted by poststructuralism in the form of postdrama to consider its possible audience effects. Their phrase "productive insecurity" describes the results of an affective technique that creates a performative rupture, when real or nonfictional elements are introduced into the theatrical frame, such that the audience experiences acute postdramatic indecidability about whether one is dealing with reality or fiction.[46] Garde and Mumford consider the impact of essential doubt on autobiographical performance. When actors reanimate testimony, audiences cannot decipher what is real and what is fiction. Likewise when the location of the performance is an actual real-world site where the actual story actually happened, audiences negotiate ambivalently between set and setting. Since these alternatives do not fit comfortably into one or other of these binarised categories, I am confounded to separate set from setting. The nature of these words and objects is uncertain. Having catalogued specific points of rupture that generate this uncertainty, Garde and Mumford turn their attention to how the affect of uncertainty is itself productive. Ultimately, they conclude that the experience is self-reflexive and that "these states encourage new and unstable modes of perceiving self, other, and representations."[47] The experience of ungraspability leads to the realization of the limited capacity of inauthentic performance to give access to reality and the real. This concept of "productive insecurity" will be central to my subsequent analyses, which apply this concept to other points of postdramatic indecidability concerning the ontological ambivalence of verbatim text, site-specific spaces, and the embodied audience-self in immersive performance environments.

Other echoes of Garde and Mumford's "productive insecurity" can be found in the work of Helena Grehan and Sara Jane Bailes, who separately also both recognize and refuse indecidability as cognitive paralysis or failure, viewing insecurity as a possibly efficacious opportunity.

Grehan, in her book *Performance, Ethics, and Spectatorship in a Global Age*, makes a fruitful connection between Levinasian responsibility and ambivalence. Grehan considers how productions compel their audiences to ethical engagement, how audiences might become involved in and respond to the work, how to "get beyond the potential paralysis of the contemporary moment."[48] Asking "What does the play want from me?" Grehan invokes Zygmunt Bauman's essay "The World Inhospitable to Levinas," connecting the dots from response to responsibility to the blended "response-ability." Levinas says that when the other calls us we have no choice but to respond. Here, performance is the other who calls us. Bauman's essay points out that the posthuman complexity of the world makes collective action impossible and freedom from responsibility is valorized: "Shedding responsibility for consequences is the most coveted and cherished gain that the new mobility brings to free-floating, locally-unbound capital."[49] Grehan looks to performance to provide a space of "radical unsettlement within which spectators may hear the call of the other (in a different way)."[50] Unsettlement arises through ambivalence. "This is not an ambivalence that means they will necessarily flounder or that they occupy a position of inertia, but instead it is understood as a productive space that allows for the ideas, traces, concepts and concerns in the performance to percolate."[51] Ambivalence in Grehan's model does not map exactly onto the same territory as the ontological insecurity embedded in postdramatic performance structures identified by Lehmann and Garde and Mumford, but rather describes a potential field of action in response to the performance. Where the two concepts do align is in their expectation that unsettlement in the audience, whether activated by an uncertain landscape of reality or by the uncertainty of real-world action, is productive. The impetus to think again, to reconsider and reassess, comes out of destabilization and disruption, irritation and insecurity. "Ambivalence is about these moments of self-recognition but also about the internal processes of doubt, anxiety, reflection and consideration individual spectators go through in their attempts to make sense of, or to respond to a work."[52] Rather than simply seeking thrills or novelty or aesthetic pleasure, Grehan challenges audiences to be more than narcissistic collectors of experience. Open to ambivalence, audiences "become people who are interested in and open to the other; they consider the ramifications of these responses beyond their own self-reflexive engagement and out into the community."[53] In alignment with Garde and Mumford's insecurity, Grehan looks to ambivalence as a profoundly uncomfortable but positive platform from which to interrogate the status quo.

Failure is directly related to insecurity. As Bailes writes, "[Failure] undermines the perceived stability of mainstream capitalist ideology's preferred aspiration to achieve, succeed, or win, and the accumulation of material wealth as proof and effect arranged by those aims. Failure challenges the cultural dominance of instrumental rationality and the fictions of continuity that bind the way we imagine and manufacture the world."[54] Ultimately the persistent failures of security as demonstrated in the performances discussed in the chapters that follow serve to call into question core tenets of the prevailing neoliberal ethos – values with assumed positive attributes like winning, independence, capability, growth, acquisition, innovation, knowing where you are, i.e., not being lost, knowing who these people are, i.e., not encountering strangers, or just knowing in general, i.e., possessing facts that are unambiguous and secured by unshakeable proofs. Even the value of security itself is called into question. Insecurity is not pleasant, in fact it is often downright dangerous, and we normally go to great lengths to avoid it. Nevertheless, security is also stultifying in its protective confines and confident assertions. Without insecurity, without doubt, there can be no change. We might also consider that although insecurity is scary, the alternative may be worse. Catherine Belsey writes, "On the contrary, I don't want truth back. Whose truth was it, anyway? What I want to hold onto is my unease, on the grounds that the banishment of anxiety is not sanity, paradoxically, so much as psychosis. Genuine madness is being certain you are always in the game."[55] Belsey echoes the claims of *Reality Hunger*, presented in the epigraph to this chapter, asserting the essential fundamentality of rational thought to doubt: "Thought is indistinguishable from doubt. To be alive is to be uncertain." And given a choice between the anxious insecurity of doubt and the questionable sanity of always knowing, I'll take doubt.

As mentioned at the outset, the core assumption of this book is that although theatres of the real ostensibly promise an encounter with stable documentary or authentic reality, this is not possible and instead these performances meditate on that impossibility and the conditions under which a singular secure real fails to manifest. Certainty of knowledge as a goal is set aside in favour of self-reflexive consideration of how can we effectively live in doubt. The plays model answers not to the question "What is real?," but instead "How did this reality (or realities) come to be?" The first two chapters are concerned with real people. *Winners and Losers* is an autobiographical performance event structured as an improvised conversation between long-time friends and artistic collaborators James Long and Marcus Youssef. What at first appears to be an amusing and satirical debate about "winners" and "losers" in popular culture and current events becomes profoundly uncomfortable, even unpleasant, as the two protagonists turn on each other. Persistent reality-markers in this postdramatic performance render it difficult for the audience to discern the boundary between reality and fiction. The result is an acute indecidability, generating Garde and Mumford's "productive insecurity." This chapter will demonstrate how the play's destabilizing strategies operate to create productive insecurity. The formal insecurity of postdrama connects thematic anxiety within the drama of middle-aged masculinity pertaining to being "not safe" or being a "loser" to the disruptive paralytic effect that compels the audience to re-evaluate the initial premise of the game and our habituated attachment to confident knowing. When the game messily implodes, we are left to ponder the question: How do we move forward (or really in any direction) in a world of pervasive uncertainty?

Chapter 3 also presents examples of confessional autobiography. But instead of professional theatre artists using dramaturgical and scenographic techniques to engender deliberate reality effects, realness here resides in a bid for unmediation, for presenting the real "raw," as it were. Eschewing displays of actorly skills, these autobiographers are "ordinary" people presenting themselves as themselves. They are recent immigrants to Quebec (*Polyglotte* by Olivier Choinière), Toronto and Kingston youth living with Down syndrome (*RARE*, created by Judith Thompson and the ensemble), and 100 demographically representative Vancouverites (*100% Vancouver* presented by Theatre Replacement after Rimini Protokoll). Through these varied encounters, the plays illuminate the means whereby two groups of strangers – the audience and the non-actor cast, the secure and the disenfranchised or marginal – are both subject to various kinds of insecurity. Insecurity is generated by postdramatic techniques and by real-world, political, economic, and social insecurity. Rather than simplistically suggesting that through this autobiographical encounter, "we" can actually get to know and appreciate "them," these selected performances consistently problematize potential points of contact. Even though we are brought into proximate encounter through autobiographical postdramatic performance, the product of our communal insecurities is a reflexive awareness of those insecurities, of all the things we cannot know or control. But rather than create a shared experience of not knowing together, *Polyglotte*, *RARE*, and *100% Vancouver* (each in a slightly different way) suggest that despite increased exposure, strangers remain strange.

Shifting from the auratic readymade presence of people and bodies, Chapter 4 turns attention to the documentary value of words as markers of evidentiary and experiential realness. *Seeds*, created by Annabel Soutar (Porte Parole, Montreal), who is arguably Canada's preeminent verbatim producer, uses testimony from interviews conducted by Soutar herself and follows the 2004 Supreme Court case that pitted Percy Schmeiser, a canola farmer from Bruno, Saskatchewan against biotech giant Monsanto. *Seeds* mixes the repetition of verbatim testimony with live video feed and green screen technology, combining the onstage real with the elsewhere real. Technological remediation is also a key feature of *300 TAPES* (Public Recordings), which uses a technique called auto-reciting. The performers listen through headphones to prerecorded autobiographical stories that they speak aloud in real time as they hear them. The tape technology allows for rewinding, replaying, and re-recording, distorting the original into something new, which might be more real. In each case, the real is refracted in such a way as to generate uncertainty about which real – the live reenactment or the recorded original – is the most real. Both plays confront the paradox of verbatim wherein a genre that purports faithful delivery of testimony is haunted by the inescapable awareness that the words are always subject to revision, ventriloquized, and remediated. This chapter considers how *Seeds* and *300 TAPES* own their self-awareness of their constructive situation, using reproductive iteration as a theme. Life is made to be copied, whether literally via biological reproduction as seeds or via technological reproduction though looped (de)generative recordings. The central question for verbatim theatre under poststructuralism is not, "Should life be copied?" but "How do we want to see life modified?"

Like verbatim theatre, site-specific performance also stakes out a strong claim to being rooted in the real world, but in this case, rather than bringing the world to the stage, site-specific performance takes the stage to the world. The two performances under consideration in chapter 5 – *Landline*, created by Adrienne Wong and Dustin Harvey, and *Garden//Suburbia*, created by Melanie Bennett and Hartley Jafine – both invite audiences to stroll through urban spaces, orchestrating events whereby audiences can tap into the psychogeography of a city or a neighbourhood. In *Landline*, each "player" is given an iPod with an audio track and connected via texting with a synchronous "scene partner" in another city. The audio in your ear guides you out into the city where you are left to wander and to follow certain cues: "Find a location that reminds you of an old friend." You are also instructed at intervals to text your partner with your impressions, questions, and personal stories. A unique "script" is created between the two audience members, who become "actors" and "playwrights." The stranger on the other end of the texting link becomes a potential friend and confidant. Yet, through this blending of real and virtual space across time zones, "here" becomes "nowhere." Audiences are prefigured as ghosts floating placeless in an urban landscape, enmeshed in a variety of land lines, both real and metaphorical. A similar insecure estrangement is evoked by *Garden//Suburbia*. A walking tour combining both live guides and audio tracks, the play leads the audience through the leafy and well-heeled Toronto community of Lawrence Park. The twist is that our guides quickly show themselves to not be entirely reliable sources of truth. Although the site we occupy is ostensibly real, the stories that reside behind the façades remain elusive. Through performative storytelling, *Garden//Suburbia* makes clear that the site of Lawrence Park (as well as the autobiographical personae of "Melanie" and "Hartley") is reinventing itself literally as we watch. The environment and the city are places of change and evolution, open to reinscription. Exploration of the interrelation of identity and place in *Garden//Suburbia* and *Landline* interrogates our attachment to physical environments, specifically in the tension between the potentially stifling security of belonging and the likewise unsettling freedom of nomadism.

The flip side of the current fascination with putting uncertainly real things on the stage is a correlative trend that brings the really real audience into the fictional frame. Immersive theatre events create complex, flexible environments and situations where each audience member has a role to play with significant freedom to make choices, thereby generating a plethora of unique, DIY theatre performances. Productive insecurity comes into play here as well since the real world and the fictional worlds of the situation unnervingly blend in the bodily perceptions and actions of the audience, which are simultaneously both real and pretend. In this case, it is the audience-self that becomes a stranger, estranged from its usual confident identity as real in a real world. Chapter 6 examines two immersive performances that configure that audience experience as a collective. One, *Counting Sheep: A Guerilla Folk Opera*, was created by Lemon Bucket Orkestra, self-described as

"Toronto's only balkan-klezmer-gypsy-party-punk super band." The performance is billed as "an invitation to experience the spirit of the Maidan, complete with song, dance, and an entire Ukrainian feast" and to get "as close as you could get to experiencing a revolution without actually putting your life on the line." The other, *Foreign Radical*, compels audiences to participate in an interactive task-based environment and reveal personal information in the context of a game, to explore themes of cyber-surveillance, political dissent, and government restrictions on movement. Both performances offer virtual simulations of the modern crises of security we fear, which remain for the moment at arm's length in contemporary "safe" Canada, yet which stalk our globalized world. The chapter argues that both plays are examples of Patrick Duggan's "trauma-tragedy" wherein oscillations between different poles of reality and fiction create an effect of mimetic shimmering, which circumvents representation and allows affective symptoms of tragedy to become manifest.

In contrast to the global crises of the coercion of personal freedom in the context of popular revolution and terrorism explored in the immersive group "games" discussed in the previous chapter, intimate, small-scale performances also trigger awareness of the audience body as real. The final chapter describes performances for one audience member that I refer to as "haunted houses," although they are not always scary. When the audience is alone, a single person confronted with an immersive experience, she becomes acutely aware of smiling, sweating, heart beating, breathing – the ordinary, usually insignificant, somatic impressions of being a body rise up, and focus turns inwards. *Everyman* (Single Thread Theatre Company) is a retelling of the fifteenth-century medieval morality play of the same name in which the solo audience member is cast as Everyman. Told by Death that God has summoned him to his final reckoning, Everyman must reconcile his spiritual accounts through confession before being put into his grave. In these incredibly heightened visceral encounters, insecurity manifests in a way that touches the existential.

In a final coda, the book concludes by considering the praxis of theatres of the real in the immediately contemporary political context of a post-truth world. In the second decade of the twenty-first century, the worm seems to have turned and the same poststructural theories of performative social realities that facilitated progressive liberal ideologies (especially around identity) also enable the primacy of feelings over facts, the burgeoning of fake news and the legitimation of conspiracy theory thinking, and the mainstreaming of white supremacy under the sanitized tag of the "alt-right." By accepting the core notion of performatively constructed social realities, the door has been opened to post-reality. How might theatres of the real respond to this new level of anxiety about representation and reality? Or is this the end for this style? From a theatrical point of view, will we see a return to a more rigid mimesis? What does it mean when performativity is ethically neutral and politically flexible? From a political point of view, how do we make good decisions in an infinitely flexible post-reality world? What is the connection between epistemological uncertainty arising from poststructuralism and recent (faux-)nostalgic desire for security, as manifested by the 2016 Trump campaign slogan "Make America Great Again" and the Brexit Leave slogan "Take Back Control." Whither theatre of the real in an age of post-reality?

2 Real People Part 1: Winning and/or Losing the Game of Life in Autobiographical Performance – *Winners and Losers*

And this is where it gets absolutely fascinating and deliciously uncomfortable. This piece blurs the line between the theatrical and the real like nothing I've ever seen, and while I'm sure the actors are, in fact, just acting (mostly ... I think ...) it nevertheless FEELS bloody real, to the point where when it's all over you feel almost garish for applauding. An experiment in realism that isn't afraid to punch traditional stage boundaries right in the dick ... this play won't be everyone's cup of tea, but if it doesn't get you thinking and talking you might be the Scarecrow in WIZARD OF OZ. Huge props to the actors, and I'd love to compare notes with people who saw it on different nights. This is theatre at its most real ... and, therefore, at its scariest.[1]

Billed as a "staged conversation" between long-time friends and artistic collaborators James Long and Marcus Youssef, *Winners and Losers* is an autobiographical performance-event where the audience is invited to wonder what the real-world dangers of this contest might be.[2] The contest that structures *Winners and Losers* is an improvisational game that Long and Youssef have invented where they debate the merits of a random list of people and objects, briskly passing judgment as to whether these are winners or losers. If Jamie declares an item a winner, the format of the game demands that Marcus counter that it is a loser, and vice versa. So, in addition to the specific item being ranked as a winner or a loser, Marcus and Jamie each win or lose the round depending on whether or not their case has been successful. The winning of a point is signalled by the ringing of one of the service bells placed on the table in front of the two debaters. And so with a little "ding!" their subjects are flippantly and speedily dismissed. Some are popular (Twinkies,

Gangnam style, Pamela Anderson) and some weighty (Truth and Rec-
onciliation Commissions, Alberta oil sands, Africa). The framework of
competition overrides any residue of polite serious decorum that these
subjects might ordinarily expect. In its tone, the debate of *Winners and
Losers* is more late-night game show than Oxford Union. But soon the
debate becomes personal as Marcus and Jamie each make the case for
why the other is a loser.

   The gloves come off and their honest mutual assessments, launched
from a position of intimate knowledge, are cruel and cutting. On the
one hand, we ought to be quite confident that this is a performance –
rehearsed, controlled, repeatable, and as such, safe for both actors
and audience. On the other hand, the strong reality effects at work
undermine that sense of safety. Our confident surety is systematically
eroded and we are indeed scared: scared that what we are witnessing
has escaped the bounds of the theatrical frame and that the actors are
at risk of real psychological harm. Even though as sophisticated the-
atregoers, we, like the blogger Kevin Reid cited in the epigraph above,
know this ambivalence is entirely groundless, we still worry. We still
experience significant concern for the safety of Long and Youssef, subject to the barbs of unwelcome truths. Even when uttered from inside a
theatrical frame, the emotionally eviscerating words still hang in the air,
their effects unknown. This equivocation is a persistent motif, featuring
in nearly every published review by grassroots bloggers and seasoned
press critics alike. Catching the performance at Festival TransAmériques
in Montreal, Paula Citron of *The Globe and Mail* acknowledges her own
uncertainty: "some words are said that cut to the quick, and the audience
is sent reeling ... [U]nsettling questions start to arise in the audience's
mind."[3] The *New York Times*'s Charles Isherwood assures himself that
"[a]lthough the final moments suggest that some serious old wounds
have been reopened, I had little doubt that after the lights went down,
these two would share another beer, and probably play quite nicely
together."[4] With his confidence in enduring post-performance friendship, it is telling that Isherwood finds it necessary to weigh in. And
even then, he counterbalances his prediction of bar room camaraderie
against an acknowledgment of real injuries done. His compatriot at the
New York Post, Elisabeth Vincentelli, is not as sure: "and as the tension
escalates, it seems the men might actually come to blows. You have
to wonder how they can do this and still go for drinks together – but
maybe they don't anymore."[5] Liz Nicholls (*Edmonton Journal*) sums up
her impressions this way: "[t]he illusion of spontaneity vs. rehearsed

acting will prove to be a deliberate source of unease, ours ... There is, of course, something kind of horrifying about this. Which is, I guess, the point of a show that is insightful, and leaves a sour taste."[6] Certainly that is how I feel about it. After watching this agonizing train wreck of a fraternal breakup, it is virtually impossible not to ask: how can they still be friends after the shockingly candid, nasty things they say to each other in the pursuit of honest evaluation? How can this go on night after night for more than two years?[7]

The audience's perception of risk of harm to the performers inheres in our belief (a somewhat ambivalent belief, but a belief nonetheless), that what we are witnessing is, on some level, real. Carol Martin cites the example of the dance marathons popular in the 1930s in her book *Theatre of the Real*, reporting that "[s]pectators were drawn to the mix of the risk of the physical effort of dancing for hours and days at a time *and* the performance of that risk. Contestants really danced, and some even died during the contests. At the same time, they performed and exaggerated their effort to create theatre for the show."[8] This dichotomous tension between the really real and the enactment of techniques in support of a strong reality-effect underpins our understanding of performances categorized as theatre of the real or reality-based performance. Emphasis placed on the material real in this genre operates not to stake claims to the absolute authenticity of original experience, but rather to draw attention to these real-world foundations so as to interrogate the processes of creating reality.

In the wake of poststructuralism, representations have become unmoored from reality, no longer owing allegiance to an authoritative origin, and in a significant reversal in priority reality is now understood as itself a representation.[9] Thinking about language and the relationship of the signifier to the signified, Jacques Derrida asserts famously, "il n'y a pas de hors-texte."[10] There is nothing outside of discourse. What he is arguing is that citationality is built on a void. Discursive signifiers lack signifieds. Each statement is entirely dependent on arbitrary reiteration for its effective communication of meaning, referring to nothing and its comprehensibility structured solely in relation to other statements. In this free-floating context, representations no longer reflect concrete authentic reality but instead have the power to create that reality. Not just one reality but a fluid multiplicity of realities. These twisted loops of simulations comprise the totality of our world. Whereas it was once comprehensible that a geographic map represented a small-scale version of an actual real territory elsewhere, this is no longer a tenable position. As Jean Baudrillard argues, "Simulation is no longer that of a territory, a referential being or a substance. It is the generation by models of a real without origin or reality: a hyperreal."[11] Representations no longer adhere to a stable origin. What was formerly valued as original or authentic has lost its priority, becoming itself yet another citation. "The whole system becomes weightless, it is no longer itself anything but a gigantic simulacrum – not unreal, but a simulacrum, that is to say never exchanged for the real, but exchanged for itself, in an uninterrupted circuit without reference or circumference."[12] We stand at a point where we recognize that there is no longer an accessible real.[13] There is no stable origin upon which representation rests. As Liz Tomlin concludes in her book *Acts and Apparitions: Discourses on the Real in Performance Practice and Theory, 1990–2010*, "[t]he emergence of the simulacrum as the new paradigm of the real marks the end of any confidence in a metaphysical certainty that might offer recourse to a reality lying beyond the ideological constructs of the spectacle, and with it comes an end to the old distinctions between truth and falsehood, the real and the fictional."[14] In this ambivalent space, we stand on a thin crust set about with crevices into which we can peer at the hollowness beneath.

Reality-based performances like *Winners and Losers*, then, are not about accessing the real as such, but about how we understand these contingent substitute constructions we take to be real, how they are created, and how they are consumed. Without a firm originary referential foundation, we are invited to consider how to live without certainty. In the pages that follow, my first aim is to introduce *Winners and Losers* as an initial exemplar of a contemporary genre of performance that foregrounds this troubling experience of a contingent performative real. I will demonstrate the specific strategies of characterization whereby the play exposes uncertainty by destabilizing the expected theatrical boundary between a character and the actual-world actor, between what we perceive to be dramatic fiction and what we perceive to be its real-world underpinnings. Second, I argue that this uncertainty, which initially seems to inhibit agency in the audience, is paradoxically politically generative through the critical unknowing that Ulrike Garde and Meg Mumford call "productive insecurity."[15] Finally, I examine how insecurity, which manifests thematically within this specific drama as anxiety about being not-safe/being a loser, extends beyond the already porous frame to characterize the audience affect of *Winners and Losers*.

Existential insecurity for the characters is reflected in an ontological insecurity that compels the audience to re-evaluate the initial premise of the winners and losers' performance-game and our habituated attachment to confident knowing.

Autobiography is a truth-based genre. As with other nonfiction genres, autobiography presumes as a core principle that there is a reliable correspondence between its representation and the world, in this case specifically, between the protagonist of autobiographical narrative and the author-creator of that narrative. This correspondence aligns representation and its original in such close proximity and likeness that the two are almost (but not quite) identical. When encountering an autobiographical storyteller, there is a strong impression that we are meeting the person herself. Performative mediation is almost (but not quite) invisible. In a seminal work for autobiography studies, Philippe Lejeune proposes to differentiate autobiography as a genre distinct from first-person novels. He auditions various criteria but ultimately only two are definitive. First, that the author, narrator, and protagonist must be identical, and second, the author-subject must be a real person.[16] He calls this social contract the "autobiographical pact." The ontological security offered by Lejeune of equating the stage persona of autobiography with its correlative real-world person is tempting but impossible in a poststructuralist milieu. Following Judith Butler, Erving Goffman, and other proponents of performative identity creation in the real world, autobiographical personae also participate in looped acts of mutual self-generation. The character-self is a performative construction, selected and shaped by its actual-world antecedent. Likewise, the actual-world self relinquishes its priority as origin, understood to also be a performative construction accreted over time by the stories I tell about myself. In this context, Lejeune's author, narrator, and protagonist can never be truly identical, lacking as they do a stable authentic original. There are by necessity gaps and inconsistencies among these performative portraits, gaps into which creeps doubt. Susanna Egan in her book *Burdens of Proof: Faith, Doubt and Identity in Autobiography* zeroes in on the problem of doubt, examining as a special case intentional impostors, people pretending to be someone else and committing what she wonderfully calls "frautobiography."[17] As she points out, imposture matters in autobiography, simply because "it promises to tell the truth and then fails to do so."[18] Egan observes that these acts of identity-plagiarism speak to a cultural sensitivity to truth and doubt. Why, she asks, does autobiographical imposture raise so much dust?[19] Paradoxically, it is exactly because of the autobiographical pact, the claim to authenticity at the core, that autobiography is especially vulnerable to mischief-making with truth and doubt. Extending the specific crisis of doubt arising from deliberate fraud, I would argue that autobiography, like all nonfiction genres, must always and unavoidably be beset by doubt resulting from its foundational poststructuralist performativity. Counter to Lejeune and Egan, who align autobiography with an essential truth claim, David Shields aligns himself with poststructuralist thinking, recognizing that all representations, even those claiming to be "non," are still representations: "The memoir rightly belongs to the imaginative world, and once writers and readers make their peace with this, there will be less argument over the questions regarding the memoir's relation to the 'facts' and 'truth.'"[20]

Shields, in his manifesto *Reality Hunger*, persuasively claims that whereas nonfiction genres are plagued with questions of what is true and what is false, what is contained and what is omitted, fictional genres are free of this worry. As he writes, "In imaginative literature we're always constrained from considering alternative scenarios; there are none. This is the way it *is*. Only in nonfiction does the question of what happened and how people thought and felt remain open."[21] Shields's identification of the pernicious doubts necessarily embedded in the truth statements of literary works like essays and memoirs is even more potent when applied to autobiographical performance as an embodied oeuvre. In place of the printed morpheme "I" standing in for the protagonist-self of the memoirist, there is the flesh and blood of the actor-protagonist herself. The basic iconicity of theatrical representation that employs the signified to indicate its own signifier further augments the epistemological doubt that Shields declares to be inherent in nonfiction. We grasp at the seeming solidity of the performing body, keen to claim it in our apprehension of it as a token of authenticity for the words it speaks and the gestures it enacts. When the innate ontological distinction between the character-I and the performer-I is compressed to near identity, this similarity is disconcertingly not the source of epistemological stability we hope for. Instead, this radical compression generates more doubt about what is "true" and, by extension, generates increased risk for all concerned – performer and audience – by opening a conduit through which the effect of fictional words and gestures might rebound on the actual body that speaks and acts.[22] For the audience, who are phenomenological witnesses to the live performance, so much is given to apprehension, but an equal, if not greater amount is withheld. Every detail, multiplying to infinity, begs a veridical confirmation, which will always be beyond my reach. The striving audience of nonfiction is mired in doubt. In the face of this epistemological uncertainty, Shields encourages us to embrace it and shift our point of engagement from "what is real" to "how did it come to be real." We are invited by him to embrace Keats's negative capability, becoming "capable of being in uncertainties, mysteries, doubts, without any irritable reaching after fact and reason."[23]

Transposition of actual-world elements into fictional-world elements is the core business of theatricality; objects staged by reality-focused performance forms will inevitably fail to fully escape the gravitational pull of theatricalization. So, in spite of appearances, reality-based theatre cannot give us access to pure unfiltered reality. Subject to the transformations of theatricality, it is a style, like Expressionism, or clowning, or naturalism, and as such has certain defining practices, which make manifest its goals. The primary strategy of the collection of practices that trigger uncertainty is a weakening of our perception of the theatrical frame. The audience is subtly and not-so-subtly encouraged by various techniques to discount the usual binocular double-vision engendered by the fictionalizing frame and instead to see the performance as an ontologically single entity residing only in the actual world. Although *Winners and Losers* was created out of improvisations and continues to feature a few improvised sections, it is a crafted, rehearsed, and repeatable performance event. It is not substantially different in this respect from any other conventional dramatic work. It seems foolish to have to say this. Yet, because of the persistent disarming devices of reality-creation employed in this performance, it seems necessary to assert these bona fides.

From the outset, *Winners and Losers* projects the outward semblance of unfiltered reality, adopting a stripped down, Fringe-aesthetic scenographic style typical of performances in the confessional autobiographical genre. The play is performed in a bare black box theatre space.[24] In the centre is a table. One chair is positioned at each end. There are two of those nickel-plated service bells – one for each of the performers – that they use to indicate a decision: "winner" or "loser." Jamie and Marcus appear casually dressed in street clothes. The lighting does not perceptibly change and the blocking is likewise unobtrusive with the two either standing or sitting side by side for much of the play. Through their casual banter the audience is easily admitted into the game. Indeed the audience is regularly asked to provide topics for debate. Each of these choices contributes to the impression that this is not a play. The set is not a set; it is just the naked theatre space. The lighting is not lighting; the lights were just turned on. The costumes are not costumes; they are just clothes. Of course, each of these scenographic elements has been subject to theatrical selection but in their likeness to the mundane they are making a strong bid to be interpreted as "not-theatre," as free of the essential duality of drama. Likewise the shared presence of audience and performers is another attempt to suggest that the necessary theatrical distinction between the real world and the provisionally real world of the performance has been erased. In opposition to these markers of not-theatre, Jamie and Marcus begin the show by ritually chalking a large rectangle on the stage floor that encompasses most of the stage space. They take turns and each completes half of the shape. I read this line as a formal container for their contest: both as a representation of a boxing ring or mixed martial arts fighting cage consistent with imagery drawn from physical combat sports/entertainment and as a physical manifestation of the theatricalizing boundary distinguishing (and problematizing) the division between actual and fictional. In the actual making of a frame, the distinctive perceptual stance of drama is reactivated. For all intents and purposes, it is a proscenium, except flat on the floor. It fills the same role as a proscenium, indicating the ontological separateness of the world contained therein. The result is a complicating tension between these conflicting signals, between elements marked as real and those same elements marked as performative.

After setting the scene with strong reality-markers and then undermining those same markers with the delineation of an actual frame, the play moves on to dramaturgical techniques that intentionally weaken the theatrical frame, seemingly using theatre against itself. One of the most common techniques of promoting the ostended actions as "real" is to explicitly acknowledge the actual-world activity of performing the play. Throughout *Winners and Losers*, Jamie and Marcus negotiate the structure of the play as they go. Jamie proposes Burt Reynolds for a topic, and Marcus demurs, suggesting instead that they play a sub-game called "Worldly Wise." Jamie counters with another sub-game "Street Smarts." Marcus agrees and off they go in this new direction.[25] The essence of this technique for creating the reality-effect is not just that they behave in a realistic manner that seems to be spontaneous, but that they draw explicit attention to the spontaneity of the action.

Having just described his own dad, Marcus invites Jamie to discuss his dad:

JAMIE: No. Not near as interesting as your dad. Let's do something else.
MARCUS: Isn't that a rule? One of us does it, then the other?
JAMIE: I thought we were just making this up.
MARCUS: Yeah, we are.
JAMIE: So let's make it up.[26]

Having established this cross-world ambiguity, Long and Youssef introduce themselves and the show: "Hi my name is Jamie and this is Marcus." "That's right, I am Marcus." "And this is *Winners and Losers*."[27] In performance, Lejeune's stacked triumvirate of roles – actor, narrator, and protagonist – finds equivalents in the playwright, actor, and character. Despite their ostensible shared singular identity, these component personae are in fact ontologically distinct. The autobiographical actor is a citizen of the actual world, that is, he is what I refer to as a world[a] person.[28] The character persona, although sharing many touchpoints with the originating real-world source, is a fictional creation (and as such is radically indeterminate as all such fictional creations are). The character lives in world[b] – a provisionally real but subordinate nested world. The Jamie and Marcus (Jamie[b] and Marcus[b]) that we meet in *Winners and Losers* can never be fully contiguous with their world[a] counterparts. However, the names "Jamie" and "Marcus" ground these terminal points, bridging the proposed equation; it is not merely that each of the playwright, actor, and character are all superficially named "Jamie" but the function of the shared name is to indicate that they are all at some fundamental level really the same person, eliding the ontological difference. We are invited to see a single identity housed in a common physical body and sharing a unique history, presence, and future. In addition to the posited ontological unity of the performer, the usual duality of the physical space of the theatre can also be collapsed in a similar way. The setting for *Winners and Losers* is in whatever performance space the event is being presented. The fictional here is identical with the actual here. Later, at a tense moment in the evening, Marcus scores some points with a telling criticism; Jamie is hurt, and his reaction is to walk out. He says he needs to go pee and leaves the theatre. In doing so, the play draws attention to the presence of the biological actor body and also frames the theatre space *qua* theatre space. In the premiere production, Jamie exited into the lobby through the same door that the audience used. Through this one-to-one correspondence, the play suggests that no transposition is necessary, and, by extension, that the theatrical frame is extraneous.

The perceptual collapsing of world[a] and world[b] in support of the reality-effect can also be achieved by the inclusion of verifiable real-world information. In addition to giving us their names, Marcus and Jamie begin the contest between them with a list of personal details.

> JAMIE: I'm forty-one years old.
> MARCUS: I'm forty-five.
> JAMIE: Married.
> MARCUS: Common law. Toyota.
> JAMIE: Mazda.
> MARCUS: Matrix.
> JAMIE: Protégé 5. Six feet tall.
> MARCUS: I'm five eleven. And a half.
> JAMIE: One hundred and eighty-one pounds.
> MARCUS: One hundred and eighty. Seven. Plus six.[29]

This goes on. In this agon of comparison, we become privy to a host of personal biographical details about kids' ages and genders, education, hometown, and current address. Some of this information will be independently verifiable for audiences who might know the performers personally. For some characteristics like age, height, and weight, we can corroborate these reported facts with our own visual assessment of the performers. They seem to be telling the truth. Since facts communicated about their world[b] personae correspond to what we can independently determine about the world[a] actors, we might be inclined to think that no transposition has occurred, and that Marcus and Jamie appear to be present here unmediated by theatrical framing.

Although they are not fully congruent terms, presence is closely aligned with realness. Conventionally, presence, like reality, is located in opposition to representation. Realness speaks to originality and the authenticity of the thing itself. Representation in this context describes a copy or replica somehow ontologically apart from that origin. Cormac Power defines presence as simultaneity between consciousness and the object of its attention.[30] Presence speaks to what is here for apprehension in the immediate moment. Presence is predicated on spatio-temporal relations; the representation is elsewhere, not here, not now. By citing the external informational characteristics of "Long" and "Youssef" and bridging those details to the stage personae present in *Winners and Losers* – "Jamie" and "Marcus" – the play aims to establish synchronous presence in support of the reality-effect. To discriminate the sources and effects of presence in theatre, Power creates a typology featuring three broad strategies: making-present, having presence, and being present. The strategy at work in the play is consistent with "having presence," Power's auratic mode of presence, which is "constructed through the fame or reputation of the actor, playwright or artwork, along with the knowledge and expectations that spectators may carry with them into the experience."[31] Often aura is generated by prior knowledge of the subject and associated with cultural value of a venerated person or object. Celebrity encounters are marked by "having presence" in this manner. But celebrity can also be a local phenomenon, that is, celebrity can be generated in situ by providing that necessary external knowledge as you go, knitting the original to the present person in such a way that they are recognized as identical.[32] Through this correlation of evidentiary testimony, the real is transported into presence.

Extending the naturalistic tradition of closely imitating actual-world behaviour, theatre of the real takes this one step further, staging the replica and then highlighting it for our attention. In this vein, *Winners and Losers* attempts a highly naturalistic acting style, with the performers speaking to the audience directly in casual language. The script actively replicates speech disfluencies that are common to everyday conversation but which are frowned upon in more formal pronouncements – these include overlaps, interruptions, pauses, non-lexical utterances like "um" and "ah," and repaired speech where the speaker backtracks to correct an error. Jamie proposes Burt Reynolds for a topic. "Any era Burt Reynolds. *Deliverance*. Burt Reynolds. *Boogie Nights* Burt Reynolds..." Not having heard him properly, Marcus clarifies: "Any Arab Burt Reynolds?"

JAMIE: No, any *era* Burt Reynolds.
MARCUS: Oh, I thought you said any "Arab" Burt Reynolds. Which I
    guess would be Omar Sharif.[33]

At one point, thinking through what the Canadian equivalent of Mexican Zapatistas would be, Jamie slips: "Who is our Zapatista? PL – No, I'm sorry, Marcus, not the PLO but the FLQ?"[34] This half-slip of a related but incorrect name mimics the way a person might speak when he is trying to articulate a fresh spontaneous idea. The play not only includes the mistake "PL – " but brings it to our attention in Jamie's correction of his slip. In the same way that Jamie and Marcus's vacillations about how to proceed from section to section or their flexibility about the rules of the game work to imply the unscripted nature of the performance, these speech disfluencies and mishearings do the same thing on a more detailed level. The usually invisible, fixed as expected script, rehearsed to be delivered as clearly as possible is instead deliberately made visible, appearing as if it were indeed open to simple failure to communicate. However, it is merely an "as if." The usual theatrical practices that contain contingency (the fixity of the script, predictability of behaviour through rehearsal) are in full force despite these teasers that suggest that they have been nullified.

A final strategy for producing the impression of reality is the use of task-based performance, that is, actually doing the thing one is doing. For some stage activities, the world^a action is not equivalent to the world^b action. The character is sleeping but the actor is reclining with her eyes closed. The character is engaged in mortal combat; but the actor is performing choreography. In cases like this, the outward appearance may be the same but the act is materially different. But for other activities, the body is actually doing what it is doing. Among the things Jamie and Marcus actually do is play ping pong. Marcus is an excellent ping pong player; Jamie struggles. Marcus almost always wins so the narrative outcome is not in doubt, but the trajectory of the ball, the movement of the performers, and the arc of the paddles exceed the bounds of dramatic repeatability. The unpredictability of the game makes the spontaneity of the real manifest: this can't be rehearsed. The literalness of task-based performance and the contingent behaviour of objects like the ping pong ball invoke another of Power's strategies of presence: being present, the literal mode of presence.[35] "Art [in the literal mode] is not enshrined in some aesthetic universe that we may magically enter by suspending our interest in the empirical world, but is a very real and tangible part *of* our world; art is an 'event' taking place in space and time, between observers and objects/performers."[36] The effect of being present is connection to the audience, which is also concurrently present. Instead of bridging Marcus^a to Marcus^b, for example, reality-effects composed by this strategy bridge the ambivalently present or real Marcus and his environs to the always real audience and its environs.

Perhaps the most influential reality-effect arises from the confluence of all these stratagems. Over and above the sense of a nonfictional encounter momentarily created by these specific practices, they also

2.1 (l–r): James Long ("Jamie") and Marcus Youssef ("Marcus") play the winners and losers game. Photo courtesy of Neworld Theatre.

operate cumulatively to cast a reality aura over the remainder of the performance, producing a wholesale reframing of objects and behaviours that might ordinarily have been read as fictional under other circumstances, but now project a sense of being really real.

The experiential corollary of introducing these persistently real elements and encouraging the audience to refuse the usual fictionalizing transposition is that, rather than engender the certainty of truth, the performance is now permeated by the epistemological doubt inherent in nonfiction. Curiosity regarding the real truth about what we are being told extends beyond the reported details in the performance and affects the ontology of the event itself. The safety of fiction is no longer limited merely to the safety of knowing what is and is not true as information but also encompasses the safety of knowing that these words and actions don't "count." When the frame becomes imperceptible to the point of being irrelevant, the audience cannot be certain of its assessment of the event as a performance. Perhaps it is really happening. Without the safety net of the theatrical frame, nonfictional doubt applies not only to the contents of the box, but also to the existence of the box itself.

More than simply testifying to the real antecedents of the performers, the reality markers catalogued above also undermine that reality by raising it to our view. This is precisely how the real operates in *Winners and Losers*. Reality-markers are generated purposefully through the persistent and varied strategies outlined above, not in support of asserting a concrete truth but rather to mobilize this indecidability. Lehmann explains further that

> [t]his self-referentiality allows us to contemplate the value, the inner necessity and the significance of the extra-aesthetic *in* the aesthetic and thus the displacement of the concept of the latter. The aesthetic cannot be understood through a determination of content ... but solely – as the theatre of the real shows – by "treading the borderline," by permanently switching, not between form and content, but between "real" contiguity (connection with reality) and "staged" construct.[37]

As Peter Boenisch notes with regard to these reflexive dramaturgies, the "situation of spectating is thus turned from the traditional aesthetic attitude of 'reception' into an act of encounter."[38] Shifting from the "what" to the "how," audience attention becomes reflexive and so we are more concerned with the construction of realities (and fictions) than with the real things themselves.

Garde and Mumford apply their concept of "productive insecurity" to describe the disruptive ontological oscillation associated with work that purports to stage the real. They identify specific politically productive outcomes of this insecurity: "[a] distinguishing feature of the postdramatic productions under discussion is the way they introduce the *volatile* and *constructed* nature of the authentic. It is our contention that such destabilisations of the authentic can be used to unfix stable and possibly oppressive perceptions of strangers and the unfamiliar."[39] Beyond the specific effect of opening up the liminal spaces of intercultural encounter with the autobiographical words of strangers, the verbatim works that Garde and Mumford consider in their selected examples also trigger acute indecidability as the audience is challenged to consider how this real testimony arrives on the stage. As much as the audience is brought to new knowledge of strangers, these productions also introduce doubt about the process of that knowing. The principal outcome of productive uncertainty for the purposes of this argument lies in the unfixing of previously stable perceptions. As Erika Fischer-Lichte notes about reality in performance, "transferring the spectator into a state of liminality ... not only destabilizes the order of perception but, more importantly, the self ... By letting such frames collide, by collapsing the dichotomy, [perceptively multistable] performances transferred the spectator between all fixed rules, norms and orders."[40] The seismic shift created in the collision of frames between the ostensibly real and its construction alters not only my specific perception of the staged fable but also my perception of the rupture itself, and by so doing, calls me to radically reassess my position in this disorienting looped landscape. Uncertainty is in itself productive and uncertainty is the thing being produced. The cogitations of doubt and the inevitable subsequent reassessment of previously cherished assumptions pave the way, not for knowing, but for questioning.

Even though the social situation of the postdramatic event rises to prominence through audience attention to the ontological precariousness and ambivalence of the theatrical frame, still "the *aesthetic* process of the theatre cannot be separated from its extra-aesthetic materiality in the same manner as one can distinguish the intentional aesthetic object, the ideatum of a literary text from the materiality of paper and ink."[41] For *Winners and Losers*, the formally-manifested aesthetic processes of audience uncertainty are not merely a free-floating experience or gimmick; they are tied to the text. Insecurity is generated structurally in the destabilization of the performance event as drama but it also manifests thematically. Far from completely dismissing the dramatic, the question of how we value safety and risk, security and insecurity, comprises, for game-players Jamie and Marcus, the central criterion for determining who is winning and who is losing.

As plainly marked by its title, at the heart of *Winners and Losers* is the controlling trope of the contest. Every exchange between Jamie and Marcus requires a determination: winner or loser. The agonistic battle for either this or that is enabled by the poststructuralist landscape. Once the real renounces (or is forced to abdicate) its priority then all the different worlds are simply different manifestations of different kinds of citations. This lack of a dominant authorizing real is freeing, allowing dynamic creation of fluid free-floating multivalent selves and worlds, but it is also chaotic in that liberation. Examining different models of postdramatic characterization, Tomlin flags this as a point of concern. Even as existing ideologies are swept away, exposed as mere representations of reality, she foresees the potential for new and equally dangerous kinds of authority to emerge.

> By disabling the authority of an objective real, a new kind of authority inevitably emerges that is now relative and subjective, as each individual becomes, in potential, the Author-God of their own narrative, resulting in the contestation of micro-narratives described by Lyotard whereby "to speak is to fight, in the sense of playing." The playing field, however [...] is not a level one, and there are losers as well as winners in the absence of objective authority.[42]

This depiction of character creation as "fighting that is playing" aptly describes what is happening in the agonistic competition that is *Winners and Losers*. Not only do Long and Youssef embrace the performative power of autobiography to create their own self-characters of Jamie and Marcus, they also attempt to corral this same performative power to author the other. In the absence of the authority of the real, characters fill that void with their own dominant representations. Tomlin (following Nietzsche) dubs them "artist-tyrants." Writing elsewhere about this same phenomenon in connection with metatheatrical works featuring characters who usurp the power of the playwright to become biographical world-makers, I took inspiration for a correlative term – "aspiring divinities" – from Anton Piatigorsky's play *Eternal Hydra* where the ostentatiously self-named novelist Gordias Carbuncle proclaims:

> God likes to own things. The very first and best of things ... And, as the Gospel of John attests, words are God's possessions. His proclamations and servants. His very life ... Words are His products above all others. They are flexible and violent and beautiful. The most useful things of all. And more fun than a bar of soap for the truly ambitious collector ... We are jealous creatures, aspiring divinities.[43]

These aspiring divinities, characters who usurp the godlike power of creating realities in nested or worlds-within-worlds or plays-within-plays, seem harmless enough in dramatic works where the "danger" is limited to fictional worlds. The ontologically ambiguous landscape of postdramatic autobiographical performance raises the temperature of the game, which may no longer be only a game. Artist-tyrants or aspiring divinities, Marcus and Jamie try to hurt each other with words as each tries to biographize the other as a loser, and himself by exclusion as the last one standing as a winner. When asked in the final endgame of the play to judge the other as either a winner or a loser, both men invoke autobiographical details to paint a portrait of their opponent. Understanding of who Marcus is is based on how Jamie describes his life and vice versa. Both portraits are framed as the candid reports of a friend but the insights are corrosive and it is a race to the bottom. But even in the initial rounds of the game, when the stakes are lower, the rules of the game compel forcible performative identity-creation of one on the other. For each person, place, or thing nominated for assessment as winner or loser, the two players must take opposing views. If Jamie says "winner," Marcus must say "loser." The rationalizations in support of their imposed view accumulate to create the image of "that kind of person." What I am suggesting here is that not only do they win "points" for winning the round, as designated by the "ding" of the bell, they also gain stature by adopting more popular or more socially acceptable views, thereby performing "winner," and forcing the other person into supporting unpalatable causes or promoting untenable views, performing "loser." For example, when Jamie claims Canada is a winner, Marcus perforce makes the case for Canada as a loser. He makes the perhaps too facile analogy between Mexican Zapatistas and First Nations people in Canada. Jamie pounces:

> JAMIE: So you are comparing a localized uprising in southern Mexico to an entire nation – no sorry, multiple nations – across an entire country. Come on.
> MARCUS: I think the basic colonial dynamic is exactly the same.
> JAMIE: This is Marcus wrapping his Noam Chomsky (circa 1996) blanket around every indigenous population in the world.
> MARCUS: Incarceration rates in Canada, First Nations people versus white people, these are shocking.
> JAMIE: What are they in Mexico?
> MARCUS: I don't know. I'm sure they're terrible.
> JAMIE: Exactly. You have no idea.[44]

Given these stakes, we can ask what it means to be a winner or a loser. "Jamie" and "Marcus" play the game with passion and conviction. Frequently, however, their assessment of something as a winner or a loser seems wildly counterintuitive or arbitrary, especially when the object under consideration doesn't seem to invite or warrant this kind of judgment. What are Jamie and Marcus's criteria? Taking some representative examples from the dozens of topics offered in the show, some core values emerge. Evaluation of winners is strongly inflected by a conception of human nature characterized by self-sufficiency, self-determination, and an ability to impact others or the world reminiscent of the Enlightenment liberalism of John Locke.[45] It is interesting to note what is not on Jamie and Marcus's list: value is not given to what is ethical, what is beautiful, what is pleasurable, what is healthy, or what is spiritually satisfying. Microwave ovens are declared winners because they are efficient, getting the job done, which is defined narrowly by the two debaters as "heating coffee." Marcus tries to suggest that the microwave is a loser because it is dangerous, and also because it only does one thing. But it is ultimately declared a winner because it does this one thing very well. Likewise, the Occupy movement is a loser because it has been ineffectual. Jamie justifies his assessment thus: "I know you cannot name me five things that are still happening because of the Occupy movement."[46] Physicist Stephen Hawking stymies the pair for a minute. "That's difficult." "It's a big challenge."[47] On the one hand, he is a winner because of his global intellectual impact. This is contrasted with the ability to "go to the bathroom by yourself." These two positions come into collision as a result of the implied foundational value system being deployed. Thriving on these conflicts, the game itself is inherently adversarial. As the show progresses, our two contestants abandon any effort to justify their evaluations:

JAMIE: Stephen Harper
MARCUS: Loser. The European Union.
JAMIE: Winner. Mick Jagger.
MARCUS: Winner. Iceland.
JAMIE: Iceland's a winner. Barack Obama.
MARCUS: Loser. Tar sands.
JAMIE: Winner. Lululemon.
MARCUS: Loser. Pine beetle.
JAMIE: Winner. Liquid Paper.
MARCUS: Loser.[48]

Representing the audience's bewilderment at some of these rulings, Marcus says, "but the logic that says – Pam Anderson is a winner and Sylvia Plath a loser – I do find that a little elusive." Jamie replies, "The big difference is that Pam Anderson is currently living in a beach house in Malibu and Sylvia Plath stuck her head in an oven."[49] And that is *Winners and Losers*'s hard outlook of Enlightenment liberalism in a nutshell. The aggressive certainty with which judgment is dispensed is a source of amazed amusement for the audience but it also makes us deeply uncomfortable. Jamie and Marcus are behaving like juvenile jerks; their judgments are too quick, too casual, mixing the trivial with the important, and turning issues deserving of our solemn consideration into one-liners. By way of an aside, it should be noted that the attitude of Jamie and Marcus here is not synonymous with that of Long and Youssef. Citron describes the two as exemplified by the recent work produced by their respective companies – Theatre Replacement and Neworld Theatre – as "left-leaning, sociopolitical provocateurs."[50] Both are very well-known actors and writers, especially within the Vancouver arts community. And so within that context, these personae will be perhaps read as ironic. Yet, even those who are acquainted with the performers and their politics may still find themselves sometimes stymied by their declarations. Citron herself notes the unsettled audience perspective in her review: "Do they really believe in what they are saying, or does one take the opposing view just to play devil's advocate?" However, assuredly, outside of their hometown context, any confidence in a deliberately contrarian stance inevitably fades.

This same logic of the economics of happiness and success is then applied to Jamie and Marcus as they offer themselves as candidates to be honestly assessed by the other as either a winner or a loser. And, as the show's promotional material notes, "because one of these men is the product of economic privilege, and the other not, the competition very quickly begins to cost."[51] Even in this age of too much information, the question of economic privilege is perhaps one of the last taboo subjects in contemporary society. People share the most embarrassing personal details, but are reluctant to admit specifically how much money they earn, how much their house is worth, how family money has affected their lives, and how much they might expect to inherit someday. Jamie and Marcus casually take on the contest of who is the better masturbator, discussing their sexual proclivities and fetishes with squirm-inducing candour, but it is the toxic accusations of the prospects of their differing financial situations that make us feel as if they have finally gone too far. Reviewer J. Kelly Nestruck claims in the opening sentence of his year-in-review article that it is difficult to shock a theatre critic and yet he reported that "this theatregoer's jaw did literally drop" during *Winners and Losers* when Jamie reveals his annual income and Marcus provides details of his inheritance.[52]

Nestruck's response demonstrates that what used to be called "class" has gone underground. Class is about one's genealogical socio-financial birthright and it is through stories about their fathers that the class divisions between the two men emerge. Marcus's story about the mythology of his father follows his father's immigration to the US on a foreign exchange scholarship, which brought him from Egypt to do his PhD in economics at Berkeley. From there, he became a fast-rising executive at the Royal Bank of Canada. He "[b]ought into a pension management company in the 1990s right when I bet a lot of people in this room started believing all the propaganda about mutual funds"[53] and as a result these smart, well-timed financial decisions provided significant opportunities and security for himself and his family. Marcus admits that his current lifestyle is cushioned by monetary gifts from his father and that he lives with the promise of a large inheritance someday. Jamie's father's story also has a mythic quality: a hardworking popular cop from Ottawa, he is playing football with his buddies, a "bunch of lawyers, doctors, big government guys," and has just received a pass when he suffers a heart attack. He "takes a knee" in the middle of the football field, and pounding his heart with his fist, he walks it off. He goes with his chums to the pub, has a pint of beer, and then finally drives himself to the hospital. As Jamie concludes, the man's heart stopped "[b]ut he never fell down. Never fell down. Sure, he took a couple of knees but he never fell down. So in terms of that, he's a total winner ... Because he survived. Somehow he survived."[54] The legacy of their fathers reaches into the present, creating an unmentionable class division where Marcus is protected by a financial safety net and Jamie is basically on his own to be pulled along exclusively by his own resources.

A significant moment occurs when the dialogic exchange of the pair is disrupted. At the point mentioned earlier when Jamie, having lost his composure, exits the theatre, Marcus is left alone. Initially he seems to be at a loss as to what to do or say next, now that his sparring partner is gone. "The game is a lot less dynamic with me up here by myself."[55] Then, to fill time, he tells us a story: "The house next door to our house – on upper Napier Street – it's *that* house in the neighbourhood ... The house is more or less falling over. 'Total eyesore.' ... It's got actual holes in the outer walls ... It's basically a de facto rooming house. I have this reoccurring fantasy about this house."[56] In his fantasy, one of the "rough guys" who lives there breaks into Marcus's house and grabs his eight-year-old son. Marcus tries to talk the man into releasing the boy. When the intruder lets the boy go, Marcus beats him violently with a baseball bat that he has been holding behind his back. Marcus concludes the story by saying, "[b]ut the guys next door aren't scary at all. They're super poor, and their bodies are bent and haggard. They collect cans and bottles for a living. When I see them outside, on the sidewalk, they immediately look down. They can't bring themselves to speak to me. One look at somebody like me, and they submit."[57] Although from a dramaturgical perspective, this extended isolated monologue is an oddity, it actually fits nicely into the emerging cluster of thematic concerns in *Winners and Losers*. Inside the frame of the fantasy, fatherly protection is immediate and physical, even excessive, as compared with the deferred, amorphous financial security of the future. In his epilogue to the fantasy, Marcus clearly recognizes that a man like that is no threat at all. The advantage he has over the rooming house men is not only one of stronger physique, but one of social status. According to the value system of the *Winners and Losers* game, the intruder that Marcus imagines lives at the very bottom of the hierarchy. Having returned partway through the story, Jamie's immediate comment at the end is "[b]ecause they're losers."[58] Winners are safe in the world. Recast from a threat to the safety of Marcus's son to himself being not safe, the intruder represents what it means to be "not safe," to be a loser. He is what Jamie and Marcus fear they might become.

The last fifteen minutes of the performance are riveting but hard to watch as Marcus and Jamie agree to put themselves up for assessment as a winner or a loser. Marcus begins by listing all the ways in which Jamie is a winner: "[s]mart, funny. A great storyteller ..."[59] But then he identifies the reason that makes Jamie indeed a loser: "your Achilles heel, your tragic flaw, what ultimately makes you a loser compared to me ... is that you always have to win. You have to win because to lose might make you feel human. Might make you feel something, anything. And as far as I can tell that's not really your thing. Human feeling."[60] Being a loser, then, according to Marcus's judgment, pertains to staying aloof, to playing games too much or too well to actually engage with the world outside the game, to engage with something real. In the next skirmish, Marcus connects this idea directly to Jamie's theatre work. Marcus accuses him of overworking in his striving for financial security, of letting his father die alone, and of neglecting his kids, letting other people raise Nora and Leo while Jamie hides in his work.

"You're always working ... We'll be away for three weeks touring and then the very next night I will see you at some bad show or some dumb work party that there's no reason to be at. Your kids are little, Jamie. This is when they need you. But I know why you're not with them. It's because spending time with your children, looking after your family – that scares the shit out of you. Of course it does. Because it means you have to be patient, you have to show compassion, you have to just be there, over and over again. It's called intimacy.[61] To keep himself safe – economically but also emotionally – according to the logic of sufficiency and self-determination of the winners and losers' game, Jamie achieves this goal by playing the theatre game.

Jamie insists that he is a winner in economic terms as defined within the fictional frame of performance. Marcus counters that by contrast Jamie is in fact a loser because by working too much and neglecting his family, he is hiding from his obligations, from his real life. Too much playing, too much staying within the safe performance frame equals losing. It is not real winning. What counts is what is happening outside the frame. Jamie is a loser because he will not step outside the frame, will not step outside the rehearsed safety of the theatre and embrace the real unpredictable risk of his family. *Winners and Losers* thus conflates the two kinds of being not safe and passes opposing judgments on these outcomes. Inside the frame, economic safety is winning; but for the audience subject to the social moment in which we read the actions of the play as (possibly) real, performative safety is losing.

Jamie's assessment of Marcus comes to the same conclusion. Jamie argues that because Marcus has already "won," because there are no risks for him, he is, in fact, a loser.

> You are such a good victim ... But it's such a bad act because, in my humble estimation, you've never been the victim of anything – real ... You've already placed yourself above it and that is frustrating for people who have experienced poverty and its many, many byproducts. People who have actually lost things ... Marcus, you are an imposter. (*to the audience*) And maybe this is what makes him so sad, that he can't share a huge part of his reality.[62]

The stinger is when Jamie calls Marcus a tourist. "I'm not going to punch you. Because you don't punch a tourist. Because tourists talk and talk and talk. They have absolutely no idea what they're saying, but they keep on talking. You don't punch them for it. No. You say, 'Stay. Spend your money. Buy T-shirts.' And then you wait for them to leave and you forget about them."[63] The implication is that Marcus is not participating in a way that matters; he is safe because he is only playing. He is protected by money as a kind of theatrical frame rendering everything inside the frame as not really real. Like Jamie, the equation for Marcus is the same. In the experiential reversal of the logic of the play's dialogue, winning then is not being safe. Both Jamie and Marcus in their attacks implicitly agree that winning is not-playing; winning is doing something for real. By communicating on parallel tracks, *Winners and Losers* invites a critique of the original terms of what makes a winner.

The play ends when either Jamie or Marcus decide that they have had enough. "Who's attacking?" "What?" "Who's attacking?" (*Marcus and Jamie stare at each other.*) "That's it." "That's it?" "We're done." "We're done."[64] Just on the brink of losing the remaining veneer of civility, one of them gestures to the stage manager and asks him to end it. With this abrupt conclusion, and Jamie's and Marcus's solemn-faced curtain call, the play offers us no solace. Ontological insecurity at the heart of reality-based theatre creates paralysis. We can neither discount *Winners and Losers* as merely fiction, as merely a thematic analogy of a fictional cosmos to our own world, nor can we act as if it is real because this is foolish; we are quite rightly chagrined at our concern. And so we are stuck. And Jamie and Marcus are also stuck. The effect is not tragic. The philosophical logic at work is not the impossible choice of Hegelian tragedy, trapping our protagonists between two irreconcilable poles, but it is something similar. We can discard our belief that the play format is real, abandoning our perception that it is a really real spontaneous unmediated encounter. (Certainly the publication of the play script supports this reassessment.) But we continue to believe that Jamie and Marcus are real. We can't discard them. Within this ontological paralysis, we are still moved. The affective lessons of productive insecurity teach us that we need to abandon core assumptions of the winners and losers game, not to be so certain in our conclusions or even in our ability to assert conclusions at all. The hyper-confident snap judgments of Jamie and Marcus cannot be sustained. The extradramatic social moment of the play turns it back on us, as our experience of ontological displacement runs counter to the value system espoused by the fictional world. Jamie and Marcus are playing the game wrong. This becomes profoundly and painfully clear in the audience experience of productive insecurity arising out of theatre of the real's generic strategies. At odds with its own protagonists, the play tells us that we ought not to play their game. We need to change our attitude and eschew judgment. When thinking about having an impact on the world either through parenting (Jamie) or through public service (Marcus) or through the creation of theatre (both), we need to recognize that these are projects that combine high stakes and deep personal investment with unpredictable and unquantifiable long-term future dividends. In the space of a snap judgment, there is no way to really know if a lifetime's work made any difference at all. Long and Youssef's performance not only calls into question how we form judgments about what makes a winner or a loser but how we play the game (or choose not to play at all).

In this way, *Winners and Losers* gestures towards the extended effect of theatre of the real in general. Productive insecurity arising out of the essential undecidability of reality-based performance thus has the potential to generate a more hesitant, thoughtful, open, inquisitive attitude in the audience, stimulating the "potential to produce reflective citizens who cannot be conscripted into an unquestioning"[65] judgment. Judgment is to be remitted in the pursuit of the security of winning, but also in the security of other neoliberal values, like growth, innovation, autonomy, individualism, or ideals of beauty. Postdramatic performances that create these ruptures call us to find new strategies for navigating the mediated and the ontologically uncertain. We are invited to embrace doubt as a moral position. Moreover, humility and caution must be exercised when every outcome is beyond our limited capacity for knowing, when the majority of the problems we face in the posthuman era – such as global income inequality or climate change – are so complex and multifaceted that we cannot compass the whole. We cannot fully understand the problem, let alone imagine a solution. It is precisely this experience of profound "ungraspability"[66] itself that structures the productive outcomes of insecurity. Lehmann recognizes the latent ethical opportunity in this discomfort.

> Instead of the deceptively comforting duality of here and there, inside and outside, [postdramatic theatre] can move the *mutual implication of actors and spectators in the theatrical production of images* into the centre and thus make visible the broken thread between personal experience and perception. Such an experience would be not only aesthetic but therein at the same time ethico-political.[67]

Being cast into uncertainty, compelled to set aside our confident know-ing, we are given an opportunity to reassess the ethical landscape. As I wrote in the foreword to the published script, we are without a reliable compass, and so "[w]inner or loser becomes impossible to declare. We might have no choice but to be scared and to live with the uncertainty."[68]

3 Real People Part 2: Insecurity and Ethical Failure in the Encounter with Strangers – *100% Vancouver*, *RARE*, and *Polyglotte*

Near the end of *RARE*, the cast responds to the prompt "You know a word I hate?" with a litany of words they have heard others use to name them: "Mongoloid idiot. Deformed. Special Ed. Handicapped ... Freak. Alien. Strange. Disabled."[1] By way of conclusion, one of the speakers, Andreas,[2] confronts the audience with another freighted derogatory word: "You think I'm retarded? Please look at yourself."[3] The effect of this direct challenge is twofold. First, it positions the audience, interpellated as "You," as distinct from the performers, and secondarily it imposes (rightly or wrongly) on this now-estranged and homogenously projected "You" a particular set of values and perceptions, expressed by what we "think." This encounter, variously configured, between "I" and "You" is a central feature of autobiographical work as the performer attempts to communicate an intimate sense of what it means to be this particular unique self to a second-person assemblage of curious witnesses.

Rooted in the values of second-wave feminism, autobiographical performance acts on the credo that the personal is indeed political, claiming space in the public sphere for previously undervalued and neglected self-stories. It is no coincidence then that autobiographical performance was from the outset, and continues to be, primarily the domain of voices from the margins, with the majority of work being produced by women, gay, lesbian, or transgender individuals, people who live with disabilities, and performers from racialized cultures. The simple act of bringing the quotidian into view through autobiography stakes a claim to visibility and awareness, saying, "I am here. This is my life." Through a series of bodily present, first-person narratives, autobiographical performers articulate their hopes and dreams, what makes them angry and what makes them fearful. They offer a rainbow of answers to the question: Who am I? By doing so, they tap into the political potential latent in performative storytelling. As I have argued elsewhere, following Deirdre Heddon (*Autobiography and Performance*), the embodied activity of autobiographical performance can have profound real-world effects as the retelling of self-stories regenerates those experiences in the subject-body where they can be reshaped and transformed. Autobiographical performers thus do not simply report on past memories but instead leverage the power of performative creation to bring into being new selves and imagine new futures.[4] Focus on the transformative impact of the journey on the character-performer herself has been a dominant strand in recent studies of both literary and theatrical autobiographical works.[5]

This autobiographical activity does not happen in isolation however. For scholars of autobiographical performance, it behooves us to consider the nature of this bivalent interaction between the "I" performer and the "you" audience. Shifting focus from the positive political potential granted to the self-storying autobiographical subject to examine that of the audience that bears witness to this generative act invites us to ask: What real-world benefits might inhere to the autobiographical audience? What challenges manifest for this audience in effecting the ethical uptake of autobiographical stories? The potential pitfalls latent in the reception of autobiographical performance are many. As Heddon reiterates, the revelation of "personal narratives might bring hidden, denied or marginalised experiences into the spotlight ... This is just some of the work that autobiographical performance might do."[6] The attention-pulling element here is the repeated word "might." Transmission is fragile and inherently unstable, its power held as contingent. Tempering Heddon's hopeful belief in the transformative promise of autobiographical performance is her awareness that in reception these stories are subject to the "dangers that include problematic essentializing gestures; the construction of limiting identities; the reiteration of normative narratives, the erasure of 'difference' and issues of structural inequality, ownership, appropriation and exploitation."[7] Bound up in the autobiographical performative statement, "I am here. This is my life." is the risk of too easily extending the presentation of a single marginalized experience into a generic understanding of all similar persons. "I am X. I am like this." leads to the false and unconscionably simplistic conclusion "All X are like this." The potential for this essentializing interpretation is unfortunately heightened in autobiographical performances that feature a collective rather than an individual, where the kaleidoscopic presentation of individual difference within the group is in competition with the essentializing tendency to perpetuate the sameness of the group as a group.

The same ontological bridge that carries theatrical impressions from the performed self back to its actual-world doppelganger activates another pitfall as performative subjects are drawn to the stage from the real world in the first place. Autobiographical performance work, which employs real people portraying themselves, presents a strong reality-effect stemming from the close association of the actual real-world self and the constructed character self. This reality-effect is further augmented when, as in the three productions considered here – *100% Vancouver* (Vancouver 2011), *RARE* (Toronto 2013, Kingston 2014), and *Polyglotte* (Montreal 2015) – the work taps into an amateur community-engaged performance context. Whereas Long and Youssef in *Winners and Losers* are professional theatre-makers who consciously employ sophisticated acting techniques to deliver the performance of a "score" that generates an affect of realness, the approach to the real taken by these productions is to bring non-performers to the stage. Since these performers often exhibit fewer traditionally recognized performance skills than professionally trained actors, they seem even more actually like themselves than a mimetic representation of themselves, no matter how adept. Lacking formal training as actors, the raw presence of these real people allows them to simply "be." Another distinction between *Winners and Losers* and these three productions is that while the autobiographical connection to the real enacted by Long and Youssef is individual and particular, exploring the singular lives of "Jamie"/Long and "Marcus"/Youssef, the autobiographical identities prioritized in these other productions is collective. *100% Vancouver* presents one hundred demographically representative Vancouverites. *RARE* explores the lives of young people living with Down syndrome. *Polyglotte* exhibits recent immigrants to Canada engaged in taking their citizenship test. For each of these productions, the one-to-one correspondence of these assemblages of non-actors to their collective identity position is their primary raison d'être.

Reality theatre strategies that make use of actual-world elements like non-actors are often used with the overt political intent of augmenting the audience's understanding of contemporary individuals and groups. The idea is that by putting ordinary people on the stage, the work can productively "generate (and then, in some cases, destabilize) an impression of close contact with social reality and 'real' people."[8] That said, a recurrent criticism raised with regard to this kind of community-engaged work that brings paying audiences into autobiographical encounters with strangers is that this fabricated meeting that has been specially marketed to sheltered elites is an inferior substitute for authentic, personal, engaged experience. The ethical instability of the situation combined with the risks of failed transmission invite the question, "Why do we watch?" Is it to gain insight into someone else's life? Is it plausible to suggest that bearing witness to another's story might lead to openness and acceptance of difference through exposure? Yet, problematically, performance is always enmeshed in the power imbalance of ostention and the gaze. At best, there is an educational profit in the second-hand exposure to another life; at worst, it is exploitative, offering a "weird" essentialized Other for vicarious, touristic consumption. Given the long, vexed history of performances of people with disabilities in freak shows and other venues that objectify and dehumanize their experiences, this risk is profoundly significant.[9] It is also important to remember, however, that this is the risk of all autobiographical performance. As recent local examples of autobiographical performance largely by non-actors, the three productions profiled here provide good case studies for the general consideration of how all autobiographical performance is entangled in ethical questions about how the encounter with actuality in the theatre is shaped and to what end. As witnesses to autobiographical intimacy, we are compelled not to shy away from Andreas's challenge and to look into the mirror of the performative encounter and to consider candidly how we arrived here. We are challenged to ask how we too might be changed by the consumption of autobiography. Who am I in my audience role? Why does Andreas exhort me to interrogate how I am "retarded"? Why does he invoke this powerfully oppressive word and how does he expect me to answer?

As Nicholas Ridout asserts, "When the promise of a direct face-to-face encounter between two human beings is made within the theatrical set-up, either the act of delivery or the act of collection is always compromised."[10] It is this feature of compromised meeting that is the primary focus of this analysis. Situated in the context of intercultural encounter, these plays illuminate general features of postdramatic autobiographical performance. The "old school" intercultural performance patterns invoked by *RARE*, *Polyglotte*, and with variations in *100% Vancouver*, serve to establish oppositional relationships between the source culture of the performers and the target culture of the audience. Framing auto-biographical performance as intercultural encounter makes the ethical imperative clear. As Helen Gilbert and Jacqueline Lo note, the challenge is "to avoid essentialist constructions of race and gender [and, I would add, disability] while still accounting for the irreducible specificity of certain bodies and body behaviours."[11]

In her book *Strange Encounters*, Sara Ahmed articulates some of the distinctive features of intercultural encounter. To begin, it is impor-tant to note that in terms of her title a stranger is not simply anybody whom we do not know. "Rather [the stranger] is a figure that is pain-fully familiar in that very strange(r)ness."[12] That is, some strangers are stranger than others. The stranger is a person in my world – known and unknown – who is, however, excluded for some reason. But this exclusion does not arise from an innocent ignorance, rather it is active, an attentive policing of the boundaries of my community to divide "us" from "them." Stranger fetishism can only be avoided by examining the social relationships that are concealed by this fetishism.[13] A key fea-ture of this social relationship is that the encounter with the stranger is marked by an irreconcilable tension between what we think we know and what we cannot know, what is shared and what is necessarily hid-den, between fixity and the impossibility of fixity. Given this unstable oppositional duality of certainty and uncertainty, how might encounter engender an ethical relationship? "What are the conditions of possi-bility for us meeting here and now?"[14] In partial answer, Ahmed first invites consideration of proximity as a key component of the encounter:

> An ethical communication is about a certain way of holding proximity and distance together: one gets close enough to others to be touched by that which cannot simply be got across. In such an encounter 'one' does not stay in place, or one does not stay safely at a distance [...] It is through getting closer, rather than remaining at a distance, that the impossibility of pure proximity can be put to work, or made to work.[15]

Holding proximity and distance in balance, the potential exists for becoming closer, permeating existing boundaries and communities, while at the same time resisting the intention to see the stranger as eas-ily assimilable, and respecting an inherent and inaccessible foreignness.

After proximity, a second feature of ethical encounter is particular-ity. Particularity, here, does not require a descriptive catalogue of per-sonal characteristics – a project that risks turning specific "this-ness" of one's body or speech into a generalized portrait. This is the error that Heddon cautions against. Instead, particularity for Ahmed speaks to the modes of encounter through which others are faced. "Differentiation ... happens at the level of the encounter, rather than 'in' the body of an other with whom I am presented."[16] From this perspective, attention is directed at the social processes that structure that difference and the separation arising from that difference, rather than on the difference itself as distinct and autonomous. The phrase that Ahmed uses to describe this active contemplation of interrelation is "the sociality of the 'with.'"[17] What does it mean to be "with"? To look but also to be seen. To look but also to fail to see. Failure of the "with" is also necessarily implicit in the ethical encounter. "There is something that remains a secret ... my missing of it, my failure to face up to it, is also an encounter with it, and a responsibility for it ... How to get closer, to take responsibility, and yet to take up the impossibility of that very gesture, at one and the same time?"[18]

In the pages that follow, I will take up the three aforementioned productions – *100% Vancouver*, *RARE*, and *Polyglotte* – as case studies of intercultural encounter with collective autobiographical strangers. The analysis will use Sara Ahmed's two core characteristics of proximity and particularity that describe the hybrid nature of the stranger to examine the dramaturgical and scenographic strategies invoked by these productions to generate and destabilize an impression of authentic connection between the audience and the performers. The combined affect of ontological insecurity (residing in uncertainty about the fictional or actual status of performed others) with epistemological insecurity (concerning what can be known about those others) becomes productive, revealing the structures of that impossible encounter with reality, exposing the framework. The encounter with a stranger, then, does not actually facilitate contact, authentically illuminating what it means to be another, but it does confront the means of encounter, and is therefore productive in its self-reflexive disruption.

Central to the way that the three productions discussed here frame the experience of engaged encounter is the claim that the performers featured are real, more real somehow than professionally trained actors. The first question to be considered then is in what ways do the performers in these plays manifest their realness? Or if absolute realness is beyond our ken, then at least a strong impression of their "real-ish-ness."[19] I think the word "their" foregrounds an essential premise about the real on stage. Theatre is made of real stuff. It is the only art form where real things pretend to be other nearly identical real things. Bodies are transformed by theatricality to become other bodies. But the real remains in the background like a heat signature radiating visible/invisible in the infrared from the embodied and ventriloquized fictional character. In phenomenological terms, the theatricalizing *epochē* of the audience belief stance brackets out the real, allowing the *noema* of the fiction to be given to consciousness. Absent but co-present, the real remains. So it isn't that some theatre has realness and some doesn't. The realness is there. The realness is inherent. The question is: "How does it manifest?" "How does it escape phenomenological bracketing in performance?" Distinct from metatheatrical techniques or from the momentary "upsurges of the real" described by Bert States whereby the usually obscured real-world materiality of staged people and objects bubbles up to the surface,[20] these works attempt to activate a sustained encounter with the real. Postdramatic work in this mode makes a bid to circumvent theatricality, to escape the gravitational pull of mimesis, and allow performers to be perceived in an extended fashion as primarily actual rather than primarily fictional.

What are postdramatic non-actors doing (or not doing)? In a seminal essay concerned with this exact question, Michael Kirby proposes five stations along a spectrum from non-acting to acting: Non-Matrixed Performance, Symbolized Matrix, Received Acting, Simple Acting, and Complex Acting.[21] The first three steps in this model are defined in reference to audience belief stance in combination with the theatricalizing frame or what Kirby calls "the matrix." Non-Matrixed Performing involves behaviour that occurs within the event-context of a performance and remains rooted in the real world, like the movement of stagehands. Only liminally present within the play, they do things without entering into the matrixed perceptual space of a fictional world. They are non-representational. The next two steps – Symbolized Matrix and Received Acting – involve no action on the part of the performer, but surrounding conditions encourage the audience to impose a fictional representation. In the first case – Symbolized Matrix – props or costume pieces present cues for the activation of the matrix. In the second case – Received Acting – representational perception is triggered by a more developed fictional context. Stage extras – like the plebeian crowd or that old chestnut of scenic spear carriers – become enmeshed in the fictional scene and fall into this subsequent category. In both situations, the audience imposes a matrixed view on a predominantly passive performer. Then Kirby changes gears, shifting responsibility for acting/not-acting from the audience to the actor. Simple Acting and Complex Acting attribute intention to the actor. As Kirby writes, "Acting means to feign, to simulate, to represent, to impersonate ... not all performing is acting ... Acting can be said to exist in the smallest and simplest action that involves pretense."[22] Willmar Sauter briskly disputes this theory of Kirby's, returning the onus for acting to the interpretive perception of the audience and setting aside any concern with the internal processes of the actor. Examining various ways in which costumes signify on the stage and in everyday life, Sauter proposes that "to embody a Jew [for example] on stage is not a matter of pretence, but a matter of signification."[23] Signification, however, is dependent on an arbitrary agreement with the receiver who reads that sign. "Only through the context of the event will [the beholder] be able to discern the kind of communication that the agent presents."[24] So just as various contextual factors activate and shape the perception of representation, likewise other contextual factors may work to deny representation, preventing the audience from imposing a matrixed view on the performers.

Autobiographical works that seek engaged encounter, such as the three considered here, invoke a variety of strategies to resist the frame, presenting the performers as "ordinary" people tasked with simply being, and inviting audiences to align them most closely with the first category of Non-Matrixed Performing. Although the participants may be rehearsed in certain routines, they do not feign. They do not attempt to represent another. Henri Schoenmakers claims that the move to postdramatic acting witnessed over the last two decades where actors do not play characters but instead present themselves as themselves "is the biggest change in Western theatre since its invention."[25] The characteristic of imitation once thought to be essential to the definition of theatre has been set aside. Reluctance to create a fictive cosmos, one of the key markers of postdrama, manifests in acting as "the actor of postdramatic theatre is often no longer the actor of a role but a performer offering his/her presence on stage for contemplation ... 'liveness' comes to the fore, highlighting the provocative presence of the human being rather than the embodiment of a figure."[26] Pulling from both ends of Kirby's spectrum, the two dominant strategies for triggering non-matrixed acting focus on either weakening the theatricalizing mimetic frame, rendering it perceptually null, or exposing the mechanisms of mimetic craft, explicitly marking the work of the actors as not feigning or doing it "badly."

Since 2002, Berlin-based artists Helgard Haug, Daniel Wetzel, and Stefan Kaegi have produced work under the label Rimini Protokoll, developing a highly regarded international reputation for their reality-based performances. A quintessential marker of the practices of Rimini Protokoll is the importation of cultural strangers to the stage; people who are "strangers" because they are foreign or insufficiently known due to occupation, class, or ethnic background. Some of their best-known works include *Crossword Pit Stop*, featuring octogenarian female residents of a neighbouring nursing home; *CallCutta*, in which audience members chatted to Indian call centre workers; and *Cargo Sofia X* – a mobile tour in the back of a transport truck narrated by the Bulgarian drivers.[27] In her study of the work of Rimini Protokoll, Meg Mumford argues that the strategic encounters orchestrated by the company "[generate] a sense of immediate contact with living people and truthful representations of their lives ... while simultaneously destabilizing that impression through overt fictionality and theatricality."[28] Such performances offer knowing through autobiographical storytelling but also problematize that knowing, drawing attention to gaps, inconsistencies, and fabrications. Competing oscillating perceptions between knowledge that is fixed and unfixed, between representation and reality, relegate the audience to an experience of uncertainty caught up in ontological hybridity. On the surface, one might expect that reality-based theatrical performances such as autobiographical performance and verbatim plays offer strong, unambiguous reality-effects, easily encouraging audiences to take what they see and hear to be a stable truth, directly transferrable to people and events in the actual world. Inherent to their form situating ostensibly real voices inside a theatrical frame, the plays "create ontologically unstable phenomena that appear to oscillate between ... authentic ... and ... manufactured."[29] This undecidability "is caused not only by the creation of phenomena that do not sit clearly within one or the other of these problematically binarised categories, but also by representations whose very nature is uncertain."[30] Confronted with this uncertain epistemology latent in these plays, Garde and Mumford suggest that the unstable "reality status" of the work rises up, displacing any conventional reading of what the play is about. Our dramatic understanding then is necessarily filtered through this disorienting audience affect they call "productive insecurity."[31] Shannon Jackson makes a similar observation in her work on social art practice, writing that "the unsettling of reality and fiction in contemporary documentary theatre provokes new knowledges but also invites reflection upon the conventions of knowing itself."[32]

100% Vancouver: A Statistical Chain Reaction

"These are not trained actors. These are everyday Vancouverites. The demographics of a city brought to life, with the stories and individuals that make up Vancouver."[33] Following in the footsteps of Rimini Protokoll productions *100% Berlin* and *100% Vienna*, the *100% Vancouver* franchise follows the same elegantly simple recipe.[34] One hundred residents of Vancouver are assembled to collectively represent the demographic makeup of the city as constituted by five key markers: age, gender, marital status, neighbourhood, and language. Each person embodies one percentile. The necessary proportions for each category were calculated from data collected in the then most recent national census in 2006. These 100 performers become what Haug, Wetzel, and Kaegi call "experts of the everyday," not because of what they do as a profession or what they have experienced in life, but because of who (or perhaps more appropriately "what") they are in the most basic, almost reductive terms. Propelled by the need to tick the right combination of boxes, casting directors made their selections, seeking fifty-one women, forty-nine men; thirteen fifty to fifty-nine year olds; three Hindi- or Punjabi-speakers and so on.[35] As the casting search reached its final stages, the demographic demands became more stringent. Because each person needed to map in precise ways onto five different aspects to fill remaining gaps, the casting directors might be seeking a married female between sixty and sixty-nine years old, whose first language is French and who lives in Kitsilano.

As evidenced by the opening quotation taken from the festival website, a strong emphasis is placed on the notion of the participants as ordinary real people; their value lies in their unmediated presence as postdramatic non-matrixed performers. And yet, even though these "experts of the everyday" were not chosen for their abilities as actors to represent fictional characters, they nevertheless have been chosen to be representational. They represent 1 per cent of the population of Vancouver. They represent 6,463 other people. They also multiply represent their applicable categories in the five controlling demographic criteria. So Selina Chew is 1 per cent out of the whole 100; she is also one of 51 per cent females; she is also one of 13 per cent who are aged between 50 and 59, one of 46 per cent who are married or common law; 1 of 2 per cent who are from West Point Grey; and one of 26 per cent whose mother tongue is Mandarin/Cantonese/Taiwanese. She is not "playing a character" but she is representational. On the back of her autobiographical program card, it says "Selina Chew is 67 (out of 100)." Arguably, these cards constitute the listing of the *dramatis personae*, linking actors to their character roles. Selina's character role is "67 (out of 100)." In this capacity, the performer-percentiles are ontologically doubled, being both themselves and other than themselves. Although this is not "acting" in the traditional sense, it is mimesis. Numbers are by their nature representational, standing in for something else that is absent and elsewhere. In addition, percentiles are special numbers; they are mathematical distillations, representing large numbers as fractions of the whole. The national census is itself an exercise in marrying individual and collective autobiography. It is an exercise in representation with (ideally) 100 per cent participation. Everyone represents themselves in a one-to-one relationship to then produce an aggregate portrait of something we can't ordinarily see, except as distilled representation: Canada. The performers do not participate in mimesis in a narrow sense, typically prefigured as theatrical imitation, but it is mimesis nonetheless insofar as mimesis is the representation of one thing by something else. As percentiles, 100 ordinary Vancouverites are reframed, subjected to the matrixed view that renders them (ambivalently) fictional. From the very outset, the core premise of *100% Vancouver*, by casting people as percentiles, both fixes and unfixes autobiographical knowledge. The result is a destabilized binocular view of the ontologically ambiguous performer-percentiles who are caught between acting "as if" and non-acting, between representation and the real.

Keren Zaiontz, drawing a connection to the hyperbolic or pluralistic quantum stage directions that mark the work of playwrights like Martin Crimp and Sarah Kane, notes with regard to *100% Vancouver* that is impossible to cast a person as percentile.[36] As she points out, the individual is always both less and more than a percentile. The performer is insufficient simply because one person is not 6,464 people. By contrast, the performer also exceeds this role because she is more than her statistics. After initially collecting and classifying each participant in terms of their quantitative data value, supplementary qualitative questions were asked. In the performance, percentiles are instructed to respond and sort themselves according to these other questions. Some enrich the bare bones statistics, asking additional census-style questions: Who has children? Who lives in a house? Who rents their home? Who is in a same-sex relationship? Other questions are more aspirational and values-driven: Who is in love? Who wants to have children? Who grows their own food? Who knows at least one First Nations person? Constrained by the scenographic protocols of the performance, the performer-percentiles can only respond to bivalent questions, positioning their bodies on the stage or raising their hands to indicate "Yes" or "No," "Me" or "Not me." And yet occasionally narratives emerge that seem to irritate the superficiality of just counting, allowing the audience to project meaning on the specific configurations. For example, when asked who is in a same-sex relationship, nine percentiles cross to the "Me" side of the circle. They are applauded by the audience and by their fellow percentiles in what can be understood fairly straightforwardly as a show of political support. Other potential stories are less transparent. After having sorted themselves according to "Who has children?" the performers are then asked "Who wants children?" The mass movement of more than twenty percentiles from "has children/Me" to "wants children/Not me" causes laughter. But the interpretation is not stable. Why do we laugh? What do we think we know? Presumably some do not want the children they have, but perhaps others have interpreted the question as "wants more children" or "wants children today." Returning to Zaiontz, she continues, "[it] is difficult to know whether questions like this were intended to mirror the limitations of the census itself, or simply to reveal the constraints of working with a large 'non-expert' cast and a transposable dramaturgy that can reproduce particular effects, such as authenticity, but cannot necessarily intervene in debates in a sustained way."[37] Both positions, of being both less and more, point to impossibility and call into question the viability of the task itself. The participants are insufficient as impersonal numerical placeholders and at the same time the attempt at richer individualized representations is also woefully inadequate. Confronted by the perceptual uncertainty of being both and neither, uncertainty that renders the ontology of these strangers indeterminate in holding two seemingly irreconcilable positions, the audience becomes stuck.

As George Pendle notes in a short essay in the show program, "[the strategy] to restore human faces to numbers, with personal biography offsetting impersonal statistics [...] appears to humanize concepts, to give texture to abstractions, but what it in fact offers is a *representation* of an abstraction that, while itself textured to the point of life itself, is still, at bottom, a representation"[38] and is not really real at all. Representations feel unsatisfying when we are trying to know something fully.

They are not as Pendle says "really real." And yet representations are needed to express that which cannot be communicated or experienced directly. Large-scale objects like the map of a city and complex information systems like demographic data for millions of people need to be processed, compressed, made more succinct. Representations allow proximity to things that are distant, but they themselves are distancing. Representation is a critical knowledge strategy and yet the knowledge that is yielded by this strategy is always essentially incomplete. *100% Vancouver* stages this indecidability between oscillating representation and the real by concurrently performing the collective city through a number of mimetically ambivalent strategies. Combining data visualizations and sequenced protocols with personalized stories and photographs, scenographic choices in *100% Vancouver* persistently bring these mutually exclusive binarised portrayals into the same view, presenting a double perspective of the participants as brought into proximity and humanized as real and at the same time distanced and dehumanized as representation.

The set for *100% Vancouver* consisted of two blue circles. One large circle on the floor provided the stage space; the other, smaller, circle, hanging vertically, acted as a screen above. Occasionally, the screen circle projected the text of the questions posed to the participants, but most commonly it showed a camera angle of the stage circle from directly overhead. The effect of this bifurcated view is to simultaneously show performers from the front as three-dimensional human figures – we can see their whole bodies and their faces – and also from above where they are flattened into two dimensions as we can see only the tops of their heads. From that view they become dots, and the focus is on the kaleidoscopic patterns created by the collective movement of those dots. In this way, the scenography precisely enacts the indecidable duplicity between human and dehuman perceptions of the performer-percentiles. This indecidability extends to how the percentiles occupy and configure this space. Without speaking, using their bodies, the one hundred answer personal autobiographical questions. When questions are phrased in such a way as to be answerable by "Yes" or "No" or asserting that the statement is true of "Me" or "Not me," the performers move across the stage to position themselves, clumping together in the corresponding zone. The circle is revealed as a pie chart. Sometimes the stage is split a second time into quadrants and the percentiles respond to two related questions. After being asked to divide the stage upstage and downstage according to being married or single,

3.1 The 100 Vancouverites featured in *100% Vancouver* move across the stage and arrange themselves according to their response to a statement that is true of "Me" or "Not me." Photo credit: Tim Matheson.

the ensemble is asked, "Who is in love?" "Who has children?" and "Who wants to have children?" Other patterns are created when the 100 line up in columns from youngest to oldest, and when they cluster around signs with the names of their neighbourhoods, sketching circles of various sizes. Through this autobiographical choreography, they become embodied infographics. In this context, it is significant that, after the regimented movement that permeates the performance, the last thing they do when asked "what they want to do with 100 other participants"[39] is dance. And so they do. One hundred people gyrate autonomously, unified by the rhythm of the music. On the overhead screen, 100 dots randomly swirl.

The dyadic questions that limit insight into the percentiles as individuals in performance are offset by more richly qualitative opportunities on the program cards. The program for *100% Vancouver* consists of a small rectangular grey cardboard box with a lid that is approximately four and a half inches wide by six inches long and just over one inch deep. Inside the box lies a short booklet of essays and 100 cards. The front of each card features a photographic portrait of one of the performer-percentiles. In addition to basic data like their name, their role – "9 (of 100)" – and their placement in each of the five requisite categories, turning the cards over, they offer a verbal autobiography on the verso to complement the visual recto, comprising qualitative open-ended questions like, "What would you like to ask 100 people?" "How do you define wealth?" "What do you see when you look out your kitchen window?" The postcard portraits follow a fairly consistent aesthetic. Although several subjects are seated at a table featuring the head and torso only, for the most part the subject is captured whole body. The subject meets the camera's gaze directly, sometimes smiling but not always. In their hands or just positioned nearby is their chosen personal object. The body of the subject occupies approximately one-third of the frame, allowing a generous glimpse of their location. These locations are predominantly domestic: living rooms, balconies, sitting on the stairs, presumably the homes of the subjects. In addition to their personal object, the subjects are posed with numbered yellow forensic evidence markers indicating their percentile identity. Their own number is the most prominent but other numbers also occupy the visual field, sometimes in order and orderly, sometimes disordered and scattered. Once again, the unique individuality of the performers is complicated by these clinical uniform numerals, a reminder that each is a number, merely one component of larger set. Likewise, just as each card features a single person, the cards, reminiscent of collector hockey cards or Pokémon cards, are part of a set. You gotta get 'em all.

This distinctive push-pull of proximity and distance, of knowing and unknowing, in intercultural encounter is in evidence in *100% Vancouver* right from the very first moment. To begin the performance, the participants enter in parade in percentile sequence from 1 per cent to 100 per cent. They file across the downstage edge of the stage following a fairly repetitive pattern. Pausing in front of a microphone, they introduce themselves. "Hi, I'm Stephanie and this is my piggy bank." "Hi, I'm Casey and this is my baby blanket." "Hi. My name is Keith. This is a poem I wrote in grade nine. I entered it in a library contest and it won." Personal objects create proximity. Any object selected is going to be a representation of identity simply by virtue of being specially

3.2 One of 100 postcards produced for *100% Vancouver*. This one is 67 (of 100) Selina Chew. Photo courtesy of Selina Chew.

selected. And yet, a significant proportion of personal objects exhibited participate directly in the generation of autobiography, including a passport, birth certificate, family photos. In addition, many objects have familial historical provenance, narrativizing past life experiences into the present to perform a self, like "my mother's nail file," "a paddle carved by my father," "my grandmother's elephant. Now it's my elephant." Proximity, as Ahmed says, is central to the affective pull of this encounter. Yet, even as the percentiles introduce themselves as individuals singly and by name, adding personal detail with their selected objects, the constrained and repetitive protocol reduces them again to discrete, sequenced, potentially interchangeable units. As demonstrated, by using actual people as data points and the imposition of strict behavioural limits on these real people, *100% Vancouver* explores the oscillating tension between proximity and distance, between human and dehuman, to generate an affect of uncertainty. Whereas formality creates theatrical distance and a sense of construction, informality underscores proximity and realness of the raw. At the end of the percentiles' concluding dance, when the music ends, they applaud the audience and the audience applauds them. Then gradually they disperse. Some exit. Some stand around. Some talk to audience members in the front row. Eschewing more typical dramatic performance conventions, there is no definitive conclusion to the event that recognizes the temporary division between art and life that makes theatre theatre; there is no moment of formal release for the actor and the audience from the fictional world of the play back to the actual world, because perhaps if we never entered into representational theatricality none is needed. This uncertainty with regard to the boundaries of theatricality in *100% Vancouver* operates as a reality-effect, suggesting that theatricality does not factor into the presentation, remaining fixed in the actual world. In addition, the failure of the frame to follow expected conventions draws our attention to the convention as such. Once again we are uncertain whether we are "in" or "out;" if we were never inside a fictional cosmos to begin with, then there is no need to exit and return to an actual world.

Similarly, in performance, given that our horizon of expectations prepared the audience for performance by non-professionalized actors, there were some not unexpected failures of acting. Rehearsals were very minimal. Undoubtedly the community context of *100% Vancouver* was a contributing factor, exerting practical restrictions on the availability of rehearsal time.[40] The performers' voices were sometimes too quiet, some stuttering with nervousness. In the opening parade, performers stooped awkwardly to the microphones. At one point, following her monologue, because she is standing close to a microphone, the audience hears Joan say disarmingly to a fellow participant, "Now what do we do?" In another instance, less obvious to the live audience, but clear in comparison of the performance to its script, speakers do not always stick closely to the documentary text; they embellish and they skip. Even though these are their own stories, the words are now at one remove from their source, having been written down and returned to their original authors as script. The effect of these obvious failures of polished performance is to increase the cumulative authenticity of *100% Vancouver* as a non-mimetic, task-based event.

In addition to the task of representing a percentile, another labour undertaken by the performers was the work of casting each other. Part of the original Rimini Protokoll performance protocol required that within twenty-four hours of joining, each person must find and recruit the next person. Notionally, participants were chosen according to how they fulfill specific demographic criteria in the "casting graph" with the idea that the cast would comprise a single unbroken chain uniting the whole city. In practice, however, this proved to be a difficult task, as the Vancouver chain would break "after 10 or 6 or 3 people."[41] In addition to breaking the rule of the chain, it proved ultimately impossible given the short time frame of 100 days to perfectly capture every demographic category fully and completely in 100 actual bodies; impossible to find precisely the right combination of actual people to represent the demographic portrait of the city. This failure is documented in the casting graphs printed in the program. There, a checkmark represented a successful match between a person and the statistic. A circle was used to represent a "non-represented statistic" – a person/percentile who was missing; for example, there were two few men in the staged representation. A circle with a strikeout represented a "represented non-statistic" – a person/percentile who was extra; for example, the actual group included one additional female and one person who identified as transgender. As Sara Jane Bailes declares, failure is productive. Failures direct attention to processes in such a way as to invite reconsideration of those processes.

> Failure *works*. Which is to say that although ostensibly it signals the breakdown of an aspiration or an agreed demand, breakdown indexes an alternative route or way of doing or making. In its status as "wrongdoing,"

a failed objective establishes an aperture, an opening onto several (and often many) other ways of doing that counter the authority of a singular or "correct" outcome.[42]

Tim Carlson, the casting director of 100% Vancouver, concurs with this attitude: "Failures in protocol are as revealing as successes showing where understanding or expectation is out of joint ... [B]reakdowns in theatrical expectations illuminate the human experience on stage in a way that theatrical convention might not. A little chaos is in order." Failure of the casting task illuminates several aspects of the proposed autobiographical encounter of 100% Vancouver that point productively not just to what cannot be known about strangers but to those processes that shape how we might know strangers. First, the demographic criteria are shown to be insufficient, as demonstrated when the designations of male and female fail to accommodate non-binary identities. In an effort to overwrite the protocols, when the performers are asked to divide themselves according to gender, one percentile moves to occupy a liminal space in the middle of the stage, effectively performing a failure of excess data. In the case of the criterion of neighbourhood, there is a lack of data. The four communities of Oakridge, Shaughnessy, South Cambie, and Sunset were not represented because the network of casting assistants and existing cast members was unable to penetrate these communities. Another problem relates neither to excess nor to lack but to granularity. Whereas some failures are made visible in performance, others are hidden. With regard to ethnicity, 2 per cent of Vancouverites fall into the category "Other," being not Caucasian, Chinese, Filipino, Japanese, Korean, Southeast Asian, West Asian, Latin American, or African. Under the census, this 2 per cent is constituted of fractional per cents combining a number of groups. When casting 100 people, it is not possible to cast partial performers, and so the particular protocols controlling the absence of fitting bodies in the production render these less numerous minority groups invisible.

Ultimately, the Vancouver audience bears witness to a failed autobiographical representation of a collective self. Through the bivalent positioning of "Vancouver" both on the stage and in the audience, 100% Vancouver complicates the autobiographical trope of the intercultural encounter with a stranger. On the one hand, the audience and ensemble participate in a shared collective identity as Vancouverites. And in this mode there is strong affinity and affection in seeing "yourself," both collective and singular, reflected in the performance. Pleasure lies in recognition of the reflection. "There I am." Somewhere on the stage is someone just like me. Perhaps one of the 100 is someone who replicates exactly my particular combination of five demographic markers. Pleasure also arises in the communal expression of civic identification. "There we are." On the other hand, it is more likely that my five markers are distributed among several performer-percentiles. None of these individuals is me. Rather, the portrait is a mosaic, offering a fractured composite facsimile of myself and of my city. Michelle Reid, reviewing the production for a local blog, writes, "I admit that I'm sceptical. After all, I see a mixed cohort of Vancouverites clutching at various objects every day, but it's not theatre – it's called riding the bus."[43] Just as some performer-percentiles represent me, the others, many others, by definition, do not. There are many strangers on the stage. As an individual I am represented and I am not; this group is familiar and also strange. This feeling ebbs and flows as I match their various responses to my own. Likewise, as a collective, these 100 people are Vancouver. Is this a Vancouver that I recognize? This inconsistent intercultural location of audience to performers problematizes the nature of autobiographical encounter in *100% Vancouver*.

Jeff Khonsary and Kristina Lee Podesva of Filip Editions, editors of the program box, write in the afterword, "[A]lthough the 100% project can never truly represent the cities it engages, it self-consciously recognizes this problem and, in the process, humanizes representation by reconnecting it back to actual life and people on a case-by-case basis. Hidden or forgotten intricacies are, therefore, made visible by the project, confronting us with our long list of assumptions and prejudices, and proving them false or at least incomplete as a consequence."[44] I think this is sometimes true but also not true. Where *100% Vancouver* humanizes representation by giving numbers flesh, it also dehumanizes by using that same flesh and blood as data points. It makes visible hidden and forgotten intricacies and also veils those same people and their stories, revealing them in ways that are unavoidably partial and ambivalent. Rather than receiving knowledge and a feel-good experience of civic affection for the city and its denizens, audience are compelled to step back. *100% Vancouver* gently shows us what we don't know and invites us to look more closely. Uncertainty arising from a destabilized real is a promising place to start. We need to face what we don't know but also understand that sometimes we can't know. In this respect, the show is not above teasing the audience. Towards the end of the show, performers are asked to move into the middle of the circle if the statement is true of them: "We have a job." "We have debt." "We have broken the law."[45] When the statement, "We have lied since the show began" is posed, 11 performer-percentiles take centre stage to confess that this is true of them.

RARE

Created through improvisational devising processes, *RARE* is the product of collaboration between lauded playwright Judith Thompson and an ensemble of young people in their twenties and thirties living with Down syndrome.[46] As in *100% Vancouver*, autobiographical storytelling by non-mimetic performers in *RARE* engenders unstable hybridity rather than confident interpersonal knowledge. Audience experience of intercultural engagement with strangers becomes productive, compelling us to accept failure and inviting us to contemplation of the "sociality of the 'with'" in a manner that takes up ethical responsibility for both the potential and the necessary impossibility of democratic encounter. Whether staging a culture of many or one, the patterns and practices of intercultural performance productively inform our understanding of *RARE*. Whereas *100% Vancouver* prefigures audience and performers together as, at least outwardly, members of a shared culture as Vancouverites, *RARE* establishes as part of its modus operandi an oppositional tension in the relationship between performers and audience. The actors ask rhetorically: "How does it feel to be us? ... Ya wanna know?"[47] This positioning of "us" and "you" explicitly separates performers from audience and makes each into a coherent and homogenous group. More than this, however, the challenge "You wanna know?" exposes the heart of the autobiographical project, revealing both its desire for contact and its uncrossable distance. Yes, the audience does want to know, but is knowledge possible and what is mutually risked in this transaction? Projecting what "you think" and what "you wanna know" onto the autobiographical audience, the play interpellates this audience as ignorant yet curious travellers seeking insight into the lives of a heretofore unknown population. At the conclusion of Jacob's song "Out There," the singer declares, "All we want is to be out there with you / So don't be alarmed."[48] In this construction, their role made manifest as a "normate" audience with limited exposure to people with Down syndrome, an audience who is exhorted to not be afraid of the performer-strangers, there is little space for audience members who share the performers' experience, who might not be afraid, who might in fact be themselves an "us" rather than a "you."[49] As Ric Knowles points out, the assumption of the target culture as a monocultural audience as well as the perpetuation of a "west and the rest" dichotomy are problematic features of outdated intercultural practices,[50] practices that *RARE* seems to reenact.

My first approach to the failed encounter through uncertainty and hybridity as thematized in *RARE* starts with the play's title. The play takes its title partly from the idea that people with Down syndrome are becoming increasingly rare in societies that permit/encourage the abortion of fetuses that test positive for this congenital condition. Down syndrome, also known as trisomy 21, is a genetic disorder caused by the presence of an extra (third) copy of the twenty-first chromosome.[51] In recent years, an increasingly reliable and increasingly non-invasive screening procedure has allowed prospective parents to know whether or not their child possesses this anomaly.[52] The combination of genetic testing and a widespread inclination towards terminating fetuses with a Down syndrome diagnosis is effectively reducing the contemporary population of adults with Down syndrome.[53] In the play, the performers invoke Shakespeare to express anger and confusion at this situation:

KRYSTAL: To be or not to be? That's a question for people who are pregnant and have found out they have a baby with Down syndrome, to keep it or not to keep it.

NICK: Exactly Krystal. You know what pisses me off? Most parents terminate the pregnancy when they find out their baby will have Down syndrome. When I was born the nurse told my mother "You know, you don't have to keep him."

DYLAN: Me too the same thing happened to my Mom.

JAMES: Me too.

[...]

NICK: And that is wrong, that is discrimination. It is against our rights to be who we are, what we are. We are unique, we're ... rare! We stand together.[54]

Then Dylan thinks about why society, represented here by the nurses, might make this suggestion. "I don't know. I think they're afraid because they don't understand Down syndrome. Maybe they are worried that there will be health problems?" Nick counters, saying "Doesn't everyone have health problems?"[55] Krystal lists her food- and digestion-related health issues and then the play goes off on this new vector with everyone listing their favourite foods.

Thus, while the production does not pursue the question of fear further in this moment, it invites audiences to think about how the kinds of discriminatory medical practices the performers describe are tied to fear. Further, the play's exchange also locates the disavowal of people with Down syndrome's human value in the mouths of medical professionals, both invoking and speaking back to medical framings of disability. Tobin Siebers, in his book *Disability Aesthetics*, helps to make sense of these framing choices: "The mental and physical properties of bodies become the natural symbols of inferiority via a process of disqualification that seems biological, not cultural – which is why disability discrimination seems to be a medical rather than a social problem."[56] This construction of Down syndrome as a medical problem goes a long way to explaining the resort to screening and abortion as a prevention strategy. The preference is to "fix, cure, or eradicate the disabled body rather than the discriminatory attitudes of society."[57]

In his plain-speaking treatise, *The Politics of Down Syndrome*, Keiron Smith, himself the father of a daughter with Down syndrome, writes:

> There is a sort of middle class fear about Down Syndrome ... Down Syndrome seems to have transformed into a metaphor; a metaphor primarily for stupidity; a shared 'other' which represents idiocy and contempt ... represents a diminution of people with Down Syndrome to something akin to sub-humanity. Where people with Down Syndrome exist in a world where they remain forever dependent, forever children.[58]

Smith continues, pointing out that culturally Down syndrome finds itself in conflict with many of the trends of late-capitalism: being unrecognized as beautiful, being outside of society, being unable to self-actualize, being dependent.[59] He argues that what potential parents fear stems from existential anxiety on the one hand as they imagine how the existence of a child with Down syndrome would threaten their vision of a satisfactory life, as laid out according to the late-capitalist values described above. And, on the other hand, fear also stems from aesthetic anxiety as again the life of a child with Down syndrome might not adhere to accepted norms of beauty and behaviour as promoted by embedded contemporary cultural values, which we must (albeit shamefully) acknowledge.[60] The fear that Dylan muses about, then, exists in the liminal space between self and stranger, and is activated by proximity. As Ahmed insists, "Fear ... does not reside positively in a particular object or sign. It is this lack of residence that allows fear to slide across signs and between bodies ... Fear works by establishing others as fearsome insofar as they *threaten to take the self in*."[61] Ahmed gives the provocative example "The nigger's going to eat me up."[62] The fear of dependency that characterizes the disability of Down syndrome is similarly transitive.

As already noted, the intercultural encounter with the stranger is a moment marked by hybridity. The stranger is both fixed as known and is also essentially unknowable, resulting in a moment of inherent epistemological and ontological insecurity. This characteristic of the general hybridity of the stranger maps directly onto the locus of fear in neurotypical adults in relation to Down syndrome imagery, featuring a specific hybridity that blends normatively defined elements of childlike social expression with adult physical maturity. In other words, normate understandings of contemporary Canadian culture's division between adult and child experiences do not fully account for critical differences in the lived experiences of adults with Down syndrome. There is a marked absence of robust social understanding, recognition, and acceptance of Down syndrome adults. Indeed, numerous books are concerned with the "transition" of twenty-somethings with Down syndrome from a dependent life at school and at home with their parents to a more independent adult life with all the responsibilities and risks that entails.[63] Not surprisingly then, this is also a key theme of RARE, where it is demonstrated as a central preoccupation of its performer-creators who inhabit that same demographic. In their speeches, the performers demand independence in employment, in living conditions, and in self-determination. They want to be adults. They want to have sex, to get married, to have children. Yet, as much as these speakers lay claim to their status as adults, their statements in this production are consistently problematized by a sense of hybridity rooted in normate conceptions of the division between adult and child, resulting in insecure identity positions.

In the opening section of the play, using a similar strategy to that of *100% Vancouver*, the cast introduce themselves with a mini autobiographical portrait by name, age, and a defining statement. Also like *100% Vancouver*, the performers are both individualized by these introductions and simultaneously distilled to components of a collective group identity.

> NICK: I am Nicholas Herd, I'm 28 years old. I'm looking for a serious
>   boyfriend. I'm ready for romance before I turn 30.
> SUZANNE: I am Suzanne. I am 35 and *don't* mess with me.
> KRYSTAL: I am Krystal. I am 23 and nobody owns me.
> [...]
> DYLAN: I am Dylan. I am 22 and I am the spirit of a boy.
> [...]
> MICHAEL: I am Michael Liu. I am 29 and sometimes I feel like Batman.[64]

Mixed with some of the more unassuming portraits – "I am James. I am 28 and I love music" – are some statements of marked hybridity. Both Suzanne and Krystal assert their power and independence, drawing my attention both to their vociferous statement and to the explicit necessity of this statement in a world where this autonomy, in contrast to most adults who assume this silently, is notably contested. Dylan expresses precisely the hybridity of a twenty-two-year-old man who embodies boyishness. Likewise, Michael, echoing the women's powerful self-characterization, does so by invoking a childlike projection onto a fantasy superhero. Two short stories demonstrate another way that the dependency/independency hybrid presents itself in *RARE*: Krystal recounts a time when, "I was at this party and suddenly there was a knife. I was scared, I was really scared, I thought I might get stabbed but I couldn't leave. I couldn't leave because I didn't know how to get home."[65] In a lighter tone, Erin is listing who and what she loves: "I love everybody! But my dad is sometimes bossy about what I can eat. Why can't I have two cheese slices? I'm an adult!"[66] In both of these vignettes, the performer's assertions are demonstrated as challenges to normative ideas about adulthood. Here, Krystal and Erin find themselves in situations – one serious and one slight – that highlight dependent relationships in their adulthood. Another example occurs when listing things they love, one cast member says "When my Dad picked me up to the sky and I felt like Peter Pan."[67] The image communicates the thrilling feeling of flying, but it also carries an intertextual reference to the boy who never grows up. As a single mention this might not be noteworthy but taken with other examples it contributes yet one more citation to a thematic montage that permeates the play.

Augmenting the verbal self-portraits and memories that position the cast of *RARE* as caught in an irreconcilable hybridity of dependence and independence, the play also scripts performances-within that also exhibit this same unstable relation. In scene four, titled "Love," the cast repeats "I love you" in several languages. Scene nine is titled "Language." In this scene, the cast displays their linguistic talents speaking various conversational phrases like "I would like to make you a GREEK salad" or "I love to eat chocolate ice cream in summer" in Greek, French, Arabic, Mandarin, and Italian.[68] Mike sings a whole song about friendship in Cantonese. The ability to speak several languages is a laudable skill and the production might have developed these skills in different directions; however, the recitation of words in other languages by rote here risks echoing the cliché of faux intellectual sophistication performed by precocious children. Along the same lines, *RARE* features numerous recitations of poetry, featuring verses by William Butler Yeats, William Blake, Emily Dickinson, and William Shakespeare as well as Odette's dance of the Dying Swan from Tchaikovsky's *Swan Lake*, demonstrations which, when performed out of context as they are here, risk being yet another showcase of precocity. From another perspective, however, these recitations speak to ability and attempt to efface difference, proposing that the speakers can master second and third languages, that they can participate in canonical literary culture at the "highest" levels. We might then read these sections as postcolonial appropriations and revisionings of the cultural property of the target culture to hear the texts afresh and to make them sing a new song. Either way, whether progressive reclaiming or retrograde mimicking, these relations rise from the child-adult hybrid and are founded on an unequal power dynamic of encounter between these two groups.

The trope that equates disability with being childlike is outdated and frankly patronizing, and yet despite the apparent efforts to suggest that the performers are capable adults, *RARE* seems to get caught up in its unfortunate repetition. In his review of the Toronto production in the winter of 2013, Robert Cushman of the *National Post* locates his review in precisely this territory, finding common ground between the audience and the performers in the experience of childhood: "[The scene between Sarah and Michael] also seems like everybody's fumbling, hopeful youth, caught forever ... The pleasures and the pains recounted and enacted here should relate to everyone's remembrances of childhood, with the confounding difference that we're experiencing here through people who, physically and intellectually, are not children."[69]

This is precisely the challenge (and failure) of proximity in encounter and the extending corollary of fear of hybridity. One way the stranger is so familiar – everyone's childhood is onstage. This is the simplicity that we must avoid. Moreover, who is "everyone"? Cushman appears to accede to the production's interpellation of "you" in the audience (and in his newspaper's readership) as able-bodied adults whose hopeful and fumbling youth is in the past. The other way, there is profound and uncrossable distance. Fear and anxiety bubble up. Cushman writes that, "it's possible – actually very likely – to approach this production feeling queasy; or, equally, with a determination to avoid that feeling." Through formal choices that do not unsettle the normate framing of the adult/child divide mapped onto dependence/independence, this ostensibly adult stranger appears childlike, where the audience by contrast does not. Nostalgia is tempered by uneasiness.

But this insecurity can (and must) be productive. "Hybridity involves the transgression and destabilization of identity."[70] It is in this destabilization that we might renegotiate the terms of identity. Herein lies a performative opportunity. Ashamed as I may be to own up to it, the fear in uncertainty illuminates my prejudices. As Meg Mumford writes in relation to the work of Rimini Protokoll, the sense of proximity to cultural strangers unfixes oppressive views and in that radical unsettling we can experience fresh ways of engaging these strangers.[71] Therefore, it is not simply a matter of accepting without question the insistent declarations by the performers that they are adults. Rather, in the "sociality of the 'with,'" the production assumes an audience of unfamiliar strangers, pressing them to experience hybridity and to reassess the value contemporary Canadian society assigns to independence as the marked feature of adulthood. How might the social sphere be reimagined so that dependence is not disavowed or faulted as a feature of being less, but instead is presented as an opportunity for the expression of our commonality? How might society benefit from valuing mutual dependence over independence? What is lost when society champions mastery and virtuosity? The same values that predicate success in late-capitalist society also seem to predicate success as an actor on the stage. In its particular dramaturgy and performance style, *RARE* also invites us to consider the relationship of mastery and virtuosity to the actor. What aesthetic ideals castigate mistakes made in performance or those moments when the façade slips?

Near the end of *RARE*, scene twelve is titled "I am nobody! Who are you?" The text of the scene is composed (mostly verbatim with a few transcriptions) of a poem by Emily Dickinson. The cast declares in unison: "I'm Nobody! Who are you?" Then Suzanne turns the question to a fellow actor "Are you nobody too?" Krystal replies, "Then there's a pair of us." Whispering and seeming pleased with themselves, the performers (and the poet) revel in this community of nobodies. Shifting to the male actors, the second stanza of the slightly altered poem opines: "How dreary to be somebody! / How public, like a frog / To tell your name the livelong day / To an admiring bog."[72] Anonymity here is figured as desirable, as long as the anonymity is collective. And yet, the central ethos of the autobiographical project runs counter to the possibility of being nobody. Charged with answering the question "Who am I?," the autobiographical performer becomes somebody and some body.[73] The extra chromosome of trisomy 21 enacts a distinctive physiognomy that triggers the spectacle of disability articulated by Rosemarie Garland-Thomson in her influential book *Staring*. In the theatre of the public sphere, people with Down syndrome cannot be nobody. Thus the autobiographical performer who is also a person marked by physical difference is doubly some body, public like a frog, telling your name to the admiring bog. By contrast, the target audience of *RARE* (cast as "the admiring bog") prefigured as "normate," is invisible in their dominant ordinariness, passing as uniformly non-disabled, as "white" in this intercultural exchange, recipients of all the privileges entailed in that position. Visibility of the body, of being some body, in performance functions as a strong reality-marker, drawing attention to the correlative actual-world existence of that body. In the same way that nudity on stage tends to short-circuit representation, bodies marked by their strange(r)ness also prioritize presence over mimesis. We might dub this phenomenon the biology of the real, where onstage manifestations of the unavoidable human body as body generate a real-world frisson. A sneeze. A coughing fit. A yawn. In the irrepressible moment of the sneeze, the real bubbles up. (I always wonder why actors don't sneeze onstage. Maybe they do.)[74] Thinking about the postdramatic peeling apart of reality from fiction, Erika Fischer-Lichte cites as a specific example a production of *Guilio Cesare* by the Italian company Societas Raffaello Sanzio that placed (in her words) "bodies on the stage that blatantly deviated from 'normal' bodies, demonstrating frailty and decay, as well as physical excess."[75] The hyper-attention directed to the simple presence of these marked bodies detracts from their mimetic potential and reifies the kinds of traditional western theatre aesthetics that Carrie Sandahl criticizes in her article "The Tyranny of Neutral." Sandahl traces how only non-disabled bodies, or those that seem so physically, are privileged as being able to achieve "neutral," the idealized condition from which fictional character can emerge. Although "neutral" is axiomatically unachievable, Sandahl demonstrates how disabled bodies, like other stigmatized or marked bodies, are inhibited by dominant training methods and aesthetics from laying claim to the position. From her demonstration of the disabled body's inability to achieve neutral flows the argument that "a character cannot be built from a position of physical difference."[76] As Sandahl suggests, this aesthetic assumes that actors with Down syndrome cannot "act," they can only "be." A central part of the attraction of an audience to autobiographical performance is a desire for access to authentic being-ness, an access that is held at arms-length by the theatrical frame. Once again, the autobiographical performances in *RARE* are caught in hybridity, mired uncertainly between presence and performance.

As Jens Roselt writes, "Real people on the stage are disorientating. You are never quite sure where you are."[77] *RARE*, despite the care and determination manifest in its preparation and rehearsal, relies on the performers' assertions of their real bodies and selves. As with *100% Vancouver*, through various fractures in normative expectations of transparent actorly skill, the majority of the performers' lack of traditional performance training is revealed.[78] Sara Jane Bailes's list of theatrical failures includes "unconvincing acting, coping (or not), awkwardness, and inability."[79] In the performance that I saw, there were several missed lines where actors called out to the stage manager for a line prompt and received the text of their line shouted from the auditorium, which they then repeated. One performer had a habit of tapping out the number of words in her speech with her fingers on the side of her leg, betraying her unique memorization technique. Also noticeable were moments where one actor would touch another on the back or shoulder to communicate the cue for the next action. I am cataloguing these observations here, not to find fault with the performers, not at all, but rather to raise to view a range of performance strategies that are not compatible with expected (i.e., trained, professional, naturalistic) standards of performance. The cast of *RARE* display a consistently vocally flat, near-monotone delivery. Songs are spoken rather than sung. The speech of some of the performers is not sharply articulated and so I admit that there were many points where

I did not clearly hear and comprehend what was being said. One performer in particular in the Kingston cast has a distinctive vocal quality; all her speeches are delivered in a shouting, seemingly angry tone regardless of the content, a characteristic that engenders a disconcerting disconnect between what she is saying and the perceived emotional attitude. Disruptions to the standard aesthetic practices are generative sites for understanding the value systems informing the aesthetics themselves. If we consider the disruptions cited above as moments of "failed" mimetic representation, we have an opportunity to reconsider the value system that labels them as such. To this end, it behooves us to ask, "What are the political effects of failure?" Bailes astutely notes that failure "exposes the economy of value and exchange through which live performance conducts its business; it offers new conceptions of virtuosity and mastery."[80] This is absolutely critical for *RARE* since how we measure skill applies here not only to theatrical performance but also to life skills and maturity. How do we judge performance success and good acting? How do we judge life success? A poetics of failure requires us to consider that failure might lie not with inferior performance but with my application of a (possibly wrong but) pervasive and implicit assessment scale that declares certain performance characteristics to be inferior. In this light, the failure may not be the performers' but mine. More than this, having opened up the values of failure to interrogation, I am now uncertain about whether these contested performance features are failures at all.

The second effect of these failures of theatrical behaviour is a post-dramatic exposure of the real. On the surface, the transparency of untutored non-mimetic acting is a desirable quality that appears to admit access to an authentic persona and an authentic experience. By nominating the amateur performers "experts of the everyday," Rimini Protokoll deflects concern from what they cannot do – act – to what they can do. The audience suspends aesthetic judgment. Indeed, "the very fact that their words do not appear spontaneous, but rather as somewhat uncertain presentations by not especially well-trained speakers, paradoxically increases their appearance of honesty."[81] In *RARE*, a costume change is used as a simple metaphor to establish authenticity by rejecting theatricality and exposing the real. Near the end, one by one, members of the cast strip off the grey smock-like shirts they have been wearing to reveal T-shirts beneath. Some of the tees display attachment to favourite hobbies or express fandom. Some others are more explicitly connected to the politics of Down syndrome. Anna wears a purple shirt with the logo from the television show *Glee*,[82] Nathan's shirt is a souvenir of his participation on a special games soccer team representing Ontario, Ashaya's shirt cheekily declares "Keep calm. It's only an extra chromosome." We are to understand that these are real tees from the personal wardrobes of the performers and that these items have been specially selected to "speak" on their behalf. Removing their uniform costumes and marking the end of performance, this striking costume change is offered to signal a moment when they seem to revert back to themselves. Just as uneven or untutored acting skills and awkwardness mark autobiographical "experts" as authentic, likewise the change from a "costume" to "my real clothes" generates the same understanding. Consistent with what has gone before in the scripted portion of *RARE*, the t-shirts are intended to communicate something about "who I really am." But now the context of the message attempts to transcend the performance proper. These examples represent an attempt to shift the rules of the game from the representational to the real, unmediated by art. That said, it is a failed attempt as I am doubtful that this is in fact even possible given the immense fictionalizing power of the theatrical frame. Indeed, as argued above, secure proximity in the encounter with the stranger is an illusion – a fraught illusion that leads to facile and condescending conclusions about how easily the stranger may escape the theatrical frame to be assimilated as "just like me." This de-theatricalizing gesture by way of a conclusion serves the same function as the dancing in lieu of a curtain call at the end of *100% Vancouver*. Both works are conscious of a need to re-cross the threshold of the fictional into the actual and yet actively suppress the initial premise of any mimetic foundation.

Polyglotte

Assimilation to be "just like me" is the name of the game in *Polyglotte*. First presented as part of Festival TransAmériques at Théâtre aux Écuries in Montreal, *Polyglotte* was created by playwright and director Olivier Choinière, winner of the 2014 Siminovitch Prize.[83] Renowned in Quebec as a key practitioner of postdramatic work (*Project Blanc*, *Chante avec moi*), Choinière's oeuvre is less well known in anglophone Canada. Intercultural encounter in *Polyglotte* is framed significantly not as a static show-and-tell for "us" by "them," but takes as a central theme the transformation of identity, staging immigrant prospective Canadians to an audience of Canadians. To become Canadian, it is necessary to study the regions of the country and the workings of the political system as outlined in the study guide but also symbols of Canada (the maple leaf, the fleur-de-lys, the beaver, and hockey) and associated rights and responsibilities of citizens. For example, page 9 of *Discover Canada* chides newcomers: "Canada's openness and generosity do not extend to barbaric cultural practices that tolerate spousal abuse, 'honour kill-ings,' female genital mutilation, forced marriage or other gender-based violence." In addition to passing the test, prospective Canadians must demonstrate "adequate knowledge of either English or French."[84] As its title indicates, language is a central preoccupation of *Polyglotte*, direct-ing not only the content, but the dramaturgical structure. Part of the inspiration for *Polyglotte* was the discovery, by one of Choinière's col-laborators, Alexia Bürger, of *The Polyglotte Method of French Conversa-tion/Méthod polyglotte de conversation anglaise* – a collection of twenty LPs containing language lessons, intended for new arrivals, and dating from the 1960s. Voiced by famous Quebecois actor and Radio-Canada broadcaster Henri Bergeron, the lessons repeat stock phrases in both French and English. Hurry up. *Hâtez-vous.* There are many people. *Il y a beaucoup de gens.* How do you do? *Comment allez-vous?* [85] With a taste for the absurd, Bürger and Choinière extract these phrases from their original source, transforming "Henri" into the voice of officialdom, questioning and instructing new immigrants at their citizenship hear-ing. This then is the core premise of *Polyglotte*. Nine prospective Cana-dian citizens – embodied here by nine "experts of the everyday," actual recent immigrants, who are actually seeking citizenship – are screened in a faux and somewhat Kafka-esque citizenship test. One by one the candidates are called to the stage from the audience by number: Can-didate number 10. *Candidat numéro 10.* The disembodied Henri, who is both formally kind and also occasionally cruelly demanding and brisk, puts them through their paces, asking questions about Canadian geog-raphy, history, and culture. Other verbatim text is drawn from the offi-cial citizenship manual *Discover Canada/Découvrir le Canada*, speeches by prime minister Stephen Harper, Quebec premier Philippe Couillard, and Queen Elizabeth II, as well as from personal autobiographical inter-view testimony of the ensemble.

Like the previous case studies of *100% Vancouver* and *RARE*, this examination of *Polyglotte* will describe postdramatic strategies that locate the immigrant performers as non-mimetic and real. At the same time, these strategies are persistently undermined by contingent uncertainty between knowing and not knowing, between proximity and distance; uncertainty that becomes productive, fostering humility in self-reflection. One significant difference is that whereas the ensemble of *RARE* asks "You wanna know?," positioning the audience as outsiders seeking intercultural insight, *Polyglotte* complicates this dynamic where the culture under examination is that of the audience as Canadians. Reversing the gaze, the effect is to inculpate the audience, and the production interrogates, in a sometimes caustic manner, the status of spectators as confident knowers.

To begin, the play primes the audience with strong cues to accept the actions on the stage as authentic. The members of the ensemble are performatively established as non-actors, as non-matrixed bodies. In support of their task-based roles, they are accompanied on the stage by two professional actors who perform duties as federal agents of the citizenship ceremony. Dressed in navy blue uniforms, these two give instructions for the official proceedings according to their fictional roles but they also serve in a practical theatrical context as stage managers, guiding the novice performers. They direct the performers where to move and where to stand. They hand out props. They also walk a microphone from performer to performer, a seemingly practical necessity that suggests that these untrained actors lack the vocal skill to speak loud enough to be heard clearly throughout the theatre space. The amplified voice of Henri issuing from the rear of the auditorium also acts a similar double role. He exerts authority through his questions and the expectation of correct answers, but he also asserts theatrical control by guiding/requiring the actors to follow his instructions. The actors are uniformly passive in this respect. They are told what to do and they do it. Things happen to them. At one point, Samira is instructed by Henri to "open the door" and "go outside." She takes a few hesitant play-acting steps. Fake snow falls from the ceiling. Henri asks, "Are you cold?" Samira replies "Yes, I am very cold." She starts to shiver. Henri then compels a performance of "being cold." "More than that. That's it." Samira shivers more and jumps up and down rubbing her arms. Then a winter coat falls from above. Henri instructs: "Put on your overcoat. *Mets ton paletot.*"[86] This pattern is repeated later when the remaining performers are likewise sent "outside" and eight more parka-style coats fall from the sky. With these supports in place, the performance works to maintain the illusion of the first time, allowing the performers to appear tentative while guiding these novice actors through their roles. But at the same time, these supports also evoke the experience of being herded through bureaucratic processing.

Throughout, the performers retain some natural hesitancy as strangers to the stage. However, it is also noteworthy that they do not improve with reiteration. What I mean by this is, *Polyglotte* had five performances in May/June 2015 and another fifteen in September/October of the same year, and despite this frequency, the performers continued to get certain things wrong or behave awkwardly, even though in a real-world context they would quickly, through repetition, learn the right way. The play stages wrong responses "on purpose" to highlight the ignorance of the "new" immigrants. For example, when the four men are instructed to play hockey and take shots on net, at least two of them are holding the hockey stick incorrectly. Clearly, by the second performance, it is not that they don't know the right way, but have been directed to continue to do it the wrong way. A similar thing happens when Somnath listens to a short poem – "I am Canadian" by John Diefenbaker – and then is asked to repeat it. When he fails, making frequent mistakes, he is chastised with a buzzer error sound effect. Part of the point is that this is an unfairly difficult task that Henri demands. But also given the potential for practice inherent in the rehearsed theatre model, one imagines that Somnath could do this successfully in time if desired. In these displays of deliberately cultivated naiveté, a gap is opened between reality and representation as the non-actors seem to be scripted to act "non-acting."

Another point of confusion is generated by the differing ontological status of the various performing bodies on the stage. The nine immigrants are engaged in a postdramatic theatre context that foregrounds task-based performance and encourages the audience to comprehend them as just being themselves. By contrast, other actors participate in more traditional theatrical representation. As mentioned, professional actors Mireille Tawfik and Eddy Wong assume the roles of the federal agents – obviously they are not really federal agents. Also near the end, one of them (in a mask) appears in full regalia with jewelled crown and floor-length fur cape as Queen Elizabeth II. The same ontological intermixing applies to Henri of the recordings. At the top of the show, a spotlighted record player on a stand occupies centre stage. On a lower shelf of the wheeled stand are the actual *Polyglotte Method* LPs, their dilapidated covers quite visible. This, in conjunction with program notes that recount the discovery of the records, supports our belief that all of Henri's speeches are drawn verbatim from the language learning records. This impression of authenticity is problematized when virtually the first thing that Henri says to us is: "My name is Henry. *Mon nom est Henri*. Please turn off your cell phone. *S'il vous plaît fermez votre téléphone*. Are you ready for the party? *Êtes vous prêt pour la soirée?*"[87] This reference to cell phones cannot be original to 1960s language instruction. So now, where we thought we were on a secure footing, we are instead mired in doubt. Everything Henri says from here on may or may not be a fabrication.

A more significant breach in the epistemological truth protocols of verbatim performance occurs in scenes nine and ten when members of the ensemble deliver several lengthy monologues. Henri begins the scene saying *"Le Canada est une beauté à nulle autre pareille. Avez-vous vérifié la facture?* Go to church. *Allez à l'église."*[88] He then invites the performers to "[*r*]*aconte-nous une histoire/au sujet/de la misère."*[89] One woman, named in the script as Safia, tells a story in French about her experience of the first day she was compelled to go to a church food bank. She arrives early, well before the doors open, but when the volunteers arrive the system is changed in an arbitrary way she doesn't understand and instead of first-come first-served, there is now a random draw and numbers are assigned to the waiting clients. The speaker ends up getting number seventy-five; she is now last and is unable to get any fruit or milk for her child.[90] Another woman, Amy, describes her daily encounters with a homeless man with whom she regularly chats. He is invisible to most people, but he is visible to her. "So I talked to him and he told me he just needed someone to look at him. Don't give money and not look at him."[91] He asks her what time it is and she finds in that moment an appreciation of her watch. "The watch was always a gift for my birthday. I love my watch."[92] Both stories peer into the space between the perception of Canada as a land of prosperity and the treatment of those who fall through the gaps, relegated to poverty and unable to access that plenty. This fracture is hinted at in Henri's absurd sequence of statements juxtaposing pride in the incredible beauty of Canada with the non sequitur asking if we have checked the bill. The message of this linguistic portmanteau seems to be: What is the cost of this "beautiful" life? Both stories present encounters between those who know the rules, those who know what time it is, and so benefit as a result, and those who don't know and so are left out. Parallel to this theme of unknowing in the speeches, the staging of the speeches themselves engender uncertainty in the breach of verbatim expectations. These speeches are long enough that I can imagine that they would be difficult for an untrained actor to reliably memorize, so it is not surprising that they are recorded. During the scene, a single performer stands in an isolating lighting special while a voiceover recording of her testimony plays. This staging arrangement communicates a unitary identity between the performer body with the autobiographical story. However, it is clear from the vocal tone that the speaker we are hearing is not the visible performer but is in fact someone else entirely. In addition, speakers credited in the speech headers in the script, Safia and Amy, are not members of the embodied cast. Voice does not equal body, despite scenography that implies that they are the same.

Out of this destabilizing audience experience of repeated moments where we are confronted with a promise of truth that slips away, *Polyglotte* applies this affect of uncertainty to our understanding of the performance's political context. The theatrical insecurity of postdramatic autobiographical performance directly informs the insecurity experienced by the immigrant-performers whose anticipated "Canada" is also revealed to be essentially ungraspable. Caught in the intercultural encounter of autobiographical performance, the audience is also figured in this equation. Throughout *Polyglotte*, the strange(r)ness to the stage of the immigrant-performers is connected to a similar subordinate marginal role in Quebec society. The cast is at a decided disadvantage both in theatrical terms and in their real-world efforts to become Canadians. In a similar manner to the audience of *RARE* who are interpellated as able-bodied persons without first-hand experience of Down syndrome disability culture, the audience of *Polyglotte* are delineated by the play as Canadian citizens, as fluent francophones, well versed in the folkways of Quebecois culture. Whereas the old-school intercultural frame of *RARE* casts the audience as curious but ignorant seekers, *Polyglotte* reverses these terms; the audience are knowing insiders; it is the immigrant performers who are seeking knowledge as they strive to pass into Canadian society both formally through the citizenship test and informally by navigating the subtle and often opaque cultural savvy of native-born Quebecers.

Question number thirteen asked by Henri is "Who is he? *Qui est-il?*"[93] The audience is exhorted by the immigration officials to answer in a loud voice as one by one the immigrant-performers hold up blank white panels. On the panels are projected what is at first a blurry face that becomes progressively clearer and sharper. These are the faces of Quebecois and Canadian politicians, both contemporary and historical. Henri gives us a catchphrase for each and the audience is challenged to shout out the correct identity before the image reaches full resolution. "He brags of knowing how to swim. *Il se vante de savoir nager.*" (Thomas Mulcair). "Be on your guard against him. *Méfiez-vous de lui.*" (Pierre Karl Péladeau). "Needless to say that he is bitterly disappointed. *Inutile de dire qu'il est amèrement déçu.*" (Jacques Parizeau).[94] Correct answers were rewarded by a chime and Henri assuring us "That's right, *c'est ça.*" It goes without saying that these clues are tricky in their ironic tone and require popular and nuanced knowledge of the ins and outs of Canadian political history and its personalities. This is knowledge that would be available to someone who lived through it, but inaccessible through official channels.[95] This is another way in which *Polyglotte* uncomfortably interpellates the audience as native-born francophones, as knowing hosts displaying our privileged and inaccessible background.

For question number ten, the immigrant cast members are instructed by Henri to "Say your lessons. *Récitez vos leçons.*"[96] They then read words and phrases projected on the back wall, sometimes in unison, sometimes individually. Like lyrics from a karaoke machine, the words change colours as they are sounded out. The first word is *"marde"* – a local Quebecois slang-crushing of the word *"merde"* – "shit." More profanities follow. In general, swear words when strung together don't make literal or grammatical sense. Beyond their generalized affect to communicate anger or hatred or frustration, the specific semiotic connotation of foul-mouthed swearing is innately untranslatable. This basic feature of cursing is compounded by the unique Quebecois canon of swear words, called *sacres*, drawn from elements of Catholic religious practice. Such constructions defy the dictionary and conventional language learning. These are words and phrases that we will not find in the *Polyglotte Method*. As a non-Quebecoise anglophone, I was acutely aware of being quite lost. In the politician face-guessing game, I was mostly keeping up, but this was beyond me. To decipher this scene after the fact, even various dictionaries and Google couldn't help me. Ultimately I resorted to consulting a bilingual friend born and raised in Quebec City. The message of the scene is clear: You can't study for this in the citizenship guide. As this reading test continues, the swear words are replaced by phrases taken from recent news – political quotes and judicial testimony. For the majority of people resident in Quebec and connected to current events media reporting, the speakers and context of these quotes would be quickly identifiable. For others, they are grammatically and contextually impenetrable. For example, the immigrants recite from the screen,

"*Les gratteux de guitars, c'toute des osties de carrés rouges la, des osties de, en tous cas des mangeux de marde.*" Upon asking my insider source about this quote, she explains that this is Stéfanie Trudeau, a police officer accused of brutality and the use of excessive force in association with the student demonstrations in the spring of 2012, during *le printemps érable.*[97] She is referred to by her service number 728. My source tellingly comments, "everyone knows matricule 728."[98] "Everyone" may, but I didn't. Taken as a whole, the scene combines several impressions. First, there is the awkward and distasteful display of compelling seemingly naive speakers to say some very rude words. Then, beyond that embarrassment, many of the statements they are asked to read aloud express sentiments from politicians and media personalities, ranging from mildly xenophobic to outright racist. Finally, there is the underscoring of being outsiders. This test is not a fair one and Canada is not such a nice place.

The selection of quotations in this scene also points to what I see as a central juxtaposition in the political themes of *Polyglotte*. Featuring statements that refer either to defences of the proposed but defeated Charter of Values[99] or to the suppression of recent mass political demonstrations, the play aligns the social insecurity of immigrants with the economic insecurity of the existing Quebec citizenry under austerity. The illusion of Canada as a safe haven of peace, economic prosperity, and freedom of conscience is persistently undermined. What people want or believe to be true about Canada is a thin illusion of advertising. When asked about their hopes, it becomes clear that each member of the cast is an educated and skilled worker unable to take up their career in Canada. Farlene was a radio announcer in Haiti; now she is a Tim Horton's cashier. Ali is a civil engineer who now works as a customer service representative for Bell Canada. Tatiana holds a PhD in comparative literature. Her current job is writing subtitles for television shows for people who are Deaf or have a hearing impairment. Their frustration at the systemic restrictions they experience is clear. Somnath is irked because he is paying international student tuition at Université de Quebec à Montreal and cannot find work because he does not speak French well enough. Regarding the difficulty in obtaining a job that matches their expertise, another performer, German, muses, "I don't know how Canadians feel about that. I don't see any reactions about that ... They say 'OK it is your choice. You decided to come here.'"[100] And yet the group remains positive on the whole. When asked, they tell Henri that they are happy to be in Canada.

As part of question five regarding "schooling, labour, education, administration, work and religious advice," Henri interviews three of the women. After each wrongly answers his seemingly absurd question: "What are ostrich feathers good for?," they are given feather dusters and told to dust the chairs while showing their good will. "*Montrez votre bonne volonté.*" While Pamela and Samira energetically pretend to dust the two-dimensional projections of chairs, Tatiana drops her duster in disgust. Henri asks, "Are you disgusted? *Êtes-vous dégoûté?*" Pamela says, "No. That's the life of an immigrant. You have to wake up in the morning and go. You have to put food on the table." Henri replies, "That's right." Samira says, "If it's temporary, I can do this kind of job, yes." Henri replies, "That's right." Tatiana says, "*Alors moi, je ne suis pas prête à faire n'importe quoi, surtout pas la boniche.*"[101] Her answer triggers the sound of the wrong buzzer. A light illuminates the now open exit door from the theatre. Henri asks, "What are you going to do? *Veux-tu partir?*" He continues, "*S'il m'était donné de choisir, je m'en irais a l'instant. Veux-tu rester?*" Tatiana replies, "*Oui.*" In the end, she takes up the feather duster and exits for the next scene.[102] Her acquiescence reads both in the actual world as resignation to doing this unappealing work, but also within the context of the play as play as agreement to continue with these ridiculous tasks, such as enthusiastically pretending to dust pretend chairs. Significantly, Henri feels that he has a choice not only to refuse the work but also to refuse to play this silly game; clearly Tatiana does not feel as confident.

After walking in the snow in their parkas, the ensemble is invited into a rustic cabin to warm up. There is a fire in the fireplace. The walls are decorated with a taxidermy moose head, animal pelts, and an institutional portrait of a young Queen Elizabeth – the kind you used to see in elementary schools. This quintessential Canadian imagery is critiqued when the performers are instructed to go to the window and look outside. The projected blinds open and a melee is revealed with video footage of protesters being sprayed by armoured police officers. Henri informs us that "The miners are on strike. *Les mineurs sont en grève.*" It seems that Henri of the 1960s refers here anachronistically to the historically pivotal 1949 Asbestos strike which drew 5,000 miners and lasted four months. Yet, the footage of the manifestation is definitively contemporary, another example in a long series of economically motivated, hostile demonstrations. (Coincidentally, the day I saw the show the second time, the news screens in the Métro were reporting a demonstration that Saturday by public-sector workers.) "Would you back the strike?"

3.3 The cast of *Polyglotte* with toboggans as riot shields. Photo courtesy of Olivier Choinière.

Henri asks. As they reply cacophonously, "Yes. Maybe. No. *Oui. Peut-être. Non.*" Henri commands them to "Double lock the doors. *Restez chez vous durant la soirée.* You are working tomorrow. *Vous avez besoin d'une bonne nuit de sommeil* ... What more can I do for your welfare? *Que puis-je faire de plus pour votre bien-être?*"[103] The ensemble hesitates a moment and then all speak at once, presumably presenting their various needs for assistance. The babble is curtailed as Henri declares, "Good night! *Bonne nuit!*" and the lights cut to blackout.

In the final scene, the cast march in formation and line up across the front of the stage. In front of their bodies, each actor holds a plastic toboggan painted white, which they rap sharply with a short baton, pounding a beat in unison. Transformed into a phalanx of riot police, they are intimidating. Aligned with the police against popular demonstrations, the immigrants are effectively divided from the audience. Their willingness to do whatever is necessary to attain their citizenship as they occupy a no-man's-land of being not-quite-yet Canadian sets up a productive contradiction, suggesting that the "un-Canadian" protest-ers are even more Canadian by their confident right to protest against their own government. This same division and contradiction is made explicit in the finale to *Polyglotte's* citizenship ceremony. Glowing from bright backlight, one of the stage manager-actors glides downstage as Queen Elizabeth. The audience is then instructed to stand. With the hopeful citizens-to-be of the immigrant cast, we repeat responsively the oath of citizenship, swearing allegiance to the Queen and her suc-cessors. At both performances I attended, the audience obediently stood and began to recite, but as the words and their Anglo-monarchist import became clear, many stopped participating. And at one perfor-mance, a full 50 per cent of the audience expressed their resistance to this exercise by sitting back down. It was a remarkable moment that underscored the insight that this choice, the choice to refuse the oath, is a luxury available to native-born Canadians that newly immigrated, prospective Canadians do not share.

Having established this particular power dynamic in the intercultural encounter, *Polyglotte* sharply turns the tables on the culturally superior audience. Henri declares, "You will love your country insofar as you know its history. *Tu aimeras ton pays dans la mesure où tu connaitras son histoire.*"[104] One of the candidates is then tasked with reading a para-graph of text and repeating it back in her own words. The text, lifted verbatim from the citizenship study guide, describes the experience of "*les peuples autochtones.*" Farlene's condensation of the complex history of genocidal persecution of Indigenous peoples mixed with some more upbeat platitudes ("*Dans le Canada d'aujourd'hui, les peuples autochtones retrouvent leur fierté et leur confiance, et ils ont à leur actif de grandes réalisa-tions dans les domains de l'agriculture, de l'environement, des affaires et des arts.*"[105]) into a few short sentences renders both the original and the repetition comically painful in its reduction: "*Au début il y avait les Indi-ens, mais les Européens leur ont donné des maladies. Ceux qu'ils restaient, ils sont allés au pensionnat. Le Canada s'est excusé pour ça et aujourd'hui ils s'en sortent bien.*"[106] In concert with allowing the audience to perform its cul-tural superiority, *Polyglotte* also reads that insider position back to the audience to expose us, reminding the audience that as settler-colonists, we too have been, in other times, immigrants.

At the very end of the play, the projection walls open like giant doors and the candidates and the audience are welcomed to Canada by the immigration officials. "Enter by this door please. *Entrez par cette porte s'il vous plaît.* Take your things with you and go home. *Prenez vos effets personnels et entrez à la maison."*[107] As we exit, the audience streams past a *tableau vivant*, composed of the immigrant-performers. In front of a human-scale projection of the 1907 painting *Jacques Cartier rencontre les Indiens à Stadaconé, 1535* by Marc-Aurèle de Foy Suzor-Coté,[108] the cast mimics the poses. Under the projected title *"Cartier rencontre les sauvages, 1535,"* the men in the cast play the French Cartier and his crew, standing erect with their standards and halberds; the women play the Iroquois, crouching in the underbrush. Stage directions in the script note: *Le public peut applaudir le tableau vivant.*[109] This is awkward to say the least. Having been previously denied the opportunity to applaud the cast for their theatrical labour, it seems polite at this point to offer appreciation and yet applause in this context is fraught. What is it that we are endorsing with our applause? The painting presents yet another intercultural encounter with a stranger and forces us to rearrange our understanding of who are the immigrants and who are the "natives"?

Through these various staged encounters, the play illuminates the means whereby these two groups of strangers – the audience and the amateur cast, Canadians and not-yet-Canadians – are both subject to various kinds of insecurity, insecurity generated by postdramatic techniques and real-world insecurity arising from an uncertain economic future and unimaginable social responsibilities. Rather than simplistically suggesting that through this autobiographical encounter, "we" can actually get to know and appreciate "them," *Polyglotte* consistently problematizes potential points of contact. Even though we are brought into proximate encounter through autobiographical postdramatic performance, the product of our communal insecurities is a reflexive awareness of those insecurities, of all the things we cannot know or control, things that are broken and are difficult to fix. But rather than create a shared experience of not knowing together, *Polyglotte*, like *100% Vancouver* and *RARE*, suggests that despite increased exposure strangers remain strange. And that Canadianness – even for those born within its borders – remains elusive.

Whereas the three productions discussed here are premised, like much conventional autobiographical work, as an open sharing of the intimate life of the self-storying subject, I am suggesting that these projects are, as all autobiographical performance is, at some level, always doomed to failure. What is being produced here is not simply confident security and socially progressive illumination. We are thwarted by failure at every turn. And as Bailes notes, failure leads to unpredictable outcomes. There is no longer a single planned outcome but a range of outcomes that are indeterminate and prolific. "Failure *produces*, and does so in a roguish manner."[110] What emerges as a product of the insecurity generated here is the need to admit and bear witness to the impossibility of knowing strangers. Critically, however, ungraspability is here a positive value. The ethical encounter embedded in autobiographical performance is doomed to fail, and perhaps that is a good thing. In the humbleness of insecurity, we are asked to strive without guarantee of success. In the combined attempt of approach between two groups of unfamiliars to establish mutually democratic exchange, we are indeed, as when Andreas in *RARE* exhorted the audience to "Please look at yourselves," pressed to turn the mirror on ourselves and interrogate our assumptions not only about him and the autobiographical ensembles of *RARE*, *Polyglotte*, and *100% Vancouver* as strangers, but more fundamentally about our own impossibly estranged desire for knowledge in autobiographical looking in the first place. "If we cannot overcome the relations of force and authorisation implicated in "knowing" itself, then is the answer *to come to know how not to know*?"[111] Productive insecurity, by exposing the politics of perception, reconciles the audience to the impossibility of really knowing unfamiliars and admits the ethical position of not trying to assimilate others through autobiographical encounter, letting strangers remain strange.

4 Real Words: Reproducing Life in Remediated Verbatim Theatre – *Seeds* and *300 TAPES*

Like autobiography, verbatim performance is a truth-based genre. Where autobiographical performance establishes its contract to reality and truth in the self-storying body of the actor-subject, bonding the narrative self to visceral presence, verbatim sheds the body, concentrating truth-value in the testimony of the originary, but now absent, subject. Autobiographical performance brings bodies to the stage to speak themselves into being; verbatim theatre brings words to the stage, leaving bodies behind, and houses authentic speech in new bodies. In this way, perhaps, we can see verbatim as a subgenre or variation of autobiography in which autobiographical words are collected at the source and transported from that initial point of live contact to the stage to be reified there in a different body. Just as staged bodies seem to activate perceptions of authenticity, so too the testimony of a witness attracts a similar sense of access to realness. As Derek Paget argues, in mediatized societies documents are vulnerable to postmodern doubt, to editing and to redaction, but "the witness's claim to authenticity can still warrant a credible perspective. This is because there is both a legalistic and a spiritual component in Western notions of witness."[1] Yet, despite the deep-seated cultural value accorded to the testimony of witnesses, verbatim theatre, like other reality-based performance genres, is still subject to longstanding and well-rehearsed concerns about its constructedness that destabilize those truth claims.

Constructive contingency marks verbatim work in two ways. First, as testimony is displaced from its initial witnessing situation, it becomes vulnerable to adaptation. Speech is stripped of its contextual situation. The priority placed on words can elide other complementary impressions like gesture, facial expression, and vocal intonation. Then, shaped for performance, the captured speech is edited, condensed, and parcelled out. After these initial reductions, verbatim text is reinflated, as it were, in performance, augmented in its uncanny possession of other actor bodies. Second, testimony is detached from reality in a more profound way at its point of origin by poststructural scepticism. Transmuted from lived experience to words, testimony is dependent on the citationality of language for comprehension. Following Derrida's influential argument, all language is citational, and meaning is arbitrary; words accrue sense only through conventionally sanctioned reiteration. There is no ground, merely an endless citational chain that stretches into the past without origin. What this means then for verbatim performance is that even the first articulation of a witness is a performative construction, its relation to an absolutely concrete reality insecure. This is the central problem of verbatim performance. Verbatim theatre in the twenty-first century is characterized by an "apparent paradox of a form that is required to rely on the real for its political authority, whilst simultaneously remaining suspicious of the very notion of the real as dictated by the poststructuralist scepticism of this particular historical moment."[2] Whither verbatim in the face of this innate paradox?

A common strategy mobilized in response to this paradox has been for performances to "own" this inherent tension by invoking self-reflexive techniques that simultaneously expose the processes of construction while gesturing through that construction to the original sources that speak to authenticity. It is a careful balancing act not to bring on the collapse of the whole structure. How testimony is handled and how that handling is hidden or made visible is central to addressing the problem of poststructural scepticism in documentary. A risk in this approach, however, is that formalist meditations that dwell on the familiar caveats around generic limitations of verbatim can displace the documents entirely and themselves become the main story. As Carol Martin notes, "At its best, documentary theatre complicates the idea of documentary and of the real, of a document, and even what it means to document; documentary theatre troubles our already troubled categories of truth, reality, fiction and acting."[3] Self-reflexive awareness at this metatheatrical level invites both creators and audiences to step back and to actively question the core principles that found our understanding of documentary value. Destabilizing the authority of the document as object and of the action of documentation restores balance and humility but it also creates a paralysis of unknowing. Given this veridical complication, the challenge is to move the conversation beyond this central epistemological instability of the form. The work of documentary need not stall at remarking the point of self-reflexive not knowing. Returning to Ulrike Garde and Meg Mumford, the first question to ask is this: In what ways might this inescapable affect of insecurity be productive?[4]

Two recent productions engage this potentially paralyzing impasse between the real and its products, employing disparate strategies to interrogate the value of representing the verbatim real through itera-tively replicating performative construction: *Seeds*, created by Anna-bel Soutar and her company Porte Parole in partnership with Crow's Theatre,[5] and *300 TAPES*, a devised work by Public Recordings, led by co-creators Ame Henderson and Bobby Theodore.[6] In the tradition of "new" twenty-first century documentary style of UK verbatim creators like Alecky Blythe and Richard Norton of Tricycle Theatre or Anna Dea-vere Smith and Tectonic Theatre in the US, Soutar adopts a journalistic approach, going into the field and into the archives to engage a particu-lar current issue. The real-life incident that furnishes the core of the play is a case heard by the Supreme Court of Canada: Monsanto Canada Inc. v. Schmeiser. In 1998, multinational biotech corporation Monsanto accused Percy Schmeiser, a canola farmer from Bruno, Saskatchewan, of illegally seeding his fields with their genetically modified, pesticide-resistant canola, thereby infringing on their patent.[7] The case became a cause célèbre for the global anti-GMO movement, raising issues per-taining not only to the patentability of a gene, but also to the right of farmers to save their seeds from one crop to the next, the protection of crop and weed biodiversity, and the overall safety and regulation of genetically-modified foods. Court transcripts, media reports, and per-sonal interviews form the corpus of testimony from which Soutar has crafted the play.

At the beginning of act two, Annabel, who appears as a character in her own play, recognizes an implicit connection between what she does as the maker of documentary theatre and what Monsanto is doing mak-ing genetically modified seeds. "To begin with, we are both in the busi-ness of ... life. We use life as raw material and we modify it in order to produce something that we then call our 'invention.' We both describe our mission as 'making the world a better place' – Monsanto by feed-ing a hungry and growing world; me by telling stories in which a mul-tiplicity of voices reflects something I perceive to be important about the world."[8] Although at the beginning of the play, Annabel starts with the question "What is life?," by the end she has shifted the terms of her query, asking, "How do we want to see life modified?" The matter is no longer framed as a question of moral volition: "Should life be modi-fied?" but rather she tacitly admits that this is a foregone conclusion and shifts to the practical how.

Where *Seeds* considers the question "Who owns life?" in light of Monsanto's bid to patent a gene, *300 TAPES* asks the same question through an encounter with blurred memories and identities "leading [the creators] to question concepts of ownership with regard to personal stories and movement."[9] Exploring this common territory, *300 TAPES* draws its verbatim roots from a different performance genealogy than *Seeds*. To generate raw material for *300 TAPES*, the three actor-creators, Frank Cox-O'Connell, Joe Cobden, and Brendan Gall were handed microcassette recorders and each tasked with recording 100 autobiographical memory monologues over a period of weeks. Each story had to be short – they are generally less than eight minutes, and average three to four minutes. The stories were recorded privately, with the actors working sequentially from earliest memory to the present without backtracking. In terms of tone, the speakers were asked to imagine telling the story in a bar or similar small-group social setting to a group of friendly strangers or new acquaintances. The anecdotes are conversational, loosely organized, and candid, often in a self-deprecating way. Returning to the rehearsal room, each actor handed his newly recorded and as yet unheard tape to one of the others, who played it back through headphones, reciting the text in real time, trying to synchronously voice what he is hearing. This technique of auto-reciting fosters a non-matrixed performance style where the technical challenge of the task keeps the performer off-balance and inhibits the creation of character. This approach to verbatim occupies the intersection between documentary and auto/biography. Seen in the work of experimental companies like Nature Theatre of Oklahoma and The Wooster Group, verbatim in this mode shifts the journalistic impulse from political issues of the public sphere to private narratives, taking everyday speech as ready-mades in the style of Marcel Duchamp to be reframed in performance as performance. Retaining speech disfluencies like "um" and "ah" and the pitched rhythms of oral language, the text becomes musical. Like Annabel in *Seeds*, the makers of *300 TAPES* take the modification of life as a given; reproduction is their principal modus operandi. As co-creator, Theodore says, "In fact, one of the inspirations of the show is the lie inherent in verbatim theatre ... A stage piece is artificially arranged. 300 TAPES is choreographed storytelling, where reconstructing and reassembling people's lives has an enhanced effect."[10] The question remains, "How do we want to see life modified?" Here, reproductive remediation happens not at the level of the genome but at the level of the phoneme.

Liz Tomlin poses a much-needed critique of the current focus of verbatim scholarship. She writes, "The sceptical climate ... has subsequently ensured that academic debate and analysis are rarely focused on the issues raised by the source material but are rather compelled to interrogate the validity of the form itself, particularly in relation to any implicit or explicit truth claims it might be seen to be making."[11] Moving beyond generic formal analysis of verbatim work and its well-understood fraught connection to the "truth," I propose to take up Tomlin's challenge and consider how the specific strategies employed to manage epistemological uncertainty operate to support (or undermine) issues, just as Tomlin says, that are raised by the staging of this source material. How does the self-reflexive ambivalence to truth of mediatized verbatim engage with the specific stories of *Seeds* and *300 TAPES*? Both productions make the case that life is made to be copied. From a purely biological perspective, this is indeed the purpose of life – to reproduce. The GMO debates suggest that there are good and bad ways to reproduce life and that in artificially rewriting the genetic text this process is not ethically neutral. Creation of self through autobiographical storytelling is also a generatively iterative process. Ethical considerations also inhere to personal narratives. In parallel with Soutar's concern with commercially modified genomes, the question of ownership of these narratives is likewise a point of interest for Public Recordings. Whose story is this and who has the right to tell it? What are the stakes for memory and identity when stories become unmoored from their original voices and bodies? Facing the ubiquity of reproductive modification and of the remediation of life by narrative, by performance, but also by technological innovation, we are invited to consider the principles that might be invoked to govern such remediative processes and also the effects of that remediation. It is useful in this light to consider what kind of social value – positive or negative, optimistic or pessimistic – is awarded to reproductive copying, characterized by splicing, mutation, and augmentation or degradation.

Reproducibility has always been a feature of a work of art and also a point of anxiety.[12] Plato, in his argument concerning ideal forms, proposes that all things exist "in nature" first as ideas, made by God who is "the real maker of a real bed, not a particular maker of a particular maker of a particular bed, [creator of] a bed which is essentially and by nature one only."[13] Objects in the world are secondary copies of these ideal forms. The carpenter is also the maker of a bed. The painter who then creates an image of the appearance of the bed is neither a creator nor maker, but merely an imitator. He is "third in the descent from nature."[14] The artist, then, is not in contact with reality but only with a second-order imitation. As such, these works are so far removed from the original, being degenerate copies, that they might, in fact, be harmful. As Elin Diamond succinctly summarizes, "What Plato distrusts is that mimesis implies difference – the copy is not the model; the character not the actor; the excited spectator not the rational male citizen, yet both occupy the same ontological space."[15] This is one of the pillars for Plato's ultimate conclusion that artists are not truth-tellers and as such should be excluded from his utopian republic.

For millennia, manual replication has been sanctioned as the province of apprentices learning their craft, amateurs taking impressions for souvenirs, and in a limited sense by entrepreneurs seeking profit. But as Walter Benjamin observes in his 1936 seminal essay "The Work of Art in the Age of Mechanical Reproduction," mass replication facilitated by technology is something new. Visual and audio recording technologies, from cameras loaded with film to microphones and recording devices using analog tapes or digital file formats, allow unprecedented facility not only for capturing the original artefact through recording but also for rematerializing that recording in alternate forms, in alternate times and places. Breaking technological replication into two phases – capture and playback – shows how verbatim performance is both similar to and different than the examples of reproduction cited by Benjamin. Verbatim performance as practised in both *Seeds* and *300 TAPES* makes use of audio recorders to collect testimony and preserve it as data in a radically different material form from that of the original event. Verbatim, as a genre, values exact replication. But unlike film or photography or radio broadcasting, the playback component of verbatim is non-mechanical as the text is voiced by human actors. It is worth considering what difference this hybrid composition of mechanized and non-mechanized reproduction makes to how we differentiate value between the original and the reproduction. Do we view the actor-reciters as working in an artisanal context or as merely playback machines in human form?

Both *Seeds* and *300 TAPES* explicitly exhibit and reflect on the human labour of copying in their verbatim presentations. As manual craft, these performance processes carry those appealing markers of authenticity identified by Gilmore and Pine,[16] bearing the unique qualities of artisanal handiwork, marked by limited accessibility in time and space and in number, being ephemeral, local, and scarce.

> Working in the American theatre today is like being a cobbler or a glass-blower in a world of e-commerce, virtual realities, political tumult, celebrity culture, illiteracy, digital imaging and cyberspace. We are like practitioners of an ancient artisan craft, anachronistic in a world of mass production and advanced technology. Only the rarest individuals today prefer their shoes handmade or their kitchen glasses handblown. We are not the medium for the masses. We are like the monks preserving a library from antiquity – that rare entity, once so prized, of a storyteller and play-ers recounting adventures for those gathered around a sacred campfire."[17]

As attractive as that exclusive and exalted image may be, we need to avoid the easy sentimentality of seeing all theatre as the equivalent of a pair of bespoke shoes. Rather, having acknowledged the context of "manual" or embodied replication in verbatim in a cultural moment that is affectively aligned against technologized mass production, one question to ask is: "What value accrues to this labour?" Other questions are: "What is the effect of the inevitable errors and imperfections that arise in the handmade copy?" "And how do these errors shape our understanding of verbatim in general as a form and specifically of the testimony represented?"

Benjamin notes that throughout history handcrafted copies were "usu-ally branded as a forgery,"[18] an accusation that curiously does not, in his view, accrue to mechanical copies. From where does this implicit nega-tive value judgment of the manual copy arise? Perhaps it is because the manual copy feels like a copy; its status as a copy is evident somehow, possibly through imperfections of the likeness. It is a copy that reveals its differences from the original and so therefore is less. Or perhaps it is the opposite; it is because the copy doesn't feel like a copy. There is in the forgery a sense of deceit. The copying process is hidden and so once it is discovered we condemn it as trickery. A "truthful" copy – truthful in the sense of being perfect and/or truthful in the sense that it con-fesses to its status as a copy – would not attract similar negative valua-tion. Anxiety flourishes when our desire for authenticity collides with the possibility of a forgery so good that we may never know the truth. Paradoxically, in a culture that craves authenticity, we are surrounded by fakes as never before. Having an informed citizenry is the founda-tion of modern democracy. However, in a post-truth world where the art (and technology) of spin has become amazingly sophisticated, traditional sources of information have become increasingly unreliable or disregarded. "Photographs are faked, ... articles in newspapers turn out to have been entirely fabricated, weapons of mass destruction cannot be found in Iraq."[19] Everything is manipulated (or can be) and in this context our default position is distrust. One important way this void is being filled is through grassroots dissemination of knowledge, through crowd-sourcing and citizen journalism. Documentary-style verbatim theatre has stepped into the journalistic void in an effort to give hearing to voices not typically raised in public and present insight direct from not-the-usual sources. But verbatim theatre does not stand entirely above the fray. In an attempt to offer access to authentic truth, verbatim employs exactly these manipulative technologies of reproduction and remediation and so gets caught up in Benjamin's concerns with the source of authenticity and his attachment to a clear distinction in value between the original and the copy, be it mass produced or hand-crafted, acknowledged or unacknowledged. Affects of authenticity, then, do not arise merely as a factor of the true content but are also enmeshed in the nature of reproductive mediation of that content, its crafted processes, and the visibility of those processes.

Mechanical reproduction can alter space. Part of the attraction of mechanical reproduction is that the copies can travel to meet the beholder in a way that the original can't, especially if there is a change of medium, for example when a painting becomes a photograph of a painting or a symphony becomes a radio broadcast of a symphony. In tension with the desire for authenticity, there is a profound "desire of contemporary masses to bring things 'closer' spatially and humanly, which is just as ardent as their bent towards overcoming the uniqueness of every reality by accepting its reproduction. Every day the urge grows stronger to get hold of an object at very close range by way of its likeness, its reproduction."[20] Reproductive technologies also alter space by bringing the object even closer than direct perception can admit, opening new enriched vistas of perception by creating enlargements of details through zooming in or slow motion. Access is at odds with presence as technology permits the transportation of the live work of art from there to here and from then to now. And it is this sacrifice of presence that Benjamin mourns. He writes that "even the most perfect reproduction of a work of art is lacking in one element: its presence in time and space, its unique existence at the place where it happens to be."[21] This quality of presence is bound up with the historical provenance of the work, manifesting in the conditions of its creation, and in the physical changes it has endured over time, as well as changes of ownership. Presence both in the present now as immediately accessible and as it gestures to the continuous life of the work (what Mariah Horner calls a "sense of since")[22] are central to the invaluable quality of authenticity that Benjamin characterizes as "aura." The reproduction is detached from the original both by technological means of copying that offer new perspectives like enlargement or slow motion and by the ability of the copy to travel and enter into new contexts in ways impossible for the original.[23] Although the reproduction has the ability to bring the work into the proximity that audiences desire, it lacks aura. To this view, authenticity is antithetical to reproduction.

As a bold corollary to this initial assertion, Benjamin seems to claim that not only does the copy lack aura, but that the aura of the original is threatened by reproduction.

> The situations into which the product of mechanical reproduction can be brought may not touch the actual work of art, yet the quality of its presence is always depreciated ... Since the historical testimony rests on the authenticity, the former, too, is jeopardized by reproduction when substantive duration ceases to matter. And what is really jeopardized when the historical testimony is affected is the authority of the object.[24]

In the age of mechanical reproduction, aura withers. Continuing, Benjamin also seems to suggest that this depreciation of the aura of the original work of art applies not only to secondary mechanical remediation but also to the primary representation of the work of art from life.

> This holds not only for the art work but also, for instance, for a landscape which passes in review before the spectator in a movie ... Unmistakably, reproduction as offered by picture magazines and newsreels differs from the image seen by the unarmed eye. Uniqueness and permanence are as closely linked in the latter as are transitoriness and reproducibility in the former.[25]

Philip Auslander makes a similar point when he notes that Michael Kirby's concept of non-matrixed representation "provided a beachhead for mediatization within artistic practices that resisted mediatization."[26] As Kirby writes, "in non-matrixed representation the referential elements are applied *to* the performer and are not acted *by* him."[27] For Kirby, and

Auslander, mediation is not mainly (or only) technological, it is perceptual. The meaning of the work as art or as performance is created by the frame of representing or recording. This suggests that there is no qualitative difference in this regard between technological remediation and perceptual remediation. Both are part of a chain of citation and representation. Verbatim speech remediates recorded testimony just as testimony remediates lived experience. What I am suggesting then, as an extension rather than a disagreement with Benjamin, is that each layer of mediation is in conversation with realness and authenticity. Just as the aura of a work of art (DaVinci's *Mona Lisa* at the Louvre Museum) is valued (or devalued) in conjunction with and relative to the real-world object it represents (a human face), so too subsequent pairs of reproduction and "original" are also likewise valued or devalued. Consider the aura of the painting of the Mona Lisa as authentic *vis-à-vis* its myriad copies on mugs, notebooks, and desktop backgrounds. In this auratic chain, each subsequent layer of remediation retains a relationship to the real and to liveness in its creation and its provenance. Talking about different locations of liveness in technological representation, such as how the televisual live is "now" but not "here," or how stadium Jumbotron replays are "here" but not "now," Steve Wurtzler writes, "The degradation of the live is compensated for by the inscription into the 'real' of its representation."[28] Which brings me to ask: Where is the original live in *Seeds* and *300 TAPES*? How is the absent real, being not "here" and/or not "now," inscribed into its representation? How do the different relative layers of realness and authenticity speak to the plays' concern with reproduction as imperative to the creation of life both in a biological and an autobiographical sense?

Until there was the capacity for recording, there was no need for the concept of liveness. As Baudrillard points out, the live is defined by the recorded and vice versa. The same might be said of related terms like "real" and "presence" and "authentic" and their correlatives "not real," "absence," and "fake." The relationship between these pairs of terms is not one of precession but is rather one of mutual dependence.[29] By definition, then, that which is live is that which can be recorded; it is the original that is subject to representation. However, in verbatim performance, the dualistic pairs of live/recorded and original/representation become tangled in a chiastic relationship where what comes to the stage "live" is the representation and what is recorded is the "original" document. Any originary live event located in the first speech of testimony, for example, that is the antecedent of the documentary recording, is absent and as such is directly inaccessible in performance. Auslander points out that rock concerts and stand-up comedy are instances where "mediatization is now explicitly and implicitly embedded within the live experience."[30] The live performance is the conduit for reification and recreation of an always and necessarily absent original live. For the audience of a rock concert or standup comedy routine, the live experience follows the recording and does not precede it, since for many the encounter with a particular musical group or comedian is first through the comedy album or podcast or radio broadcast or digital streaming equivalent. Not only does the live come second, already mediatized, but, like a film, the original live event does not even really exist as such. The live event that underpins the oeuvre of a popular musical or comedy performer is not contiguous with the recording, which is composed of edited and re-sequenced fragments performed specifically to be recorded. And so is a record of an event that never was. Verbatim theatre, too, is a genre where mediatization is embedded in and predicated by the live performance. Verbatim re-enactment purports to be a reliving (or re-enlivening) of a recording. A significant difference for verbatim is that although, like the concert or the stand-up comedy event, it is the re-enactment of an absent prior live, the intermedial recording that predicates its authenticity is rendered inaccessible. Whereas the treasured CD or MP3 of a song or sketch comedy routine anchors the bridge to the real for the concertgoer, the testimonial recordings foundational to verbatim are acknowledged, acknowledgment that is essential to the truth claims of the genre, yet these archival recordings (for the most part) remain unheard by the audience.

Realness in verbatim theatre is held in tension between these two poles, between the absent lived historical real and the re-lived real of the re-presented representation. In the autobiographical performances of *Winners and Losers*, *100% Vancouver*, *RARE*, and *Polyglotte*, these two sites of realness cohabit in one body, as self-storying performers re/embody their own experience. And as previously argued, this generates in the singular autobiographical body an ambiguous ontological duality, fostering for the audience perceptual insecurity where the "self" is both present and absent. Verbatim theatre leaves the body behind and attempts to transfer that "self," that lived historical real as text. In this respect, absence is a key feature of the genre. But likewise, citationality, the representation of that absence, is also key. It is a core assumption of poststructuralist thinking that everything is citation and "there can be no sense of a pure or authentic original to which the notion of adaptation can refer."[31] *Seeds* and *300 TAPES* absorb this poststructural-ist ethos as story, dramatizing its implications in form and in content. Just as we cannot sensibly talk about the original signifier attached to its signified in language, we cannot sensibly talk about original DNA. All DNA is citation. Likewise, there is no authentic originary self. Each story is a new version, and each is as legitimate as the one before as the self is accreted in reiterative performance over time.

> The crisis of an embattled self is over, because any sense of a central point or fulcrum for being or from which to evaluate experience has disap-peared. The metaphysics of presence, which orientated us to experiential time and space, is no longer meaningful; the self has no location as such, no witnessable presence to which we can coherently respond ... The self appears in myriad locations, untamed by criteria of authenticity.[32]

Being unmoored in both space and time, all selves – narrative and genetic – constitute different ontologically equivalent types of cita-tion; none take precedence. In the pages that follow, I will move to look at these two selected performances more closely, examining various dramaturgical and scenographic strategies employed by the artists to consider how the formal operations (and frustrations) of absence and presence in verbatim performance are leveraged thematically to com-ment on the plays' issues.

First, how do *Seeds* and *300 TAPES* engage with absence? One place to start is with the titles of both plays. For *300 TAPES*, the paradox of present absence resides in the tapes themselves. The title draws our attention to the tapes that exist on the stage as historical artefacts. In their racks and in the hands of the performers, the tapes as artefacts are visible and tangible, recognizable and attractive as containers of original testimony voiced by original witnesses. The data is present right there in those little boxes and yet they remain profoundly inac-cessible and silent. Occasionally, in the play, the real does bubble up and the stories on the tapes spill out. When Joe's headphones come unplugged we hear a tantalizing fragment of a phrase, before the plug is restored and the sound is quickly stuffed back in the box. Sound cues sometimes overlap with the live replicating voices to let us hear the sounds of tape hiss, rewinding, or "osculating" room tones.[33] A sound cue dubbed "Slate 3" is an audio collage constructed from the declared names and date stamps in the opening seconds of each tape. Even these teasers themselves are mediated, recordings of the original moments of anecdotal autobiography which, although raised to our attention, still remain hidden. The thing itself is necessarily obscured, but we can see and experience absence by what surrounds it, like the gravitational signature of a black hole. This performative lacuna and the indirect focus on that empty space is a key feature of verbatim performance.

In *Seeds*, likewise, the real bubbles up indirectly through metaphorical pointing to absent realness by substitutes. In the frenetic prologue, one of the actors dressed as a lab technician in a white coat holds up an egg; he then cracks it into a pan placed on a hot plate. An overhead camera captures the egg, displaying it on the large upstage screen in all its glorious realness as it sizzles. Like States's dog on the stage, the egg is a source of phenomenological fascination in its fictionally resistant en soi. The egg is a seed. Other seeds also feature as metaphorical markers of the present absence at the heart of *Seeds*. In scene fifteen, as Trish Jordan, the Monsanto rep, is outlining the evidence against Schmeiser, *"A bag of seed falls from the sky, landing next to [her] with a loud thump."*[34] These both are and are not the actual seeds that were subjected to testing to prove their specific resistance. Another point of ambivalent absence relates to the fact that Annabel Soutar was pregnant with her second child during the research phase of creating this verbatim work. In the premiere of *Seeds* in Toronto in February 2012, actress Liisa Repo-Martell, who played Annabel as The Playwright, was herself in the second trimester of her pregnancy as she performed the role. Here, the actual pregnant body of Repo-Martell points to the absent original of Annabel, in the manner of all verbatim performers. In addition, the obvious realness of Repo-Martell's own body carries phenomenological excess triggering the effect of en soi and drawing attention to the ambiguous fictionality of her own seed. This effect is magnified when at the beginning of act two The Playwright has an ultrasound screening of her incipient baby. The screen fills with the black and white footage of an in utero fetus. The inescapable question (at least for me) is grounded in the real world: Who is this? Is it Annabel's daughter? Liisa's son? Unless it is a CGI fabrication, it really is some real baby somewhere. Again, as with the frying egg, the audience is enraptured by the resistant realness of an object that is not easily subsumed into the fiction. These seeds presented in this context are members of that very rarefied class of theatrical objects that resist mediation and come to us as is. They remain raw. And by trafficking in a profound presence of realness point to other "raw" objects that are absent. "Objects only become present in themselves when this total context [of the theatricalizing frame] is somehow broken or disrupted."[35] The effect of these objects is that in the same way that excessive remediation distracts us from the outcome and we get caught up in the process, resistant lack of mediation does the same thing. These selected objects get hung up in world[a].

As Andy Lavender writes, "Theatre has always traded in nowness, and at various points in its history has developed new ways in which to heighten the spectator's awareness of the present moment."[36] Connected to this sense of now-ness is the corollary sense of here-ness. The resistance of these objects to fictionality and their determination to assert their actual-world materiality points to the here and now of the theatre event. These objects participate with the audience and with actors in the immediate work of making theatre together. This is not the aura of real presence of autobiographical actors. This is not the presence of charisma. It is Power's "literal mode of presence," being present rather than having presence. These objects are more like *Winners and Losers'* Jamie and Marcus's ping pong ball, which expresses "being present" in itself, than like Jamie and Marcus themselves, who "have presence." Power recognizes that presence is typically at odds with representation, not contradicting Derrida's dictum that there is nothing outside of representation. This line of thinking echoes Benjamin's assertion that the copy has no aura, no autonomous value in presence, but Power goes on to argue "that presence is *a function* of theatrical signification. To understand how presence is staged we must look at how theatre (re)presents its illusions."[37] To this view, "presence is not something fixed that theatre has but is the subject of a constantly shifting interplay between theatrical signification and the context in which a performance takes place."[38] In this context, these objects, in resisting theatricality, carve out a certain quality of realness against which other theatrical representations are tested. They also, as mentioned, stand in for, and assert their presence in contrast to, other ostensibly ontologically equivalent real things that are absent. Extending Kristeva's idea via Diamond regarding the viscerally present body as the locus of the hysterical true-real that destabilizes mimetic truth,[39] these objects also have the potential to express a similar disruptive realness that (impossibly) precedes signification.

Beyond these stubborn objects that resist representation to point to the real, representation is also a tool to counter absence, literally making that which is absent, re-present, present again here and now. Both *Seeds* and *300 TAPES* establish narratorial, scenographic frames, positioned in an intermedial ontological space between the testimonial real and its fictional repetition, that foreground the processes of verbatim. These frames make present the process, effectively replacing the absent original with a new present. There is now a new real: it is the act of representation that is present. The document is absent; documentary is present. Presenting metaphors for construction, these frames depict the spaces of the procreative work of remediation. Annabel's exploration of the story of Percy Schmeiser is framed by the setting of a laboratory where white-coated lab technicians bustle about with their experiments and peer into microscopes. Two dominant features of the set are the green Astroturf floor and the large screen extending the length of the upstage wall and rising from just over the actors' heads to the grid. Within this space, the stage is cluttered with rolling chairs, workbenches with articulated swing-arm lamps, illuminated racks of yellow flowering canola seedlings, computer monitors, shelves with glass vials, and moveable metal tray tables. This world of the laboratory inserts an intermedial performative space where the actors of the ensemble become, first, lab techs, who then subsequently assume multiple roles as the people in Annabel's account. In the prologue, these lab techs buzz around Annabel. They interrupt what she is saying to give her words when she pauses. Annabel is offered the aforementioned fried egg on a plate; just as she moves to eat it, the entire table is whisked away. In the conclusion of this section, Annabel offers an apologia for what she perceives to be the unfinished nature of the work: "So I'd like to begin this evening in a spirit of ... humility ... by saying that ..."[40] We never find out what it is that Annabel wants to say as she is interrupted by one of the technicians who confidently pronounces: "One thing we know for sure: DNA holds the key to life."[41] And then off the play goes, with a brisk positivism into scene one, beginning with the recorded transcript of a television commercial from Monsanto. In this opening, Annabel seems harried, pressured by the techs, moving more quickly with the story than she is ready for. They are building the fictional play world around her, scripting her into it. In the very last moment of the play, the techs, having again shed their character costume pieces, stand in their white coats, arrayed near the seated Annabel. Again she offers a disclaimer: "But I am just one person" (*The PLAYWRIGHT looks at the other actors onstage.*) "Not really."[42] In addition to gesturing towards the laboratories of Monsanto, this stage space is the laboratory for making a play where the ensemble of lab techs, assuming various characters, are the building blocks of Annabel's story: the A, C, G, T nucleotides that recombine to produce the narrative sequences of genetic code in DNA.

Getting a glimpse of the work at the cellular level, this scenographic frame displays the remediating process of theatrical reproduction.

The scenographic space of *300 TAPES* also represents a place of play-ful mediation and reproduction. Arranged in a circle divided into seg-ments, the set resembles the inside of a microcassette tape spooler with its spoked wheels. Magnified exponentially, we are inside the machine. Suggesting the teeth of a cassette spool, the floor is marked with six white chalk rectangles equally spaced around the perimeter of a circle. The three actors' chairs and their three hanging racks of cassettes are aligned with three of these rectangles. The audience surrounds the set in a triangular arrangement. As they recite their stories, the actors move around the space in a consistent circular pattern, sometimes looping the entire space, sometimes moving stepwise from station to station. The cassette racks move along hanging tracks and can be repositioned, pulled by the actors. At the beginning of the performance the floor is clean, the black paint only marked by the six chalk-filled rectangles. But as the stories unwind, the actors track through the chalk, leaving trails of white footprints as testimony to their serpentine paths. If the space indicates the wheel with its teeth, the actors are the tape. As the play progresses, the actors move their three chairs closer to the cen-tre of the tape wheel, creating smaller circles, and bringing the actors closer together, shrinking the acting space. The effect is to suggest that there is less and less tape on the spool. In addition to actualizing the cassette mechanism writ large, the environment of *300 TAPES* exhib-its those tapes as objects. At various points in the performance, often between monologues, the three actors perform what they call "tape box choreography" which involves gestural routines of clicking the plastic tape cases open and shut, shuttling tapes and cases in and out of their pockets, winding the tapes with their fingers, slamming closed the lids of the cassette players, and so on. Drawing attention to the materiality of the tapes themselves, the actors, like Annabel's lab techs, emphasize the labour of verbatim recombination.

In addition to the figurative embodiment of testimony by the ensem-ble, *Seeds* also subordinates the documentary process to the fictional realm through a kind of deictic pointing. In act one scene six, Annabel interviews Tony Creber, a lawyer for BIOTECanada. He enters the scene talking: "Believe it or not, I believe in fairness." Annabel, scrambling behind him, says "Wait, wait, wait. I need to turn it on. Can you say that again?"[43] He repeats this same statement into her digital audio recorder. This quick interjection effectively foregrounds the recording process, illustrating another method whereby the actual-world work of creating the play is recapitulated inside the fictional frame. In *300 TAPES*, the moment of recording is overtly re-enacted at a couple of points when the actors begin a story auto-recitation with a declaration of the date stamp and title – "June 19th Dilly Dallying." Near the end of the third loop, a voiceover track plays chopped up fragments of these normally unheard stamps: "June 19th. This is the first version of this story." "... recording on June 20th" "Brendan Gall. August ... " "This is Frank's story number four." In addition to pointing to the documentary process of capturing testimony, this is a very rare explicit marker in the play that names the performers, equating the bodily present auto-reciters with the labour of their absent aural autobiographical counterparts.

"In memory, as in history, the past cannot exist beyond the construction of those in the present," observes Tomlin. Thinking about how the past travels into the present, she cites the Wooster Group's "long tradition of performers who are 'haunted by those absent others whom they reference.'"[44] This sense of possession of the actor by the character inherent in all theatrical performance is heightened in the auto/biographical relationship of the present verbatim reciter to the absent testifier. Overt theatricality places quotation marks around the characters, making them visible and marking the space occupied by these historical ghosts. When theatricality is minimized or effaced through normalization, the ghost is elided into the actor. In *Seeds*, the character of Annabel is exempt from the layered liminal ontology of the lab technician ensemble. Instead she is subject to a more traditional transposition, where she is portrayed by Repo-Martell both in the framing world of the laboratory as our narrator-guide, and in the next nested fictional world, where she plays her historical self as the interviewer in the recorded encounters with her various witness-subjects. Verbatim truth conventions and the lack of overtly signposted mediation encourage our sense that through Repo-Martell we have access to the original person of Soutar. Jay David Bolter and Richard Grusin identify two "logics" of remediation that shape our preoccupation with contemporary media: immediacy that is characterized by transparent mediation and hypermediacy characterized by opaque mediation. The transposition in which Liisa Repo-Martell presents Annabel tends towards transparency. This is not to say that we naively believe Liisa to be Annabel but rather that the remedial interface of the actor-character transposition is so familiar that it effectively disappears from our awareness. Inside the appropriate audience belief stance, we are able to look through Liisa and provisionally see

Annabel. The character of Percy Schmeiser shares this quality of transparent mediation with Annabel. Unlike the other witness-subjects of Annabel's interviews, Percy is not portrayed by the lab tech "code messengers." He moves directly from the actor Eric Peterson to a historical character generated by Annabel's edits, seemingly skipping the interstitial level where the mediating work is being done. In the final tableau, when Annabel acknowledges the ensemble, asserting that this is not just the work of one person, Percy rests downstage right in his armchair. It is as if he is not on the stage at all but at home in Bruno or is Annabel's projected image of him there now. This aloofness from mediation results in a different "feel" for this character, rendering him both solid in terms of his real-world immediacy and at the same time distanced from the play-making process. It feels at times as if the other characters are interacting with a ghost. It is as if Percy is the recording itself coming out of the machine. He is very real but not real here.

By contrast, Cox-O'Connell, Cobden, and Gall are both real and here, ("Frank," "Joe," and "Brendan" are also here insofar as their recorded autobiographical stories are contiguous with their present selves) and yet, the actor-character transposition evident in *Seeds* is problematized by the rules of auto-recitation in play in *300 TAPES*. The effect is still one of immediacy through transparent mediation, as with Annabel and Percy in *Seeds*, but it is achieved not by an easy transposition that facilitates a seemingly unencumbered conduit between the actor and his or her real-world correspondent. Instead *300 TAPES* sets up conditions to disrupt transposition so that direct connection does not exist and indeed to suggest that it need not exist. The devising rule of *300 TAPES* that required the initial speakers to hand off their privately recorded tapes to another actor for recitation in rehearsal is extended into performance, thus dispersing autobiographical testimony into different bodies. So for example, the story "Dilly Dallying" is told by Joe in the first and second loops, but by Frank in the third loop; the original speaker of "Dilly Dallying" is Brendan. The story that recounts, in order, all of one boy's childhood Halloween costumes, is recited simultaneously by all three actors. It is not revealed in performance whose costumes these actually were. The effect of this switching and sharing is to sever the usual autobiographical ownership of the recited story from a historical body or self. This sense of disconnect is further strengthened by our awareness that the original author is present but may or may not be the speaker. As the versions of the stories swirl, the history of these three becomes one, a fragmented collage of quotidian middle-class Canadian boyhood of men of a certain age, "a composite portrait of that nameless [generation] wedged between X and Y,"[45] replete with hockey, summer camp, walking to school, first kisses and breakups, a decade of Halloween costumes, parents, siblings, neighbours, casual mischief, and the usual embarrassments and wonders of growing up.

Like the character Annabel, with her tape recorder and her questions, who re-enacts Soutar's initial investigations, the actors in *300 TAPES* perform their participation in the labour of documentary creation. In addition to the later work of auto-reciting the pre-recorded stories, their dual role in the original documentary task as both testifier and recording witness is captured on the tapes and re-performed inside the production. As self-reflexive testifiers, the three men editorialize on the stories they are telling as they are telling them, drawing attention to the gap between the younger protagonist-self of the story and the current speaker. One way this happens on the tapes is through associative digressions. Starting off with one intention, the meandering speaker sometimes ends up elsewhere. In "Halloween," Brendan adds being a scuba diver in grade three to his list of costumes. He recalls that he went out "with my mom and dad. They went together with some other people, which was a weird anomaly. They did not hang out at all, so they must've been having a good week or something. It didn't last. But I went as a scuba diver."[46] Another tactic of the testifier is editorial commentary by the present speaker that is at odds with what the younger self knew or felt. "I don't feel like that costume was so great ... I went as ... Man! ... I thought I did better but I didn't. I had bad Halloween costumes ... What the fuck was I doing?"[47] Something in the act of speaking memories opens space and the speakers learn as they are talking. The act of speaking in this context invites secondary consideration and what you think you had or were is perhaps not the case upon reflection. Further in this vein, the testifiers also backtrack reflecting on something that didn't in fact happen – "but I think at the last minute I decided that was dumb so I didn't wear it"[48] – and so non-events are recorded at par with those events that did transpire. The gap between past and present selves manifests in acknowledgment not only in knowledge or understanding between the two but also when the present listener acquires insight through the immediate act of testifying, adding a revealing metacommentary that bridges both testifier and documentarian. At the end of the tape "Daisy," Joe talks about his younger adopted sister Daisy and their relationship: "Ya. It's kinda interesting in my stumbling through after story telling talking about her is probably a little bit more revealing than the stories themselves. So it goes. Uuuhh. Yep."[49] In the sedimentation of current thoughts on past memories, we are reminded of what we already know, that even the "original" documents are products of the moment of capture; they are not direct copies of history. One cannot escape the current moment. In these self-reflexive interstices, past and present, testifier and documentarian encounter each other.

Another way that the labour of the recording process is reflected in the tapes is in moments of meta-awareness of the speaker as documentarian. This is evident in the inclusion of extra-testimonial comments on the mechanics of recording, both those that are intentional as in the recitation of names and date stamps or creating a title for the tape, and those that are unintentional, arising through errors, memory problems, and contingency in the recording context. Often the tapes begin with self-talk about the plan of what to talk about: "I am going to try to go through and remember everything I went as for Halloween. So ... I think the very first Halloween that I remember going out, my mother made me a sunshine costume."[50] The self-imposed stare of the red recording light adds subtle pressure to accurately log the documents and makes the speakers trip: "This is Frank on Toronto 18 ... er ... Toronto 18th? What the fuck? This is Frank on August 18th ..."[51] Each of the speakers at different points takes note of their own uncertainty about the stories, the factual content but also the scope: "When I was five years old which is the end of kindergarten, beginning of grade one. I could be wrong."[52] "I'm obviously forgetting a ton of Halloween costumes. That's alarming. That's like five costumes. What the hell else did I go for. Clearly I dressed up every year for Halloween. I should remember that."[53] It is also worth recognizing the stories that manifest as silence, the stories that don't get told. First of all, there aren't really 300 tapes.[54] Second, only about a dozen tapes are heard in the show in some form or other. Finally, some remembered "episodes" inevitably get skipped over. One rule of the devising process required that each actor record his memories in sequence from earliest memory without backtracking. Memories arise but, presenting themselves out of sequence, they must be excluded: "What else? So many things ... So many wondrous things ... uh ... none of which I can think about right now ... or remember. Huh."[55]

Another way that the work of deictic pointing to the initial documentary process is accomplished in *300 TAPES* is through literal re-performance of that labour via a kind of gestural verbatim where specific prior movements comprise a potentially iterative vocabulary. Like Annabel's recorder, the recorders of *300 TAPES* exist both elsewhere in the past in world[a] as a tool of documentary capture and they appear here and now, also in world[a], as part of the playback apparatus. The transmission of an original object from there-then to here-now acts as a potent bridge, linking these two poles. Like broadcast recording technologies, like live video streaming, focus on the recorders as a single object in both real locations functions as a transparent broadcast medium, effectively eliminating temporal and spatial gaps. A complication in this trans-mission process, however, is that these objects, like autobiographical bodies, have a dual ontology. These "autobiographical" props are both actually themselves comporting their lived history and also represent-ing that previous existence in world[b]. Beyond their immediate use as props in the role of recorders in the fictional world, the recorders are actual objects with provenance: cued up with tapes ready to record, held up as microphones for recording, cuddled while speaking, but-tons pressed, lids flipped. The physical work of handling the cassettes is also re-performed, becoming a parallel verbatim text that is codified into repeatable "dances" or sequences. During the devising process, the Public Recordings company crafted and documented twenty of these sequences. For example, one sequence nicknamed "The Original" goes in part like this:

Hit rewind; Recorder in right hand
Cross to box
Look at recorder; waiting for it to stop; with recorder door facing up
Open, Flip so "tape speed" faces up.
"Ash it" [tap like a cigarette]; close it
(Take out tape with left hand)
Recorder to back pocket (right hand)
Switch tape to right hand
[...]

Step out with left foot
All cross into centre – chin scratch (right hand)
"Oh shit I forgot" (left fast stop, pivot right)
Back to box; hands on knees
"Oh no I was right"
Cross to Box
Pick up tape – right hand (dummy)
Drop tape (dummy)
[...]

4.1 Frank Cox-O'Connell in *300 TAPES*. Photo courtesy of Ame Henderson. Photo credit: Trevor Schwellnus.

In this manner, not just text but also the movement of cassettes and recorders along with the actor bodies are performed verbatim, replicating not just the content of narrative documents but also the documentary process as a site for reproduction.

The cumulative effect of this attention to the liminal space between the original document and its performed duplicate is simultaneously a recognition and an effacement of the manipulations inherent in the documentary process. Both effacement and recognition contribute to the generation of the desired authenticity effect. In their survey of how digital media strive to render the user interface transparent, Bolter and Grusin suggest three techniques for making the creative mediating agents disappear from our active perception.[56] One, remediation as holistic. In this mode, transparent mediation happens all in one step. Television broadcast presents this kind of seamless presentation to the point where we refer to the broadcast of a temporally concurrent event as being "live." Two, transparent remediation as automatic. The replication of visual perspective by photography is rendered immediate in this way. The chemical and mechanical processes involved express an automatic character that elides both the process and the artist. And three, transparent remediation where agency is deferred; that is, the work necessary for remediation is done at a distance. Computer drawing and drafting works this way. A lot of work has been done but it is being done elsewhere long in advance of our encounter with the remediated artefact.

Each of these strategies I have identified above in *Seeds* and *300 TAPES* are strategies for creating a sense of authentic immediacy through transparency. They are examples where agency is deferred or set at a distance. Here, the remediating work of documentary is ontologically relocated away from Soutar and recomposed in the lab where it is now the work of fictional doppelganger "Annabel" and the white-coated acting ensemble of embodied documents. Likewise, the remediating work of Cobden, Cox-O'Connell, and Gall is divided and recombined among their disparate selves as testifiers, documentarians, and playback reciters. In this way, the work of documentary theatre, the selecting, editing, and arranging that significantly opens a critical differential gap between world^a history and the world^b performance, has been transmuted to world^b becoming a fictional version of itself. This then is a very effective strategy for repositioning and deflecting the inherent concern with veracity in documentary. Soutar and the *300 TAPES* ensemble acknowledge that this remediating work is being done and show it to us, rather than hiding it from us. Hidden, it becomes a locus of interest, inviting the audience to actively consider the weighting of truth and bias in the labour of verbatim creation. Not only is this labour rendered visible but its ontological situation has changed. As part of world^a, this labour is inaccessible to us. It is unknowable and therefore can be a cause of concern. Relocated to the fictional construction of world^b, it is complete in the way that all fictional worlds are complete in and of themselves. Whereas the actual world is always wholly determinate with every detail complete, fictional worlds are by nature not fully determinate, that is they are full of holes where they do not accurately map the actual world in a one-to-one copy.[57] However, in our experience of the fiction, we do not perceive this indeterminacy as lacunae to be filled; we just recognize that these elements are simply not part of the fabric of this complete-in-itself fictional world. The overall effect of this strategy of inserting an intermedial frame-world that houses the labour of remediating life into performance is that both productions encourage this remediation to be transparent and stable. We can see what is being done. It is fully comprehensive and fully visible, thus the mechanism "disappears." In the case of *Seeds*, we trustingly read the results as an authentic transposition. In the case of *300 TAPES*, we are encouraged in the attitude that it doesn't matter; authenticity, that is, the precise location of the bridge from representational to the real, becomes irrelevant as a feature of our experience.

One of the reasons that Annabel finds questions about genetically modified foods so pressing is that, as she notes, "our perception has changed." She exhorts us to look. "My fear, though, is that if we don't look for this ... this ... this ... [...] This phenomenon ... yes, the *phenomenal* aspect of life, we won't see it. Because it's not that reality, or *biology*, or *life* has changed since Watson and Crick – it is our *perception* that is changing."[58] Before James Watson and Francis Crick articulated their theory that DNA works as a kind of blueprint for reproduction, we were only able to view the working of reproduction by its effects. In terms of our knowledge, we were essentially residents of the mid-nineteenth century with Gregor Mendel, tracing the paths of heredity in plants by counting numbers of offspring plants with green peas and those with yellow peas. Another connection in the analogy between verbatim theatre and the genetic modification of organisms is their reliance on new perspectives opened by technology. Seeing life in a new way allows us to tell new stories, but also presents new obligations of epistemology for the audience-consumers of those stories. Technology changes at what level we can "know" something. Powerful microscopes allow us to see life on a very minute scale so that we can see the organism or we can read its DNA. For geneticists, there are now new biomolecular books to read and to write. Likewise, we understand the fluidity of identity creation through autobiographical narrative in new ways. New selves are waiting to be written. For Cobden, Cox-O'Connell, Gall, and Annabel, the digital recorder in their pockets allows them to capture not just words transcribed in writing but also the vocal quality of the lived words. Access to the material of life is likewise expanded through this change in scale afforded by technology. *Seeds* gives us one generation. *300 TAPES* accelerates the processes of hereditary replication, giving us multiple generations. Over time, the fidelity of subsequent copies is eroded through mutation and new forms evolve.

Ultimately, these processes of genetic change become the thematic point of focus for both productions. Form speaks to content. When verbatim theatre attempts to address its central essential tension between the truth-contract with historical lived testimony and the constructedness of theatrical re-enactment by foregrounding that construction process, it becomes vulnerable to accusations that the stories of the witnesses are being displaced by the story of the documentarian. Tomlin clearly articulates this critique of the self-dramatizing process: "The shift from public information to private narratives raises the stakes for the ethics of performance because the citation of testifiers, as distinct from the citation of testimony, can too easily become the representation of testifiers, whereby the 'self' of the other is reconstructed by the performer for the purposes of the artistic project."[59] Too much emphasis on the work of construction tends to unbalance the narrative of verbatim towards the collector-processor of testimony and away from the source of testimony. I want to argue here that both *Seeds* and *300 TAPES* manage to avoid this pitfall by placing their focus not on the journey of the verbatim artist-journalist – the "white knight" at the centre that Tomlin counsels us to avoid – but instead on the mechanism of the documentary itself. Thus, verbatim in these two plays is not just a formal structure but resides at the fulcrum of the work where it participates not just in a meditation on form but is itself thematized as content. *Seeds* and *300 TAPES* are about unending citationality or reiteration as the means for mutation, degradation, evolution, and change. In this way, the process is the protagonist. As Josette Féral writes, "performance gives us a kind of theatricality in slow motion ... giving the audience a glimpse of its inside, its reverse, its hidden face"[60]

On the one hand, making the labour of crafting verbatim work explicit and visible is an effective strategy for addressing the central tension of the genre, caught between its allegiance as a truth-based form and its necessarily aesthetic construction as performed. On the other hand, the re-performance of this labour itself is a representation, enmeshed in fictional worlds. In act two scene five, Annabel self-reflexively dramatizes her own process and marks a particular point of frustration. Seated at her own kitchen table, she debates whether or not to include the testimony of Dr Vandana Shiva, an Indian environmental and anti-globalization activist. Annabel's difficulty is that Shiva's views regarding the dangers of consuming genetically modified foods are unsubstantiated, as far as Annabel can tell, by peer-reviewed science. In performance, Shiva, embodied by ensemble member Bruce Dinsmore adorned in a sari and earrings, stands upstage left separated by a square of light from the more naturalistic setting of Annabel's kitchen. From this position, she interjects the comments that Annabel is thinking about editing out. In the scene following, ostensibly an interview with Dr Ann Clark, other characters crowd in contributing their own views, disagreeing with each other and trying to influence Annabel's opinion. Historically, this group melee did not happen. Testimony was collected individually, then spliced together to create this fray. But rather than a debate between actual people, I am suggesting that this moment is an uprising of post-editing fragments. Bits of testimony are competing to be selected by Soutar/Annabel for inclusion in the final text. It is another moment where the process of documentary creation is re-performed inside a subordinate fictional world.

Whereas *Seeds* chooses as its dominant approach splicing together fragments of dialogue, *300 TAPES* displays reproduction through loops. The play is structured in three acts or three loops; each loop repeats the same stories and gestures. At the end of the play, the actors reset for a potential fourth loop. In its reiterative loops, *300 TAPES* displays multiple generations of speaking-recording-speaking in sequence and we witness an accelerated reproductive process. In addition to simply re-speaking recorded texts through auto-reciting, the actors also make new copies of the texts inside the performance. During the third iteration of the story recounting the one child's lifetime history of Halloween costumes, the actors form a circle. Gall wears his headphones but hands his machine to Cox-O'Connell, who speaks into the microphone; Cox-O'Connell's machine is in Cobden's hands and Cobden speaks into the microphone; Cobden's recorder is in Gall's back pocket. Gall speaks but does not record. The effect of this arrangement is that each actor is hearing a version of the story, but also simultaneously voicing a new version of the story – sixth generation, seventh generation, eighth generation. Verbatim text moves from generation to generation through technological re-recording using the machines but also through human recording and playback in the three-act/three-loop structure of the performance. A basic rule of the game dictates that any new material arising spontaneously in an early loop is to be incorporated verbatim into subsequent loops. If an actor coughs or stutters in the course of a speech, then this sound or action is "recorded" and is repeated in the next iteration. In one of the archival videos of the performance, during the story "Dilly Dallying," Cobden accidentally (?) disconnects his headphone cord from the machine when putting it in his pocket, and the sounds of the tape are heard briefly; he then scrambles to reconnect the plug, cues up the tape again and continues; an action sequence that became necessarily embedded in loop two – performed again by Cobden – and in loop three – performed by Cox-O'Connell, re-performing the ethos of capturing live action and remediating it through reproduction. All the ephemera of live performance – errors and flubs, choreography that is out of sync, or double takes of "oops I forgot," – must be repeated and so are neatly absorbed into the new loop, becoming representational in the next round, genetic mutations that become part of the basic DNA of the offspring.

In performance, the mediatized scenography of *Seeds* and *300 TAPES* amply illustrates this new perception, immersing the audience in a hypermediated experience. The opposite of the immediacy proposed by transparent mediation, hypermediacy presents an excessively mediated, self-conscious style. Through layering, fragmentation, and distortion, we are reminded of the ineffable mediating frames that stand between the viewer of the work and the original experience it represents. Bolter and Grusin recognize the desire for the real at play in both kinds of remediation but mark their different sources: "Transparent digital applications seek to get to the real by bravely denying the fact of mediation; digital hypermedia seek the real by multiplying mediation so as to create a feeling of fullness, a satiety of experience, which can be taken as reality."[61] That is, the layered and multiple media presenting an opaque interface deliver the authentic but in a different way. Here, the authentic lies in our real experience of the media, in the pleasure we take in the meta. Excessive hypermediacy indirectly "reminds us of our desire for immediacy." Playful and subversive, it compels us to consider our lack.

Lawrence Grossberg, writing about audience perception of authenticity at rock concerts, connects the playfulness of hypermediacy to what he calls the authentic inauthentic. The authentic inauthentic arises when performativity is not only explicitly acknowledged but made to be self-referential. You know that I know that you know that this is a performance. "Authentic inauthenticity says that authenticity is itself a construction, an image, which is no better and no worse than any other ... The only authenticity is to know and even admit that you are not being authentic, to fake it without faking the fact that you are faking it."[62] Grossberg argues that within the context of the live performance of popular music, authenticity lies in sound rather than in sight. As distinct from the recording of a song, it is only in the live situation that one can see the actual instrumental production of the sound, as well as the correlation between the emotional timbre of the voice and how that labour is marked on the singer's body. The principal element of value in the live concert is not the visual spectacle but the live production of sound. Grossberg also argues that sound has a more authentic phenomenology than sight, since sound is experienced as a fully immersive environment as opposed to sight, which is unidirectional. There is also more of a sense that sound is beyond control, washing over you and entering into you. During site-specific audio walks where you-the-audience-member roam actual-world environments while listening to headphones, you are in the visual space, but the sound is in you, psychoperceptually in the brain space between your ears. The sound quality of *300 TAPES* attempts to replicate that aural landscape. By contrast with the authenticity of the ear, "[t]he eye has always been suspect in rock culture, after all, visually, rock often borders on the inauthentic"[63] with its elaborate costumes, spectacular effects, extravagant personae. Thus, Grossberg argues for a two-channel perceptual model, balancing authentic aurality with authentic inauthentic visuality. Although he is talking about the culture of rock music, this same pattern is discernible in how authenticity manifests in verbatim. First, like popular music in concert, oral testimony is also a genre premised on an ideology of the authentic; the essential raison d'être of the event is an opportunity to access realness. Second, like rock music, that authenticity and sense of realness is located dominantly in aurality, through the musicians and through the witnesses. The pairing of rock music with television in the creation of music videos parallels the pairing of oral testimony with theatre in the creation of verbatim, linking two media of authentic aurality – music and testimony – with two media of acknowledged performative visuality – television and theatre. This dichotomous mapping may be overly simplistic in its application to verbatim performance in general but it does productively open avenues for thinking about visual hypermediation in contrast with bids for aural transparency of mediation in *Seeds* and *300 TAPES*.

The strategy of authentic inauthenticity need not necessarily lead to visual excess. Rather, it is the knowing wink, that any construction is a construction. Authenticity is always performative with any staged element "achiev[ing] and maintain[ing] its effect of authenticity by continuously citing ... the norms of authenticity for its particular [genre] and historical moment, and these norms change along with changes in the prevailing discourse of authenticity."[64] Andrew Goodwin observes that, for example, "within the established codes of rock music, the act of 'revealing the machinery' rarely involves making the narration visible, but instead is a *guarantor of authenticity*."[65] He cites the pervasive music video mise en scène of the rehearsal room or warehouse space. The rehearsal room or warehouse is a (clichéd) maker space for a band; this is where (we imagine) the real work of making music happens. *Seeds* and *300 TAPES* present the metaphorical maker spaces of a laboratory and a tape recorder reel, but notably, *300 TAPES* also overtly resides in the literally real maker space of a theatre. The theatre does not disappear. Theatre in the round ensures that we can see fellow audience members in their role as audience members visible through and across the performance space. We can also see Anna the sound operator and Trevor the lighting operator. The floor is standard black Masonite. The walls are visible. A structural pillar is incorporated into the blocking. The actors wear "street" clothes and sit in crappy theatre chairs. And in this way, *300 TAPES* manifests a "slacker" not-a-design design, gesturing to the authentically inauthentic theatre as theatre.

Hypermediality in *Seeds* also manifests in authentically inauthentic design elements. One use of the large upstage screen in *Seeds* is to display imagery that helps to communicate the location of the scene. Rather than visually replicating the original places, creating the pictorial documentary equivalent of verbatim copying, the screen tags each scene with a kind of distorted shorthand, an iconic visual quip. The Schmeisers' kitchen features two outsized partial windows flanked by a section of patterned wallpaper also at a very large scale relative to the actor bodies below. The office of lawyer Terry Zakrewski is depicted by a beige wall adorned by framed diplomas, which distort as they recede quickly away from the viewing plane. Scenes with Monsanto public relations representative Trish Jordan are marked by an enormous partial image of the Starbucks mermaid logo. Another example of hypermediacy in the scenography of *Seeds* arises in the use of the screens for broadcasting live video feed of the actors. When characters address the journalistic media, onstage tripod-mounted video cameras operated by the lab techs capture their images to be projected above. In addition, these shots never replicate the frontal view afforded the audience; instead they render our doubled perception as almost Cubist, contrasting the live actor with a mediated extreme side or reverse angle. As with the static setting imagery, the original archival visual material of the televised footage of the speech or press conference is notably not used. Although the use of screens and the framing of Soutar's interview subjects as expert talking heads evokes the truth-claims of televisual documentary on the one hand; on the other hand, by making visible the cameras and their operators and by layering the live actor with the screen actor, it taps into the playful disruption of hypermediacy. Liz Tomlin points to this interplay, noting its power, where the spectator's perspective shifts "between, on the one hand, the performance of construction on the stage and, on the other, the filmic performance on the screens in a highly charged strategy for deconstructing the representation of the real whilst highlighting its powerful and ideological potential for persuasion."[66] The window or screen of remediation is marked as such and we are acutely aware that the ontology of liveness of image on the screen, usually an indicator of immediacy and intimacy, is undermined through this process of re-capture, re-recording, and re-presenting as patently a third-order representation. It is also noteworthy in this context that these zoomed in close-up images are remediated as black and white. Black and white imagery bears cultural associations with newsreels perhaps or with archival footage and so acts as a truth marker, but as a corollary to that impression, the alteration of the original, now broadcast in black and white, also marks the image as remediated.

The vivid green colour of the stage floor serves a specific remedial purpose, providing a contrasting background for the special effect of chroma key compositing, also known as a "blue screen" or in this case as "green screen." Returning to Bruno, Saskatchewan to talk to Percy Schmeiser's neighbours, Annabel phones the house of Schmeiser's employee Carlyle Moritz. Moritz's wife answers, telling Annabel that Carlyle cannot come to the phone; he just went out. Upstage behind Annabel, one of the lab techs pulls a toy tractor on a string along the floor. Out of the blend of this live image together with a prerecorded landscape, the screen shows us a tractor rolling through a green field alongside a road. On the one hand, this technology has the potential to offer us a compellingly transparent, but faked reality. On the other hand, as it is staged here, the processes and vagaries of the technology are exposed in such a way that they act as a hypermediated experience. In addition to the dual interplay between the real object and its video counterpart, distinguished by their contrasting scale and angle of perspective, the compositing of the two video paths is far from seamless here. First the tractor rolls through the meadow, its tow string clearly visible, until it bumps into the giant shoes of the technician. Finally the camera is pulled away before fully fading out, and the screen image is blurringly jolted. Whether intentional or not, the result is authentic engagement with the workings of green screen remediation. This process of blending two real but disparate inputs to create a novel compound image is parallel to that of genetic modification, filling in spaces with data imported from elsewhere.

Hypermediation in *300 TAPES* arises principally in the processes of auto-reciting. Like green-screen technology, auto-reciting is also premised on the hybridity of the live and the recorded to create something new. A core characteristic of hypermediation as it draws attention to overt or excessive mediation is the adding or layering of frames. Bolter and Grusin give the example of the way television screens for news broadcasts are broken up into multiple panels, often featuring split screen images and a ticker-tape "crawl" of headlines or other facts across the bottom. By marking up the window, the window itself becomes visible. The window, previously transparent and unremarked, becomes discernible in the experience of hypermediacy as does the perceptual work of seeing through it. Auto-reciting operates in a similar mode by marking up the usual invisibility (or in this case inaudibility) of the text as text. Auto-reciting displaces the assumed authority of the text; text is unsettled as performance draws its textuality to our attention. Like an actor carrying a book of *Hamlet* (or Annabel's binders of court transcripts stored in the baby stroller), *300 TAPES* makes the text physically present through a kind of friction. The technical challenge of auto-reciting opens a gap in the usually seamless automatic process of coding, decoding, and recoding of text. This friction that expands or slows the process acts as a reminder that presence in writing (or in this case magnetically encoded analog sound) is difficult to locate. Using the example of a shopping list, Derrida points out that the sender of the shopping list is not congruent with the receiver, even though you may be writing to yourself.[67] In this respect, *300 TAPES* evokes Samuel Beckett's *Krapp's Last Tape*. As Elinor Fuchs writes about the play,

> Beckett ... uses the mechanical device of the audiotape to rupture both the fabric of presence on the stage created by the actor's alignment of voice and gesture, and the seeming presence of life to itself with its seamless "now." The audiotape, an unsettling juncture between voice and writing, present and retrospect, saves voice as inscription, as writing, but also stands as an image of the problem of writing itself.[68]

As with the seeming co-presence of Krapp and his younger taped-selves, the three actor-reciters of *300 TAPES* and their only slightly antecedent taped-selves also experience this rupture of presence. The formerly uni-fied and coherent narrativized autobiographical self breaks into parts; parts that are able to speak to and through each other. In addition to opening this juncture between temporal versions of the "same" self, *300 TAPES* further disrupts our notion of self-storying by refusing to put the voice back into the same body. Rents in the fabric of presence are multiplied as the stories migrate from body to body in such a way that autobiographical "ownership" or synchronicity between narrative self and the somatic experience of the body become disconnected.

Another way that the stories of *300 TAPES* are hypermediated is through error. As argued in the previous chapter in connection with the work of Sara Jane Bailes, failure exposes the mechanisms of con-struction, inviting reflexive awareness on the failed illusion.[69] In this context, that shattered window or screen functions as hypermediation by revealing the now broken glass. Playback errors are an inevitable part of the semi-spontaneous nature of *300 TAPES*. Headphones get unplugged, cassettes are dropped, actors backtrack on choreography. However, because one of the devising rules of the production requires any "error" to be repeated in subsequent loops, errors need not be taken as faults but are merely new information – a mutation in the code – to be replicated into the basic structure. Mutations also arise when the performers ostensibly reciting or gesturing in unison drift out of sync. At the beginning of "Halloween," the three reciters take time to align their tapes and press play simultaneously. Despite their effort, the coor-dination is not precisely perfect. And so their recitations inevitably vary with lags and delays, some slight extension of vowels or pauses that create minor variances. It is difficult to describe but the effect in perfor-mance of the overlapping speech flowing together and then diverging and then recombining in unison again is mesmerizing and musical. The most pronounced results of looping mutation feature in the distortions that arise as the reciters create and re-speak generations of tapes. "Hal-loween" has seven generations. The overall effect of reiterative human playback is that the words start to break down into disparate syllables and other non-semantic noises, ultimately becoming gibberish. They also become more musical, rising and falling in pitch. Intonation also varies with the sounds (and some identifiable words) being elongated or delivered in truncated staccato. Some clear phrases are interspersed with breathing, sighing, growling, buzzing, and repeated stuttered words: "that that that." Through this mediated game of broken tele-phone, words evolve into other words; "sunshine" becomes over seven repetitions "ship of a sand." At one point in the seventh generation of "Halloween," the speaker blurts out "I don't know what that part was" as (presumably) the recorded text becomes incomprehensible and his powers of oral imitative transcription momentarily fail him. Consistent with the attitude of the production, I think it is important not to see this breakdown as loss, or at least not only as loss. Something of the original sense is lost certainly as the generations go on but something new and unexpected emerges in its place.

In her exploration of the question of whether there can be a feminist mimesis, Elin Diamond follows Luce Irigaray's ideas about mimicry to imagine a playful but alienating mimesis generated specifically through multiple distorted reiterations. Quoting Irigaray, Diamond writes, "To play with mimesis is ... for a woman, to try to recover the place of her exploitation by discourse, without allowing herself to be simply reduced to it."[70] Diamond continues, "This move from 'subordination' to 'affirmation,' from 'play' to 'recover[y]' pushes the irony of multiple reflection into dialectical struggle. Mimicry can function, in other words, as an alienation-effect."[71] Mimicry as mimesis is overcharged through endless repetition and deliberately distorts the original to create space, and to talk back against strict control of representation. It manifests in the production of "a funnyhouse concatenation of irreconcilable selves ... Forms with 'false offspring.'"[72] This seems to be to be an accurate description of what is happening in the looping distortions of *300 TAPES* that engender narrative progeny that are both like and unlike their "parents"; a fecund production that is both subversive and joyful. The attitude throughout the production is that these "errors" of replication are not failures but are "natural" aspects of reiterative reproductive processes.

More than merely structural features of hypermediacy, performing, reciting, lying, misunderstanding, and breakdowns of communication are recurring motifs of the stories themselves. In the story "My Little Ole Baby," the speaker recalls the time when at just five years old he wrote a song about his baby sister that had similar lyrics and a similar melody to a pop song that was popular just afterwards. (The doppelganger song is "I Can't Dance," produced in 1991 by the UK band Genesis.) The story highlights this coincidence and the outrage of his child-self that someone else had copied his song. This pop song is to his mind an imperfect replication of his song, caught somehow in the zeitgeist. In the show, when he can't remember the name of the band, one of the others blurts out "Genesis." Provocatively, he also notes that

"I think there is a recording of me singing it." And so this new recording is also a replica of that remembered long-ago recording. His own historical memory of the event is inevitably coloured by his experience of hearing the recording since then. It is even possible that this recording (and the pop song by Genesis) have reshaped his memory of the song itself. Sometimes the memory of a photograph can replace the memory of the event and it is difficult to be certain which one is authentic, as the replica overwrites the original. Between the original song, the recording of the song, and the popular Genesis song, it is difficult to determine the order of genealogical precedence for the song that is recorded, and subsequently auto-re-sung in the production. As a key motif, this notion of dispersed uncertain ownership resonates in this anecdote but is recognizable as a feature of the whole production.

Along the same thematic lines, another tape presents a metacommentary about the failure of hybridizing live and recorded performances, not in auto-reciting but in karaoke. Cast in a school review as Elvis, the speaker is embarrassed when, instead of the expected eight beats on the click track as an introduction, the audio operator starts the tape late and he only gets four beats. His opening vocals get clipped by the song's first chord. He thinks he has made an embarrassing mistake and that people are laughing at him. In retrospect, he realizes that people were more likely amused by his pint-sized golden Elvis impression of "Heartbreak Hotel." At the end of this story on the tape, Frank does an imitation of the click track and his singing and the recorded instrumentation to show us how it should have gone and sets the record straight.[73] The story "Getting Dumped" also points to a kind of reiterated speech and its failure. In an effort to reconcile with a summer camp girlfriend, the speaker (with the assistance of an older counsellor) crafts and rehearses a speech designed to get her back. On the tape, he describes how perfectly he delivered it. But it fails to change her mind.[74] The anecdote captures the mawkish emotion of preteen love in the speech and also its curt brutality in her monosyllabic "No." It also perhaps provides a counter-commentary on the theme of imperfect iterations, demonstrating that this meticulously rehearsed and most perfect replica failed in its aims. As a complement to stories about failed recitation, there are also stories of breakdowns in representation where listeners fail to understand what is being shown or communicated. In "Daisy," after meeting his new sister, adopted as an eleven-year-old from China, for the first time, Joe launches into a long speech of welcome and asserts his love for her. His ardent effort to connect is deflated as he recounts when she responds, "I don't know you say."[75] Brendan documents a common Halloween problem: that people fail to recognize his costumes: "I had to tell people who I was a lot. I remember that."[76] Of course this is what autobiography is: telling people who I was.

Beyond thematizing error and uncertainty, misfires of transmission or reception, one story in *300 TAPES* stands out as an example of fabrication, not lying, but actual fabrication as creative making. In the story dubbed "3 Flights," Joe-Brendan recounts flying from Toronto to Montreal, to Toronto and back to Montreal in one day for various work projects. He concludes this account with "and that makes me the best ever ... That, and ..." And then his thoughts spin off, imaging all the marvelous art projects that he will create. He is "gonna" to do a carbon footprint project that involves walking around on carbon paper or perhaps in shoes made of carbon paper. He is "gonna" to write a book about the intersections between hacking and dancing. He is "gonna" screen print the bottom of a skateboard with the word "Taliban" and present it to celebrity skater Tony Hawk. He is "gonna totally reinvent the colours pink and grey."[77] This story is unique among those included in the performance plan in that it is not historically autobiographical but rather performatively projects that self into the future, with all the things "I'm gonna do." And by association who I'm gonna be, i.e., "the best ever." In the context, then, of *300 TAPES*'s concern with change through mutation manifested both in its form and in the content of the selected stories, this future-oriented embroidery demonstrates the results of those mutative changes. It is also interesting to note that for each of his proposed projects, Joe-Brendan also accounts for its documentation as a blog or a book or a presentation at "an obscure arts festival in Afghanistan," or as a film on a website. His projects are both the work itself and (like so much live art) its documentation. Like the tapes and their data in *300 TAPES*, documentary representations of the event are as much part of the work as the original live action. "3 Flights" eschews the attachment of verbatim to a real-world historical past, and by doing so in the context of the other stories, neatly encapsulates the play's investment in the fecund possibilities of reiterative replication, where the stories become unmoored from autobiographical ownership, from semantic sense, and from reality.

Ostensibly, the core business of verbatim theatre, as a reality-based genre, is authenticity and epistemological security. The intent of the form is to transport the historical real to the stage. In practice, however, as mentioned at the outset, direct transference of the document by verbatim work is inevitably compromised by poststructural scepticism embedded both in the vagaries of performance praxis and in contemporary understanding of the impossible relationship of representation to an absent real. The question then of how to employ the features of this (epistemologically flawed) form in support of particular issues has been answered in different ways by *Seeds* and by *300 TAPES*, although as demonstrated the two plays share many stylistic and thematic elements. The presence of objects with a high degree of en soi that mark the absence of the document, paired with techniques of transparent and opaque mediation, suggests a particular view of how we are to assess the epistemological stability of these stories. In the case of *Seeds*, elements of transparent mediation give us an impression of direct access to Annabel's research, but also laminated onto this is the overpowering authentic experience of how the research was accumulated, selected, and modified. The play is structured in such a way as to allow the transference of real historical experience directly to the fictional reflection. Although we are shown the mediating processes at work, they are constrained in certain ways that allow them to be quickly effaced, rendering an immediate experience of Annabel's story. We don't doubt what we have been told; we doubt the epistemological project itself. Looking at the other half of the scenographic equation, the persistent hypermediated presentation paradoxically communicates through its delivery of more, more, more data that although this may all be true there is still more that remains to be known. Ultimately, Annabel's search for truth comes up empty. As she unearths more of the story around Percy Schmeiser and how pesticide-resistant patented Monsanto seed ended up in his fields, Schmeiser's claim that the unwanted seeds blew in from a passing truck makes less and less sense to her. Poking around, Annabel talks to someone who gives her the name of a local farmer who, he says, sold Schmeiser the GMO seeds illegally. When Annabel tries to interview this mystery person, she cannot make contact. He refuses to talk to her. Despite everything she has learned, despite the hundreds of hours of recorded interviews and the thousands of pages of court transcripts and media reports, this one piece of information is beyond her ken.

Importantly, the ambiguity of the play's conclusion does not lie in a sense that all the evidence has been presented and we are invited to draw our own conclusions. Rather, the openness of the ending tells us that the evidence, any evidence, will always be incomplete. It is impossible to transcend the limits of what we can know. The pregnant

Annabel, at her obstetrical appointment, is asked by the ultrasound technician: "So, you really want to know?" "Yup." "Well, it looks like you got yourself another little girl in there."[78] On the screen above is projected an ultrasound video of the fetus. This hidden life, made visible through technological remediation, is now a thing we can know. Formerly there were things that we weren't responsible for because we didn't know. But now, as Benjamin notes, "[b]y close-ups of the things around us, by focusing on hidden details of familiar objects, by exploring commonplace milieus under the ingenious guidance of the camera, the film, on the one hand, extends our comprehension of the necessities which rule our lives; on the other hand, it manages to assure us of an immense and unexpected field of action."[79] Despite our advancing technology, we still can't look inside the seed DNA to really know what is going on, we can only see outcomes. The same is true for Annabel's view of Percy. We can't see inside to really know what he did or what his intent was; we can only see the external outcomes of these hidden workings. Annabel says: "But for me there is one irrefutable truth about Percy: his resistance ignited a worldwide narrative about GM seeds that continues to sprawl in contradictory directions even today."[80] The recent history of modern science furnishes a long list of things that were great until they weren't: leaded gas, thalidomide, dioxin, PCBs, DDT. What we don't know is: Does genetically modified food belong on that list? This is reminiscent of philosopher Nelson Goodman's problem of projectable predicates. The classic example is "All emeralds are green." All the emeralds I have ever seen are indeed green, but can I say that this is definitively true of all emeralds? Is it a defining feature? Alternatively, Goodman offers another statement: "All emeralds are grue." That is, all emeralds are green until some unknown future time or circumstance when they could be either green or blue. So the question for us is: Are GMOs green or are they grue? The debate offered by *Seeds* is invigorating. The play gives us large doses of authenticity both in our transparent engagement with the historical real and through the enervating stimulation of hypermediation. But even in this overcoded experience of the authentic, the end is an epistemological stalemate. The lesson of the play is how to live with the full knowledge that we can never fully know.

This uncertainty is a feature of *300 TAPES* as well, where despite exposure to personal stories recounted "directly" from original audio documents, remediation destabilizes epistemological knowledge that allows us to connect the representation to its originary reality. As with all autobiographical encounters, which purport to offer access and connection, Brendan, Joe, and Frank remain essentially strangers to us. Not only can we not know them in the present, as evidenced by genetically modified foods in *Seeds* and the problem of Goodman's green/grue emeralds, we cannot know their future either. In the first story of *300 TAPES*, "Dilly Dallying," Brendan recounts a time when as a small child he got stuck crawling into a drainpipe: "Think about how you got there, and the fact that you did get there. And that if you really think hard about it probably means you can get out of there."[81] Yes, probably. Despite past evidence of lived experience and of scientific inquiry, the knowledge of the future remains probabilistic. Another point of commonality between the two plays rests in the ethical relationship between autobiography and first-person biography. What happens when you give your story to someone else? In *300 TAPES*, the stories and their associated identities become blurred. It is impossible to determine "who" this is. Rather than grapple with the ethics of appropriating other people's stories and by extension their experiences and their identities, *300 TAPES* suggests that this appropriative blending is to be expected and perhaps even embraced. Autobiographical correspondence or ownership is not relevant here. As the creators remark in their program notes, "As we all listened to these stories, we realized that there were overlaps and synchronicities between them." These narrative similarities were augmented by the looped, recombinatory practices of the devising rules for the production until "eventually everything you remember seeing and hearing is undone and reprocessed into something new."[82] A process that is not unlike genetic reproduction, giving away your "self" through copies of DNA passed from parent to child.

Significantly, neither production is creating clones. As "verbatim," they are failures. By introducing human factors – errors and other imperfections – into the copying process, *Seeds* and *300 TAPES* disrupt the ostensible fidelity of verbatim. Benjamin, perhaps, has nothing to fear from these copies being not fully mechanized. In the context of the proliferation of mass produced identical copies, these obvious forgeries seem quaint. The crux of the argument here is that verbatim as a form, as it is employed by *Seeds* and *300 TAPES*, has value that lies elsewhere, apart from claims to authenticity and truth. Mutation is a necessary and inevitable part of remediation. Change is part of representation. This change is not necessarily "growth" or "progress" – not in the sense of a neoliberal good; nor is it degradation and loss, or at least not as negatively associated with those words. It is just change. Is it good? We can't be sure. Maybe. Aura, located in original testimony, is lost, but new kinds of presence manifest. The child does not lack aura for being part of an endless citational chain. The real becomes newly located in creation, in new organisms of genetic modification and in new stories of retelling and narrative modification. Cormac Power writes, "theatre perhaps realizes its potential as a viable artform when it asserts itself not in terms of presenting the 'live' real or a purely fictional, but as a site where reality and unreality overlap to reveal their mutual instabili-ties."[83] At this site of overlap where different relative levels of reality are manipulated is the point where process becomes visible. Baudril-lard, thinking about the nature of simulation, argues that in a society dominated by hyperreality, signs have changed from reflecting reality to disguising reality. "The territory no longer precedes the map, nor does it survive it. It is nevertheless the map that precedes that territory – *precession of simulacra* – that engenders the territory."[84] He continues, "no more mirror of being and appearances, of the real and its concept. No more imaginary coextensivity: it is genetic miniaturization that is the dimension of simulation. The real is produced from miniaturized cells, matrices, and memory banks and models of control – and it can be reproduced an indefinite number of times from these. [The operations of simulation are ...] nuclear and genetic, and no longer at all specular or discursive."[85] Arguably, *Seeds* and *300 TAPES* are functioning at this molecular level both in the sense of genetic and phonemic manipula-tion and yet they resist the creation of an indistinguishable hyperreal by managing to restore imperfection and mutation. The human playback restores a feeling of realness, perhaps not to the source, but instead to the process and then to the source indirectly as part of the chain of citationality. Realness resides not in the document but in the shared act of documentary, in the active consideration of its mutative processes, when the process becomes the story; not an impossible clone of experi-ence, but a story-child, simultaneously both recognizable and distinct from its testimonial parents.

5 Real Space: The Insecure Geographies of Site-Specific Audio Walks – *Garden//Suburbia* and *Landline*

Under Mount Pleasant Bridge, Melanie looks for a place to "leave naughty secrets on the wall." Before she can make a mark, Hartley stops her: "What about graffiti bylaw chapter 485?"[1] After debating the legal and aesthetic merits of graffiti versus art murals, Melanie proposes a solution: "Then we'll draw a frame around it to make it art."[2] Without a frame, it is graffiti; with it, it is art. Walking in Whitehorse, the voice in my earbuds invites me to create my own frame and reconfigure the ontology of the world: "Look around. You may want to think of the other people you see as the technicians moving scenery and props around backstage, or as other actors getting ready for their next cue."[3] Without a frame these are just people in the street; with it they are performers in my private drama. This is the conventional power of theatrical transposition at work. But in the case of site-specific works like *Garden//Suburbia* (Lawrence Park, Toronto) and *Landline* (Whitehorse-Ottawa and elsewhere), the frame and the cognitive labour that makes it manifest has been relocated into the quotidian world. Leaving the precinct of the theatre proper, the fully determinate actual world substitutes for the piecemeal materials of stage sets. And it is this actuality that both fosters a strong reality effect, the most perfect realism, and concurrently undermines that stability through that same quality, as the hyperrealness of the world as set, exceeds its boundaries and overflows the frame. Like testimony, actual-world space – the notion of being "here" – resides in the cultural imaginary surrounded by an aura of authenticity. We are literally "grounded" in shared singularity where "what it seems to be" maps precisely onto "what it is." And so the space of here stakes a strong claim to being a firm marker of the real. And yet, in the same way that the truth-value of verbatim performance work is complicated by the displacement of speech over time, the authenticity of site-specific is complicated by displacement of space through similar processes of fracture or unsettling.

Tracing a genealogy of site-specificity, Miwon Kwon locates its point of origin in a "dramatic reversal of [the] modernist paradigm."[4] Profoundly indifferent to its spatial context, the ethos of modernist sculpture proclaims itself to be "transportable, placeless, and nomadic"[5] with its neutral pedestal or base and semiotically silent gallery space. In the late 1960s and early 1970s, this thinking was challenged by minimalist art that asserted a new priority on the environment of the work, on the materiality of its context. "The space of art was no longer perceived as a blank slate, a *tabula rasa*, but a real place."[6] Michael Fried, in his influential 1967 essay, "Art and Objecthood," condemns this novel relational attitude of the art object to the embodied experience of viewing it, calling it "theatrical."[7] And so it is. Moving out of the theatrical equivalent of the institutional gallery setting, out of architectural theatre proper, and into the world, theatrical site-specific work takes this relational encounter as its defining feature. Site-specific performances

> rely, for their conception and their interpretation, upon the complex coexistence, superimposition and interpenetration of a number of narratives and architectures, historical and contemporary, of two basic orders: that which is of the site, its fixtures and fittings, and that which is brought to the site, the performance and scenography: of that which pre-exists the work and that which is of the work: of the past and of the present.[8]

Within this mode of intersection and interdependency, a productive friction between elements characterizes the form. "Site-specific art frequently works to *trouble* the oppositions between the site and the work."[9] Longtime makers of site-specific work in the UK, Mike Pearson and Clifford McLucas, usefully distinguish two basic dialogic elements as the host and the ghost. The host is that which is *of* the site. The ghost is the constructed scenography and performance, which is temporarily *brought to* the site.[10] The audience is the witness, invoking a kind of relational trinity that constitutes the performance work. Beyond haunting the host site, the ghost of the ephemeral performance brought to the site may activate other ghosts that are of the site, their invisible yet puissant presence palpable in the visceral, almost spiritual, frisson of the freshly apprehended site. The activated attentiveness of the audience to the site wakes these impressions. It can become hard to distinguish the host from the ghost as Cathy Turner notes: "clearly the work fakes its own 'ghosts.'"[11] Turner also remarks that "neither site nor performance is fixed or graspable, yet both seem to be glimpsed in passing."[12] Turner characterizes the interaction of ghost and host not as a clash of what is "brought to" and what is "of," what is a visitor to the site and what is indigenous, with one subsuming or colonizing the other, but recognizes that the work arising through the transgressive, defamiliarizing, and sometimes incoherent intrusion of the ghost upon the host can be mutually co-creative.[13]

In the performative intersection of this mutual encounter of host, ghost, and witness, the site is discursively generated. No longer exclusively a physical location that is grounded, fixed, and actual, the site is now understood as primarily discursive, characterized as ungrounded, fluid and virtual. As with other performatively conceived poststructuralist entities, the site is unmoored or unhinged from a secure foundational authenticity, activating uncertainty and contingency around its ontological status as real or representation. "Although the site of action or intervention (physical) and the site of effects/reception (discursive) are conceived to be continuous, they are nonetheless pulled apart."[14] A central question for any analysis of site-specific theatre in this context is how the potential for responding to current spatial concerns and the emplacement of contemporary selves is shaped by poststructuralist spaces and landscapes that are unsettled, ambiguous, and insecure.

"A sense of place is a virtual immersion that depends on lived experience and a topographical intimacy that is rare today."[15] Lucy R. Lippard, in her book *The Lure of the Local*, observes that "few of us in contemporary North American society know our place."[16] "The word *place* has psychological echoes as well as social ramifications. 'Someplace' is what we are looking for. 'No place' is where these elements are unknown or invisible ... some are being buried beneath the asphalt of the monoculture, the 'geography of nowhere.' 'Placelessness,' then may simply be place ignored, unseen or unknown."[17] Non-land-based people, for whom migration and multicentredness are the principal denominators of their relationship to place, are caught between belonging and nomadism. On the one hand, there is a nostalgic impulse to retrieve a lost sense of place, a sense that this feeling can be recovered by moving slower or even staying still, by occupying spaces on a smaller scale, or through direct face-to-face exchanges that link people to the land they inhabit. Belonging contributes to feelings of security, but belonging is also oppressive in its borders and constrictions. On the other hand, the privilege of mobility – and it is a privilege – is freeing. Possibility is a wide, open horizon. And yet, nomadism brings with it insecurity. This need not be a negative valuation. "Uncertainty, instability, ambiguity and impermanence are taken as desired attributes of a vanguard, politically progressive artistic practice ... [However,] to embrace such conditions is to leave oneself vulnerable to new terrors and dangers. At the very least, we have to acknowledge this vulnerability."[18] Unmooring oneself from place is both liberating and deeply unsettling. Caught in this tension, contemporary global nomads – both those who migrate by choice and those who are compelled to seek refuge in search of safety – belong everywhere and nowhere. Kwon suggests that perhaps there is a third way: "Countering both the nostalgic desire for a retrieval of rooted, place-bound identities on the one hand, and the antinostalgic embrace of a nomadic fluidity of subjectivity, identity, and spatiality on the other ... new model of belonging-in-transience."[19]

This chapter brings together two recent site-specific works – Melanie Bennett and Hartley Jafine's *Garden//Suburbia*, set in the Lawrence Park neighbourhood of Toronto, and *Landline*, a site-generic work mounted in a series of paired Canadian and international urban locations, created by Dustin Harvey and Adrienne Wong – to explore this idea of belonging-in-transience. What does it mean to be me here? Poststructuralist site-specific work, which combines vocabularies of authenticity and attachment (connection, presence, wholeness, and synthesis) with vocabularies of constructedness and insecurity (gaps, partiality, layering, and absence), presents a rich context for exploring the interactions of contemporary selves with place. The interdependence of environment to identity championed by nineteenth-century proponents of an objective, worldly realism is complicated as the set and setting approach the absolute limit of near identity. By combining autobiographical storytelling with pedestrian journeys through particular sites, the selected plays question the possibility of a secure relationship of self to place. In a parallel process to the other theatres of the real considered in previous chapters, site-specificity witnesses an ostensibly secure claim to the realness of here being overturned by performativity, instigating insecurity about how we know ourselves spatially. In the end, both plays invite productive consideration of the ambiguous ontological position of the self and our interconnectedness with others in fluid spaces that affectively render its inhabitants both knowable and anonymous, and here and nowhere.

A common feature of both *Garden//Suburbia* and *Landline* beyond site-specificity is their use of personal audio to multiply worlds and further complicate the already fractious relationship between what is here and what is not here, between presence and absence. Provided with MP3 players from the outset, audience members occupy sensuous aural spaces as well as physically tangible spaces. Whereas vision is linear – we see what is in front of us, sound is all around us; it is an environment into which we are immersed. Explaining the physics behind the spatiality of sound Brandon LaBelle says,

> Sound is *always* in more than one place. If I make a sound, such as clapping my hands, we hear this sound here, between my palms at the moment of clapping, but also within the room, tucked up into the corners, and immediately reverberating back, to return to the source of the sound ... the materiality of a given room shapes the contours of sound ... At the same time, sound makes a given space appear beyond any total viewpoint ... Thus what we hear in this clapping is more than a single sound and its source, but rather a spatial event.[20]

The idea of sound as immersive permeates the linguistic imagery associated with it and is "conveyed in aquatic tropes of oceans, bathing, drowning, swimming, floating, and so on."[21] Sound moves and flows.

Not only is sound a spatial environment, a place with a distinct geography that is tonal rather than topographical, it is also an unstable space marked by insecurity. The distance between the source and the sound is often attenuated, and as a result, our apprehension of sound is unmoored from both meaning and origin. As LaBelle notes, "the auditory provides an escape route to the representational metaphysics of modernity by offering a slippery surface upon which representation blurs and the intractable forms of codified order gain elasticity. For the acoustical could be said to function 'weakly' in its elusive yet ever-present signifying chains, its vibrations between, through, and against bodies by slipping through the symbolic net of the alphabetical house."[22] Labelle continues,

> Seeing is believing. The visual "gap" nourishes the idea of structural certainty and the notion that we can truly understand things, give them names, and define ourselves in relation to those names as stable subjects, as identities ... By contrast, hearing is full of doubt: phenomenological

doubt of the listener about the heard and himself hearing it. Hearing does not offer a meta-position; there is no place where I am not simultaneous with the heard.[23]

The third key quality of sound in addition to its encompassing spatiality and its phenomenological uncertainty is that "sound is intrinsically and unignorably relational."[24]

> Sound occurs among bodies ... Sound is produced and inflected not only by the materiality of space but also by the presence of others, by a body there, another there, and another over there. Thus, the acoustical event is also a social one: in multiplying and expanding space, sound necessarily generates listeners and a multiplicity of acoustical 'viewpoints,' adding to the acoustical event the operations of sociality.[25]

The environment created by sound is the product of the interrelated presence of the auditor and the object that is the source of the sound. But also, as Seth Kim-Cohen observes, it is shaped by the situation, consisting of time, context, expectation, and memory.[26] Situation is the site. Canadian site-specific audio artist Janet Cardiff connects the phenomenological experience of the body in audio-space to shifting perceptions of realness.

> The way we use audio makes you much more aware of your own body, and makes you much more aware of your place in the world, of your body as a 'real' construction. What is reality and authenticity if not that? If you give someone hyper-reality, then they have more of a perspective on what's really real. You are hearing the sound behind you, and you know it's not real, but you want to turn around and look for it.[27]

Like site-specific locations, headphone aurality also invokes a kind of secure expectation in the accurate correlation between what we see and what we hear, creating a sense of an autonomous real world. Past experience with audio guides in art galleries, museums, and on historical walking tours primes us to accept the voice in our ears as a trustworthy repository of factual information. And yet, these auditory counternarratives evoke alternate possible worlds that coexist with the ones that we can see. Our senses are divided as our embodied experience inside the "site" is troubled by another competing "world" that takes root between our ears. Both *Garden/ /Suburbia* and *Landline* explore this interplay, creating gaps where insecurity creeps in, exploiting opportunities for productive reassessment of our established modes of world-making.

As a style of representation designed to communicate impressions about the world to a reader or audience, realism is founded on certain core principles. Emerging out of the ideals of the Enlightenment, the realism of novelists such as Richardson, Defoe, and Dickens is based on an unspoken agreement with the reader that there exists an autonomous, extra-textual, actual world to which the work of art refers and corresponds. It is this work of referring and corresponding that constitutes the core of the realist project. As Ian Watt notes, "The novel's realism does not reside in the kind of life it presents, but in the way it presents it."[28] Moving beyond simple praise for successful lifelike representations of the world in realist work, analysis of realism as a style (among other styles) invites consideration of this constitutive process of how signs are deployed to correlate with the reality in the background. It is this double transposition from life itself to some kind of communicative medium and back to something like life again that constitutes the central challenge of realism.

Thinking about how one changes life into something life*like*, Roland Barthes (in his *S/Z*) considers a variety of literary strategies or codes whereby, through the arrangement of textual devices, the author can create a convincing illusion, recreating an image of the real world in the mind's eye of the reader. For example, Barthes's code of actions involves taking advantage of the recognition by the reader of common contiguous sequences from everyday life, such as answering the phone or walking to the corner to mail a letter. The shared experience of the world between the real-world reader and the fictional character cements the solidity of the realist illusion; the reader fills in the gaps in the narrative with her own experience. The author fosters this fellow feeling "by stressing at every opportunity the *compatible* nature of circumstance, by attaching narrated events together with a kind of logical 'paste.'"[29] The success of this particular strategy is dependent on the identification of a familiar lived experience across worlds.

Émile Zola, in his essay of first principles, "Naturalism on the Stage" (1880), looks to the success of the realist novel for those definitive characteristics that he wishes to bring into the theatre. He calls for the dramaturgical style of realist plays to emulate the novel:

> I am waiting until a dramatic work free from declamations, big words, and grand sentiments has the high morality of truth, teaches the terrible lesson

that belongs to all sincere inquiry. I am waiting, finally, until the evolution accomplished in the novel takes place on the stage; until they return ... to the study of nature, to the anatomy of man, to the painting of life, in an exact reproduction, more original and powerful than any one has so far dared to place upon the boards.[30]

While a novelist in the realist style depends on a bag of literary tricks, like those described by Barthes, for imitating the sensory experience of the real world by careful arrangement of the printed word, the theatrical *metteur en scène* has at his disposal the actual material of that real world itself. In support of realist dramaturgy, then, the theatre holds the potential to generate a corresponding realist scenography. Zola himself can barely imagine the full extent of the gap between print and the stage; as he notes with regard to the state of stage scenery, "It is only painted pasteboard, some say; that may be so, but in a novel it is less than painted pasteboard – it is but blackened paper, notwithstanding which the illusion is produced."[31] From blackened paper to painted pasteboard, from painted pasteboard to three-dimensional scenic elements like tables and chairs on the stage, from tables and chairs on the stage to leaving the theatre building entirely and moving out into the world – at each step, the perceptual gap between the fictional world and the actual-world materials of its construction gets smaller and smaller, until in the case of site-specific performance, it reaches (almost) identity.

A question that I return to regularly in thinking about the genealogy of theatres of the real concerns this contested space between the use of actual-world materials in the service of creating an ontologically doubled theatrical world and the postdramatic impulse to eschew that doubleness, insisting that there is only a single object, that indeed identity has been reached and the site is itself. This is the gap between realism and the real. Marvin Carlson, in his book *Shattering Hamlet's Mirror: Theatre and Reality*, delves into precisely this territory by tracing the historical lineage of realness in the theatre. Carlson brings his encyclopedic knowledge to bear, ranging widely over centuries of historical theatre practice, gathering, and then sequencing manifestations of staged reality. He begins his third chapter devoted to the reality of space by noting that while the bodies of the actors and the words they speak "are always susceptible to some 'bleeding through' of their nontheatrical reality, the same cannot really be said for the general physical surroundings of the actor."[32] Traditional stage spaces are firmly separated from the real world, both physically and in our social understanding. The ontological separation of fictional worlds from actual worlds necessary for theatrical perception is underscored by the enclosed architecture of the theatre building. Beyond the architectural confines of theatre structures, scenographic norms have also kept the real world at bay. The general practice in European performance traditions from ancient Greece through the eighteenth century has been to adopt spatially neutral staging, allowing dramatic locations to remain indeterminate, that is, to be nowhere in particular – an impossibility in the actual world.[33] It is nineteenth-century Naturalists like Zola who advocate for historically or locally accurate three-dimensional staging in the interests of supporting a rationally determined, objective depiction of human nature. Victor Hugo in the preface to *Cromwell* asserts that "exactness in the matter of locality is one of the most essential elements of reality ... The place where this or that catastrophe occurred is an incorruptible and convincing witness to the catastrophe; and the absence of this species of silent character would render incomplete upon the stage the grandest scenes of history."[34] As two-dimensional scenery is replaced by three-dimensional furniture and walls with doors and windows, Carlson follows this impulse for exactness to David Belasco, "perhaps the most famous champion of realism in scenic environments,"[35] who imported entire rooms of actual-world elements directly to the stage. It is perhaps the apotheosis of realism. But even this amazingly hyperrealistic style remains rooted in theatrical duality where the real-world objects perform as other fictional equivalents. Thinking about realism and the real inspired by Carlson's survey, the question is: Is the relatively contemporary shift to using real-world nontheatrical locations as theatrical sets, the theatrical correlative of "going on location" for a film, part of a continuous spectrum of realism extending back several centuries or is it something of a different quality altogether? Carlson seems to suggest that it is continuous in that real-world environments become almost inevitably subsumed by potent theatricality. He writes, "audiences have come during the past half century to accept the ability of theatre to claim almost any real location, as it can almost any activity, as part of its domain."[36] To this view, real-world environments stand in as sets, participating in the dualistic perceptual construction of a fictional world. This thinking might apply both to locations that stand in generically – Shakespeare out of doors where the trees in High Park might stand in for the forest of Arden – or specifically – as historical re-enactment where St Paul's church in the *New Founde Lande Trinity Pageant* in Trinity, Newfoundland stands in for its own nineteenth-century self. Environments, to this view, serve as Barthesian reality effects co-opted in their self-similarity to foster the illusion of reality. On the one hand, this argument shows that this is nothing new: the real is an extension of the values and practices of a long historical arc limning a philosophy of realism. On the other hand, the palimpsestic whisperings of the specific world[a] location performing autobiographically can be quite loud. The drive towards the singular ontology of postdrama, where the real speaks as itself and avoids being overwritten by theatricality is something new(-ish). The attempt at presentation of the thing itself as itself, positioned outside of the theatricalizing frame, challenges the paradigm of realism, being phenomenologically overcharged with its essential realness.

Taking issue with the argument that realism is too stable, ossifying its representations into inescapable, unchanging absolutes, Stanton B. Garner Jr argues instead that realism is critically unstable, betraying its instability in the "paradox" of the event as real. The core of this argument is that the materials that have been co-opted to constitute the realist illusion will always themselves be the most real thing on the stage. Garner starts from the relationship of realism to the senses. Realist stagecraft seeks to enforce the separation of the dramatic world and the audience, relegating each to separate ontological and experiential spheres.[37] The fictional world is closed off as an autonomous illusion. This strong separation creates a paradox whereby the illusion of the real is generated by the employment of actual-world materiality and the concomitant suppression of that materiality. "As its own paradoxical name suggests, illusionism carries within itself the means by which the real is constructed and an instability with which its fictional autonomy is continually threatened."[38] Quite rightly, Garner notes that this impossible tension between dramatic fictions and their actual-world constitution characterizes all forms of theatre but reveals itself with particular complexity in the theatres of realism and naturalism. Garner compares the approaches of Strindberg and Zola on this issue. Whereas Strindberg seems to acknowledge the impossible limit of verisimilitude, recognizing that "nothing is more difficult than to make a room look like a room, however easy it may be for the scenic painter to create waterfalls and erupting volcanos,"[39] Zola seems to endorse allowing the fiction to overflow its boundaries into the real world, creating a continuous shared space with the audience. Garner then connects Zola with the affective turn towards the body and the senses. He paraphrases "Naturalism on the Stage," picking up Zola's suggestion that the great naturalistic evolution has to do with the gradual substitution of physiological man for metaphysical man. "Realism, in this sense, opens the theatrical body, the fact of its embodiment, and it foregrounds the sensory exchanges between bodies and between body and setting."[40] As illusionism "ingests" materials of the real world, those materials also rebel against that consumption. As Bert States says, they assert their own en soi, and sensuously reach out to the phenomenologically engaged audience as real. Garner describes the realist stage as "a sensual field held in check, pressing up against the restrictions of the play's realist aesthetic, longing to break through the repression of the conventions to which it subscribes."[41] Hesitating on the brink of this breakthrough, Garner's realist theatre does not quite fracture the strong theatrical convention of the ontologically dualistic frame. But this is indeed where realism becomes leaky and where the singularity of postdramatic space comes to be. Theatrical conventions of fictional world-making weaken when the sensually rich real-world materials are engaged by a phenomenologically attuned audience – an audience that Misha Meyers calls a "percipient" rather than a participant.[42]

Garden/ /Suburbia

If the primary intent of realism is to present in art an accurate representation of the world as we perceive it, then a work of autobiographical site-specific drama offers one of the most extreme examples of this style, as the fictional mise en scène is constructed from exactly the persons and objects that it seeks to represent. Examples of site-specific autobiographical performance are plentiful in the US and the UK. As a case in point, Deirdre Heddon, in her seminal book *Autobiography and Performance*, devotes an entire chapter ("The Place of Self") to those autobiographical performances where not only does the performer perform as herself, but the locale is likewise co-opted to be both set and setting. To be "located" as an autobiographical performer is to be situated figuratively as a gendered, sexed, and raced subject, but in the case of site-specific work it is also to be embodied in and through specific spaces.[43] Heddon cites key works of the genre, such as: *Bubbling Tom* (2000) by Mike Pearson, a guided tour of Pearson's childhood home in Lincolnshire; Phil Smith's *The Crab Walks* (2004), which also returns to the locales of his childhood holidays on the beaches of Devon; and Bobby Baker's *Kitchen Show* (1991), which invites the audience right into Baker's own home, where she shares with us her strategies for surviving the travails of domesticity. In Canada, *Garden//Suburbia: Mapping the Non-Aristocratic in Lawrence Park*, conceived by Melanie Bennett, created by Bennett in collaboration with Hartley Jafine and Aaron Collier, constitutes a rare domestic example of the breed.[44] Under the tutelage of our guides "Melanie" (Bennett) and "Hartley" (Jafine), both residents of the area, *Garden//Suburbia* takes the form of a group walking tour of the exclusive Toronto enclave. Alternating live narration from our guides with pre-recorded audio tracks heard on personal MP3 players, the show provides commentary on community landmarks filtered through Melanie and Hartley's own autobiographical engagement with these sites.

With this example in hand, it is my intent here, first, to describe and assess the strategies employed by *Garden//Suburbia* in the erection of its fully determined realist façade, and then to consider the inherent instability of this façade as its realism acknowledges its own undoing. The ostensible aim of realism as a genre is to create an illusion of the world, an illusion so persuasive as to be absolutely transparent. Transparency, in turn, is a hallmark of knowledge and clear seeing, as it ostensibly shows us the truth of things. As Kirk Williams argues, "If the truth is empirically obvious, and all performative gestures or strategies are doomed to failure, then social or economic re-invention is equally impossible ... Naturalism as aesthetic strategy is profoundly conservative and deeply antipathetic to change."[45] And yet, in the intense correlation of the world itself and its verisimilar representation, realist performance paradoxically sows the seeds of its own failure. By investing so heavily in the facticity of representation – that is, by insisting that set *is* world and character *is* performer – an autobiographical site-specific performance like *Garden//Suburbia* opens up a space to interrogate realism's facticity and ultimately question the relation between the surface representations available to our senses and the "actual truth" of things. Further, by breaking apart the determined fixity of the realistic mise en scène and thus prompting us to question our epistemological foundations in the world, *Garden//Suburbia* reinvests in the performative power to change the world as it is (or seems to be). Just as the autobiographical subject is open to imagining new versions of herself through performative self-storying, so too the site of that performance can be re-imagined.

A key feature of nineteenth-century realism is the articulation of a metonymic relationship between what a person is and what her environment is. We can see this pattern in operation in the urban perambulations of Charles Dickens's alter ego, Boz, in his *Sketches by "Boz."* In the story, the stroller extrapolates his observations of inanimate objects or personal details such as clothing to a larger understanding of a person's life – both past hardships and future prospects:

> What he sees at first are things, human artifacts, streets, buildings, vehicles, objects in a pawnbroker's shop, old clothes in Monmouth Street. These objects are signs, present evidence of something absent. Boz sets himself the task of inferring from these things the life that is lived among them. Human beings are at first often seen as things among other things, more signs to decipher, present hints of that part of their lives which is past, future, or hidden.[46]

Casting himself as a kind of archaeologist of the present, Boz is able to deduce from a person's dress and demeanour his whole way of existence. We see this same pattern at work in *Garden//Suburbia* as we are led on a tour of the houses of Glengowan Road, our narrator conflating the names of the inhabitants with their house numbers:

> #54 is iconic Canadian, like the Roots brand. Quality. Longevity. Comfort. Embodies a distinctive look synonymous with a casual, athletic, hip and outdoor lifestyle. Total nature lovers and own more canoes than cars ... #51 is more of a Ralph Lauren type. Sturdy and long lasting. You know. The kind of style that will always be in. (Married. 1 boy. 1 girl. Oh and a golden retriever.) ... #47 is laid back casual. Lululemon, you know. Does yoga, eats organic, has goji berries and almonds handy for a snack. (Their children can do no wrong).[47]

The frequent name-dropping of popular brands (lululemon, Ralph Lauren, Roots) and fashionable cultural trends (goji berries, yoga, golden retrievers) taps into Barthes's reality effect, using his cultural code to create a web of citation in support of the realist illusion. These are things in the real world that we recognize as accurately mirrored in the realist depiction of the fictional world. But beyond this, these citations provide a shorthand to certain values. What you wear leads to what you eat and how you raise your children. To this view, each person may be defined entirely by his or her material situation – a central tenet of nineteenth-century realism.

This association of inner life with the outer trappings of that life forms the basis of much consumer culture today, which promises me a beautiful life along with my beautiful shirt, or shoes, or paint, or car. It is also a core belief of the classical stage realist project, however, that one's context (economic, cultural, political, educational, etc.) produces modes of behaviour, and thus, by showing individuals in specific contexts, one can reflect on the social justice of that context. In this way, Enlightenment ideals of individualism become tied to social ideals of equality and freedom from arbitrary rule. As Erich Auerbach writes in praise of Balzac,

> He not only, like Stendhal, places the human beings whose destiny he is seriously relating, in their precisely defined historical and social setting, but also conceives this connection as a necessary one: to him every milieu becomes a moral and physical atmosphere which impregnates the landscape, the dwelling, furniture, implements, clothing, physique, character, surroundings, ideas, activities, and fates of men.[48]

For the nineteenth-century realist, environment and identity become almost synonymous. In *Garden//Suburbia*, Bennett and Jafine parody this equivalence explicitly by replacing the names of the inhabitants of Glengowan Road with their street numbers.

Consistent with the preoccupation of late-nineteenth- and early-twentieth-century realism with social justice and economic oppression, *Garden//Suburbia* is also interested in the materialist context of a community and how the physical trappings of that community reflect the inner lives of its inhabitants. Like the impoverished London haunts of Boz (Dickens), Lawrence Park is also a kind of ghetto, albeit an upscale ghetto, riddled with class assumptions. (It is one of Canada's most affluent neighbourhoods.)[49] In *Stroll: Psychogeographic Walking Tours of Toronto*, Shawn Micallef refers to John Barber once calling "North Toronto, the area around Yonge and Lawrence ... our city's only real ghetto (a rich white one)."[50] Micallef continues,

> I worked up here for a while and met some of the nice ghetto denizens. They shop at the upscale supermarket Pusateri's, send their kids to Upper Canada College and, when giving me a ride to the subway, they would point out fancy homes where important wives had left important

husbands. As with so many Toronto neighbourhoods, it functions like a small town, where everyone knows everyone and gossip flows through the streets."[51]

Micallef's characterization may be a bit pat, but his too-cute characterization of this neighbourhood registers the clichés that Bennett and Jafine alternately enforce and puncture.

This is where realism rises up against itself. As Laura Levin observes, in the context of the specific site, "We become all too aware of the world's facticity, its stubborn refusal to adhere to the theatrical illusion."[52] The hazards of outdoor performance – barking dogs, sirens, people on bicycles who ride through the scene – take on a heightened meaning in the site-specific context. The hyperrealist illusion is persistently interrupted by the material of its own making as these actual elements are overcharged and refuse to be assimilated peacefully into their fictional roles. Thus the "everyday" material that contributes to our impression of reality becomes a kind of excess, escapes perceptual control, and disrupts rather than reinforces the reality-effect of the performance. The material of the realist illusion overflows its bounds, exceeding its fictional role and becoming real again. Williams identifies an anti-theatrical tendency in Naturalism which assumes "that there is an empirically verifiable subject of that discourse, or, to put it more bluntly, that it is possible to see a coherent, autonomous 'self' behind the seductive veils of theatrical dissimulation"; however, "theatre is never more theatrical, more metaphorical, than when it attempts to transcend its own conditions of representation."[53] This is precisely the bid made by site-specific theatre as this genre takes the ideals of realist representation to their logical extreme, immersing the audience in a seemingly fully determinate environment. But by doing so, it stages its own failure. At every turn, as we are led through the planned "garden suburb" of Lawrence Park, we are confronted not with the security of knowledge in transparent representation, but with our uncertainty. Indeed, we know too much, and it is inside that knowledge that our fallen awareness takes root. For there is so much more that we do *not* see, do not hear, and cannot know. Far from being fully fleshed out, every corner illuminated plainly, the play's world is paradoxically one of lacunae, a world of secrets and shadows. And so, after tasting the apple, our epistemological foundation has been irrevocably altered. Like Adam and Eve, we are cast out from our innocent certainty of being able to equate the word with the world. The illusions of realism have become unmoored from their actual-world grounding. Yet, in their new, sadly wise self-referentiality, words have become powerful, able to create new alternate worlds and selves out of their own performative declarations.

Garden/ /Suburbia embraces these inevitable fluctuations and substitutions to look under the surface of Lawrence Park, to question the implicit determinism of realism (in which location equals destiny), and to suggest alternate versions of this community. The world of Lawrence Park, authored by Bennett and Jafine (and their pseudo-fictional alter egos "Melanie" and "Hartley"), is by necessity distanced from any kind of extra-performative "truth."[54] As in much realist performance that speaks against its own realist strategies, our impressions of the world in *Garden/ /Suburbia* are communicated on two competing channels. On one channel, the audience receives the strong impression of a faithful pictorial realism, emanating from our 360 degree phenomenological impressions of the site and from the promise of an autobiographical account. On the other channel, the play taps into the inevitable post-structural breakdown that accrues to hyperrealist representation and undermines that realist illusion. Bennett and Jafine preface their performance by invoking it in the first stage direction as a "process of interpellation,"[55] and this is the approach that *Garden/ /Suburbia* takes to the realist expectations created by its site-specific context. By speaking into, speaking around, and speaking against the established discourses of the Lawrence Park community, the characters of "Melanie" and "Hartley" actively undermine any socially deterministic veneer to scold us, "Don't judge a book by its cover." While seeming to endorse the creation of a verisimilar façade, both characters productively use the material of that creation against itself, unravelling the strategies of realist representation to create new, alternate realities. Hartley and Melanie take different approaches to this deconstructive reworking: while Melanie digs under the surface, bringing unseen worlds to light, Hartley laminates new facts on top of old, fostering the proliferation of multiple worlds.

After we are welcomed to Lawrence Park and given our "Lawrence Park Survival Kits,"[56] Hartley's voice on track one of our MP3 players introduces us to the local library.

The George Herbert Locke Memorial Library. What's to tell? It was built in 1949 in memory of the second chief librarian of Toronto. Nothing exciting. I suppose I could tell you it's the place that once housed a vast archive of photographs, letters, deeds, and maps specific to Lawrence Park. The entire collection was stolen a couple of years ago and it remains a mystery as to who did it. The librarians say the objects were of little monetary value ... But to local historians, the missing archive is considered a theft of the crown jewels of memories.[57]

Delivery of this speech as recorded audio, instead of as live direct address by our guides, adds significantly to the tactical repertoire of realism in *Garden//Suburbia*; the mode of delivery stages Hartley's voice as an authoritative and reliable narrator in the style of a museum audio guide. The speech itself, however, is anything but authoritative. Initially the voice is not sure what to tell us beyond the name of the location. It offers one fact and then concludes it was "Nothing exciting." Continuing, Hartley suggests weakly, "I suppose I could tell you ..." Finally, after this vacillating opening, our guide tells us how the whole historical archive pertaining to Lawrence Park was stolen. Apart from leaving us wondering whether this report is indeed true or not, the effect of this revelation is to sweep away in a symbolic sense any factual foundations of this community. Uncertainty abounds. Even the identity of the thief is flagged as a mystery.

Hartley then shifts from the history of the community to his own personal history in this place. But instead of offering us one story, he offers us two. His first characterization of his younger self is as a keen student spending hours in the library, cramming his head with Reaganite foreign policy, conjugations of French verbs, and Shakespeare.[58] As a result, he wins early acceptance to Yale – the very picture of the successful offspring of professional privilege. Then he confesses that he has been lying to us, rejecting politics as incomprehensible, French verbs as confusing, and Shakespeare as uninteresting. Next, Hartley tells us that the library was his refuge on the day he ran away from home. Not brave enough to do something really rebellious or dangerous, he flees to the library and waits for his dad to come pick him up. Why did he run away that day? The reason offered aligns Hartley with the thief of the archives: "It was because I was accused of stealing from my step-mother. Not money. Or jewellery. Or her car. Or her phone. Or anything else of value. It was facial soap. Fucking facial soap ... (*Pause.*) Why would I steal it? Why would I even want to steal it? But when I was accused you would've thought I stole the crown jewels."[59] Something is stolen. Something without intrinsic monetary value and yet something considered to be "the crown jewels" – Hartley uses the same phrase to describe the stolen archives and the missing soap. Hartley, in this account, both is and is not a thief. This story sets up Hartley's deconstructive modus operandi: without a repository of documentary evidence (photographs, letters, deeds, maps, or soap) tying present objects to their past, those present objects become unmoored, weightless. Fictions rush in to fill the void, and one story is as good as another.

"Lies" in this context function, then, as a performative remoulding of one's self in the world in order to create a new self and a new world, and from this new situation to open up other possible scenarios. As the tour continues, the local sites become less and less about their own real-world history. More and more they revert to painted pasteboard, becoming the scenic backdrops for the performance of self, a fictionalizing layering or multiplying on top of the original, real history. When the tour reaches the entrance to the Alexander Muir Memorial Garden, the story that Hartley offers seems patently a lie – and yet the "truth" of the world that our guides have been offering has already been persistently questioned inside the frame of *Garden//Suburbia*. Indeed, the truth may not be out there at all. Hartley begins, "Alexander (Ari) Muir was born 1905 to Rachel and Issac Muirgold. They anglicized their family name to Muir when they arrived here. His family immigrated to Toronto from Budapest in the summer of 1919, right after the end of the first world war."[60] A very plausible biography, but Melanie objects: "FACT. The Protestant Alexander Muir passed away in 1906. FACT. Muir was from Scotland, not Budapest."[61] As the two competing biographies of Alexander Muir emerge, it becomes increasingly clear that Melanie's seems to be the truth. Her Alexander Muir is the renowned composer of the anthem "The Maple Leaf Forever." Hartley's biography of Muir soon runs afoul of the realist strategy of non-contradiction – first Muir is Muirgold, then later Muirstein. This Jewish-Hungarian Muir is also a two-time winner of Wimbledon in 1926 and 1930 – not impossible but increasingly implausible. Finally, Hartley claims Muir as his great-grandfather, and his interest in the figure becomes clear. By performing an alternate biography for Muir, Hartley bifurcates the world, interpellating uncertainty and inserting a new (albeit fictional) immigrant history into the dominant narratives of white, Scottish Lawrence Park. In this way, as the immigrant Muir overcomes his outsider status to achieve success in the vocabulary this community understands – athleticism (playing tennis at the local elite club, winning at Wimbledon) and the arts (first violin, but then as composer of a prideful national anthem) –

5.1 Melanie Bennett as one of the autobiographical tour guides in *Garden//Suburbia*. Photo credit: Ren Bucholz.

Hartley too finds space for himself in this community in which he both is and is not at home.

Whereas Hartley is a native son, raised in BVG and UCC, Melanie is a new arrival who shares his sense of imposture in her identity as a Lawrence Park resident.[62] In contrast to Hartley's strategy of filling gaps and proliferating multiple alternative worlds where he might find himself reflected, Melanie's strategy is to strip away surfaces to reveal the secrets underneath. It is through these exposures and juxtapositions that Melanie limns an autobiographical account of her journey from pink-collar working-class to her present situation as a socially mobile member of the creative class. At the first landmark on our tour, Melanie responds to Hartley's story of the library, underscoring her difference from Hartley by declaring that she was thirty years old the first time she entered a public library. Like Hartley, she identifies the place as "a refuge,"[63] but her library is not this library. In the subsequent episodes

of Melanie's autobiographical account, she breaks with the realist correlation of the site-specific environment. For Melanie, a newcomer to
the neighbourhood, the places of Lawrence Park act as metonymic substitutes rather than indices to the real; that is, they do not stand in for
verisimilar, specific locations from her personal history, but instead act
as a realist stage set for her self-engendering performances.

From the library, Melanie leads us to a sandbox. Building sand
structures and tracing lines in the sand, Melanie begins her own life
story: "Once upon a time there was a girl who ..."[64] Out of this classic opening, Melanie constructs her personal Creation myth. Etching
pictograms in the sand, Melanie sketches the story of a conventional
but confined woman who works as a secretary to privileged professional men, is happily married, tends to her house and her garden,
but yearns for something more: "Sometimes she would feel guilty
about daydreaming about silly things like becoming an actor or a
teacher or a violinist or a dancer."[65] At the story's climax, the woman
collapses in the middle of an elementary schoolyard. The imprison-
ing house-cubicle-box Melanie has sketched in the sand is obliter-
ated. Then, as Melanie tells us, the woman "[lay] on the pavement
with a throbbing stomachache, [and] gave birth to herself as she
stared up at the sky."[66] She returns home and articulates her desire
to apply to university.

Breaking with the expectations of site-specificity, this children's playground is not the actual (i.e., literal) setting of Melanie's story in the
present. It is not doubled: there is no sandbox inside the fictional frame.
Rather, using the more typical technique of theatrical transposition,
this playground represents another playground elsewhere, many years
ago. Outside the fictional frame, the sandbox functions as a blank page
or canvas, ready to be inscribed with signs of an incipient world. The
wooden frame of the sandbox literally replicates the theatrical frame,
containing the world of the story. And, in the generation of her autobiographical self-story, Melanie opens herself to a performative feedback
loop: experience lived once by this body is relived again. Melanie jumps
into the sandbox, lying down on her back, repeating the same epiphanic
gesture the woman in the story enacted in that long-ago elementary
school playground, giving birth to herself again today. The doubling
of Melanie as the protagonist of her own story (who is experiencing
all this for the first time) with Melanie the narrator, who writes in the
sand and enacts that same story (and who has already lived through
this scenario) invokes the power of performative self-telling to create

a new self. In Melanie herself, we have before us the fruits born of that moment.

The archive of a life, the words of Melanie's autobiography are, in the sandbox section, erased, but the story transcends the etched symbols, re-entering her body through her actions. As Melanie re-performs her self-reinvention, her evolution is documented not in the written word, but in notes that live undercover almost to the point of invisibility. It is autobiography by stealth. "Turn to track 9 as I want to tell you something I don't want the people here to hear,"[67] she says. Then, as the audio track rolls, Melanie begins to stick pink phone-message slips to spectators' clothing. The polite business phrase "While you were out" printed on the message slips is, whispered in our ears, at first secretive, but then gradually evolves to become aggressive and accusatory. These are not just trivial things that happened while you were out, but unseen changes in social class to which Melanie's employers (and the audience) are guilty of being oblivious:

> While you were out, your son's school called and said he wasn't feeling well. While you were out, Mercedes Midtown called and said your car has been serviced and asked if you'd like a courtesy pick-up ... While you were out, I took a 3-hour lunch to go shopping with the $50 gift certificate you gave me for Secretary's Day ... While you were out, your business colleague sexually harassed me because you told him I was into it. While you were out I found Winners so that I can afford the same designer clothing as your wife ... While you were out, I got an education and now create PowerPoint presentations for my own career instead of yours. While you were out, I obtained some cultural capital and know more than you do about art and literature.[68]

Significantly, these insights come to us not via our astute perception, but only because we get "insider" information. Literally "inside" us as Melanie's recorded voice penetrates our ears, resonating inside our heads, the phrase "while you were out" underscores the fact that we missed these things the first time and are only hearing about them after the fact. They are upheavals that would remain invisible to us otherwise – and usually do. The intense pictorial realism of site-specific autobiography proves to be just a surface: we seem to have it all, but in fact we are almost entirely in unknown and unknowable territory.

This sense of the unknown and unknowable is tied to a dynamic cycle of creative destruction and destructive creation as Melanie and Hartley lead us down the western boundary of Lawrence Park – Yonge Street. Track three features the voices of both Hartley and Melanie as they alternate telling stories of Yonge Street, past and present. Hartley's narrative delivers, at least superficially, the expected historical guide, informing us of the street's cultural significance: "Formally known as Highway 11, Yonge Street is the longest street in the world running 1,886 km from Lake Ontario to Lake Simcoe. A conduit connecting two large bodies of water. The site of Canada's first subway line. The artery separating the East from the West."[69] The name "Toronto" is attributed by them to an Iroquois word meaning "a place where trees stand in water." "Except they don't," as Hartley notes. "At least not here."[70] The place where trees do stand in water is not at the south end of Yonge Street but rather at its north end, "1,886 km north of here."[71] Whether any of this is true or not is beside the point; the lesson that we learn is that there are things we cannot know, that beneath the fiction of the reality-effect is more fiction, stories beneath stories.

In counterpoint to Hartley's account of the origins of Yonge Street and of the name "Toronto," Melanie marks the changes along the route, noting what was there, what is there now, and what will be there soon after what is there now is demolished. She apostrophizes each section with a cadence: "Life. Death. Transience." and "Build. Demolish. Transience."[72] Transience is an intriguing word in this context. As audience-strollers, we are transient – that is, we are in motion – but the sites we traverse wouldn't seem to be, or at least perhaps not at first. Through the reiteration of the word "transience," Melanie places emphasis not only on the instability of verifiable "facts" about the environment, but on the ephemerality of the environment itself. Through its performative storytelling, *Garden//Suburbia* makes clear that the site of Lawrence Park – as well as the autobiographical personae of Melanie and Hartley – is reinventing itself literally as we watch.

Site-specific theatre is an act of social geography. It asks the question, "How do we live in space?" It behooves us then to ask with regard to *Garden/ /Suburbia*: what is the audience's lived experience of the space? How do we understand that phenomenological experience in a metaphorical or thematic sense? With our "Lawrence Park Survival Kit" bags clearly visible, we try to blend in, to be unobtrusive in our strolling. But despite our efforts to pass as locals, our grouping as an audience brands us unquestionably and uncomfortably as strangers. In its depiction of a community and its stories, the play presses on this question of what it means to "belong" to a physical environment. The image of Toronto as the place where trees stand in water is prescient: it allows us to recognize that we are not an audience that circulates through a fixed environment, nor are we citizens circulating in a city whose stories have been established as facts before our arrival. The ground is not stone but water. The environment and the city are places of change and evolution, places that in their new world[b] incarnations are open to re-inscription. *Garden//Suburbia*'s exploration of the interrelation of identity and place interrogates our attachments to our physical environments, paving the way for an escape from our own embedded material determinism. Environment is not heredity, as the early realists believed; through autobiographical self-storying it becomes possible not just to change my own story, but that of my self-reflexively fictionalized environment as well.

Landline

Like *Garden//Suburbia*, *Landline* is also concerned with the creation of a metaphorical or thematic experience of a phenomenologically engaged audience located in real-world space. But whereas *Garden//Suburbia* explores the disconnect between environment and identity, promoting in that gap an ethos of flexible and generative performance of place, spatiality in *Landline* is not about re-imaginings of what might be here but about the affective invocation of what is not here. If *Garden//Suburbia* is about multiplicity of presence, with many overlapping stories concentrated in one neigbourhood, *Landline* is more singularly introspective in its contemplation of absence and displacement across vast distances.

Performed at a number of festivals both in Canada and internationally since 2013, *Landline* occurs simultaneously in two cities. Past Canadian pairings have included Vancouver-Halifax, Ottawa-Dartmouth, Whitehorse-Ottawa, and Calgary-St. John's.[73] Combining a radio play with text messaging between two geographically distant correspondents, *Landline* blends traditional site-specific audio walk with an audience-improvised text. Before the performance proper begins, each audience member is given an iPod and the cellphone number of a "scene partner" in the opposite city. We press play on the iPod in precisely synced coordination so that we listen to the audio track simultaneously with our distanced partner. Then audio-tethered audience members move out singly to roam the city. *Landline* is site-generic rather than site-specific and audience members choose their own wandering routes within a limited radius. As the play progresses, audience members are prompted at various intervals to text questions, impressions, and confidences to the other person.

Perhaps surprisingly for a site-engaged work, time is a prominent feature of both *Landline* and *Garden//Suburbia*. As a group tour, there is an extranarrative push in *Garden//Surburbia* that is about managing the audience as a group. Tourist/tour guide behaviours are implicitly followed. We know to follow the leaders and to stay with the group. We are also told "Please turn off cellphones before entering" the memorial garden. "Please stay on the pathways, as we don't want to ruin the lawn."[74] Other instructions function as stage directions for the performance, coaching the audience as to their tourist roles. "Listen now to Track 8." Invitations to complete specific tasks or join in audience participation call-and-response games fall under this category as well. Anxiousness about the time seems to be a tonal feature of *Garden//Suburbia*, as we are told, "We really should keep moving, we need to stay on schedule."[75] Controlling time controls the behaviour of the free-range audience in lieu of traditional theatrical architecture: "We have a schedule to keep. For the next five minutes, take some time to explore the gardens, take a nap under a tree, talk to a stranger, collect various rocks, flora, and fauna, clean up any trash you see lying around, carve your initials into the sandy walkway."[76] Time constraints in *Garden//Suburbia* are actually about space and movement through that space. This also happens in *Landline*, as for example when we are given a task to complete or prepare for the next instruction: "You have one minute, so act quickly. When you are happy with your spot, simply stand by."[77] Distinct from practical managerial cues, synchronicity is thematically central to our experience of time in *Landline* and so there is a different kind of external push, evidenced by the frequent countdowns. After pushing play on our iPods at the very beginning of the performance, the first thing we hear is "This is your five minute call." Each subsequent minute is also counted down. Then from ten seconds to "Hello. Welcome to *Landline*."[78] The effect of this tightly synchronized temporal control is that both scene partners occupy a shared "now," both in a literal sense, in that we are hearing the same things at the same times, but also in a metacognitive affective way, since we are acutely aware of this link, even across time zones where one participant might be walking in daylight and one at night.

Space is also constrained in *Landline*, but much more loosely. Space is inscribed. It is a circular container. We are told at the beginning that "this experience today will last one hour" and that at the end we will arrive back where we started.[79] In addition to our iPod, our other key prop is a hand-drawn circular paper map slightly larger than seven-and-a-half inches in diameter. I estimate the scale to be 100 metres for every half inch. By this calculation, our play world is 1,500 metres in diameter or about twenty minutes walking from edge to edge. The circle-shaped map makes tangible this sense of an enclosed world, and contributes to those qualities that mark belonging – boundaries, being "inside," security, knowing your "whole world." According to George Lakoff and Mark Johnson, "our ordinary conceptual system, in terms of which we both think and act, is fundamentally metaphorical in nature."[80] Certain ontological or orientational schemas that describe our physical situation in the world are extended through metaphor to help us to organize that world, imposing value systems and shaping the world to a particular perspective. This relationship of inside and outside is one of these patterns, what Lakoff and Johnson call the container schema. Humans are containers. We have an inside and an outside. The surface of our skin is a boundary that separates the two, separating what is "me" from what is not "me." This condition is so profoundly affecting that we impose this cognitive orientation on other physical objects, environments, and experiences that surround us. Activities are frequently described as containers – "She fell and so she was out of the race." States of being are also described as containers – "They are in love." "He is in trouble."[81] Significantly in this context, but perhaps not unexpectedly, theatre is also rife with container metaphors, specifically attached to the creation and maintenance of fictionality – "getting into character," "falling out of character," "entering into the illusion," "breaking the fourth wall." The immersivity of site-specific performance doubles down on the application of the container metaphor since the audience enters the space of the fiction not just conceptually but physically. Alignment between the conceptual framework of the schema and my experience of the world is comforting and contributes to a sense of security and "rightness." By contrast, discomfiting insecurity is the result when these patterns become unaligned, or in this particular case, when the normally assumed boundaries of the container are breached or blurred.

In spatially-located audio walks, we are in the world, inside the container of the map. But also, and perhaps more disconcertingly in the context of the container metaphor, the audio guide is inside us. As mentioned above, sound is an encompassing external spatial field in which I am immersed. It is a site. But the particular aural-spatial situation of wearing headphones complicates this orientation, positioning the worlds created by the narrators of *Landline* and *Garden//Suburbia* inside me, between my ears and behind my eyes. "Well built stereos and well built auditoria [and high-end earbuds] are designed so as to maximize an immersion in sound. I am surrounded by the symphony which at an optimal peak is so total that I find it difficult to tell whether it is 'in the middle of my head' or 'out there' – the usual inner and outer distinctions become blurred."[82] Peter Salvatore Petralia calls this "headspace," noting that this use of headphones subverts physical space, and co-locates all the dimensions of architectural space into the listener/participant's brain.[83] The audio track is the ghost and I am the host.

Keren Zaiontz, writing about the relational alterity between audience and performer in bluemouth inc's *American Standard* and *How Soon Is Now?*, describes the ambivalence of the audience as both container and contained.

> In this divide, space is typically understood as autonomous from those subjects who occupy it – a distinction anchored in the assumption that the stage is an empty vessel for the art. However, if a stage subject ... is simultaneously in more than one location, then the container overflows, so to speak, its contents dispersed everywhere. This dispersal of the subject into every space implies that bodies are not distinct from the containers: quite the opposite.[84]

That same feeling of overflow and dispersal is at play in *Landline*, as the perceptual feature of headspace aurality is further complicated by blending locational soundscapes between its two cities. I may be in Vancouver but Halifax is in me. During a section titled "Field Recording," I am informed that "the sound you are hearing in your headset is the sound of our parallel location."[85] Visual cues compete with acousmatic aural cues to assert the presence of here. "Not only does the stereo sound physically reconstruct space within the heads of the audience members, but the visual interplay between what they imagine and what they see on stage creates a tension that forces a constant revising of the experience, a constant questioning of what is real."[86] The boundary between self and the environment is rendered intimately permeable. Subverting the efforts of my senses to construct a single stable place, the effect of this duality is an uncertain grounding.

In *Landline*, the audio guide is a kindly but authoritative voice in my head. "Like any audio guide this track comes with instructions so listen carefully, and act promptly ... Take a deep breath."[87] We are addressed firmly in the second-person imperative: "Allow yourself to simply drift. Obey your instincts. Follow the most inviting path ... Try to make the most of the adventure."[88] One effect of the use of second-person voice is that it creates an "inner gaze," and "softens the focus of the audience/participant and places them at the centre of the work."[89] This strategic placement of attention on the audience at the centre also aligns with the exhortation to invest effort. It places the onus on the participant not only to be attentively attuned to maximizing the experience, but to creating that experience in the first place. As is common in much work of this kind, the audience is co-opted as a theatre-maker. Claire Bishop, who writes extensively about the methods and ethics of employing ordinary people as the raw materials of art practice, is reluctant to include immersive and interactive audiences into her category of delegated or outsourced performance. Considering participants as autonomous individuals making their own path through *Landline*, I am inclined to agree with her thinking; however, insofar as the participants act under instructions to create the experience for their scene partner through texting, I think they do fit her defining parameters. Delegated performers "undertake the job of being present and performing at a particular time in a particular place on behalf of the artist, and following their instructions."[90] They are asked to perform as themselves and not to adopt a persona. The treatment of these individuals "treads ambiguously between coercion and collaboration ... an approach in which the artist's predetermined premise or structure unfolds with the unpredictable agency of his participants."[91] By no means is this a negative critique of the performance, but is meant to highlight the built-in tension in the work between freedom and restriction both in space and in action, as we are reminded, "I will give you a direction, but how you play the scene is of your own making."[92] Moving the participant to creative action actually restores a more conventional host-ghost partnership where the city site is the host and my body-self possessed by the spectral text is, not merely a witness anymore, but is the ghost – or alternatively a host for the ghost – that is brought to the site.

The casting of the audience-percipient as not only active but as an actor is underscored by the overt theatrical framing of *Landline*. Divided into "acts," the play announces each new act: "Act One ... Lights up."[93] Throughout the experience, ambiguity is maintained as to whether the participant is being addressed as audience or as performer. It is not always clear which side of the frame we are on, watching or being watched. Being out in public attending a performance makes us also a spectacle for passersby. Certainly the *Garden//Suburbia* tour group, with our branded Lawrence Park Survival Kits, is offered to locals as performative just as we are watching them. The animals in the ethnographic zoo look back at us. Strollers in *Landline* are somewhat more unobtrusive, and yet, we are marked as out of the ordinary with our maps and our pinned-on badges that declare "Can't Talk. I'm in a Show." Even the phrase "in a show" is cleverly ambiguous as to whether one is in a show as audience or as an actor. We are caught and held in a liminal space between being ontologically real as a member of the audience or representational as a ventriloquized performer enacting a role as instructed by the script. Act two concludes with "Lights out. You may want to think of this moment as a scene change."[94] A scene change is of course a world[a] event; a momentary but conventional gap in the flow of fictional worlds that exposes the mechanism of construction. People on the streets are configured as "the technicians moving scenery and props around backstage, or as other actors getting ready for their next cue."[95] An odd thing happens as the representational frame momentarily dissipates and we are again watching a real-world event, but with a twist, as we are interpellated into a theatre. This is not the real world of the city but the real world of a theatre at work making a city, evoking the metaphor of the *theatrum mundi*: "You may think all the world's a stage, and we are merely players. / Confession: I hate Shakespeare."[96] The city is the set. The same insecurity of the realist ethos, evident in *Garden//Suburbia*, is apparent in this moment. In the same breath that *Landline* displays the city as the epitome of hyper-realistic scenography, it undermines that vision, exposing its excessive nature as representational construction.

"Allow yourself to be carried away. / You may want to think of this moment as blocking."[97] Again, action for the percipient-performer is figured in theatrical terms, as blocking, denoting the pre-scripted movements of actors on the stage. The locus of control is situated in the performance itself as performance. Ventriloquized movement is a thing that actors do. It is representational. You move not as yourself, but as if you were someone else, somewhere else. Through this prescription, attention is directed inwards to the labour involved in the performance of the score. I start to apply consciousness to how I walk. Fast or slow? What should I look at? What would it feel like to cross the

5.2 An audience member in *Landline* walks through the city accompanied by an audio track and also by a "scene partner" who is an audience member in another city via text messaging. Photo courtesy of Dustin Harvey. Photo credit: Mel Hattie.

street? I notice the pavement, my shoes, my legs, and feet, the weight of my bag, and my hands in my pockets. These are thoughts that are not usually part of my regular awareness when I am in the world. I become intensely, but not unpleasantly, mindful of my phenomenological engagement, the position of my eye/I in extension in the world. The instruction to follow a random stranger for a block or two compounds the same effect. Detaching the percipient-as-walker from personal will further focuses attention on walking itself, handing control of intention or "meaning" to the person being followed. My job is to just "be." Finally, we are told at regular intervals by our private narrator to "Take a look around."[98] "May I suggest you take notice of the place you are in."[99] Also: "Look up." "Notice." "Observe the city as if you were seeing

it for the first time."[100] And naturally, "Please be mindful of the traf-
fic."[101] Mindfulness both of phenomena and how those phenomena are
apprehended invites entry by the percipient-walker into a self-reflexive
attitude reminiscent of the phenomenological *epochē*, as described by
Edmund Husserl.

Following in the footsteps of Descartes's *Meditations*, Husserl asks
how we can know that the world exists. He applies the *epochē* to
remove from consideration all doubtful material. But ultimately, the
cognitive bracketing required by the *epochē* functions not to determine what is definitively true but rather to set aside the entire debate.
As a first step in the phenomenological reduction, bracketing is all
about managing belief and doubt. To shift from the natural posit-
ing attitude into the phenomenological attitude, one needs to set in
parentheses belief in the world as real, leaving to one side concerns
about what is real. This first-level reduction of the theatrical experience runs parallel to Coleridge's dictum concerning the willing suspension of disbelief. It is not a question of belief or disbelief but
suspension of the question, entering into a perceptual stance where
we consciously elect to remit judgment. Inside the phenomenological
attitude, what is perceived of the world is reduced to mere perception; sense data only. This bracketing places the stage/world as perceived by the subject into the realm of phenomena. The stage and its
contents become pure mental objects, existing only in the consciousness of the apprehending subject. The objects of the real world that
stand behind the received phenomenal impressions continue to exist
(probably) but the subject can only access them as phenomena (as
noemata). "The whole concrete surrounding life-world is for me, from
now on, only a phenomenon of being, instead of something that is."[102]
Appearances are all there is and phenomenology is literally the study
of those appearances.

Now, phenomenological bracketing is not normally the way we
approach the world. Husserl describes two states: natural reflection and
transcendental reflection. In the natural mode of reflection,

> I am aware of a world, spread out in space endlessly, and it time becom-
> ing and become, without end. I am aware of it, that means, first of all, I
> discover it, immediately, intuitively, I experience it. Through sight, touch,
> hearing, etc., in the different ways of sensory perception, corporeal things
> somehow spatially distributed are *for me simply there*, ... whether or not I
> pay them special attention.[103]

In this quotidian state, the input of the senses and their role in creating actuality are not questioned. This is how we move through the world ordinarily. It is through the special attitude engaged by bracketing that we enter a state of transcendental reflection. "Only in reflection do we 'direct' ourselves to the perceiving itself and to its perceptual directed-ness."[104] Phenomenological reduction leads to a mode of self-reflexive perception where the act of perceiving (*noesis*) is itself made available as an object of perception.

What I am suggesting, then, in relation to *Landline*, is that the various strategies oriented towards sensory mindfulness described above oper-ate to shift the consciousness of the audience-walker to that of one who is dominantly a percipient. We bracket out concerns about distinctions between actual and fictional, focusing on the flow of phenomena and on our own processes of apprehension. In that mode, Husserlian *epochē* not only brackets out concern with whether or not we are witnessing reality, but also disallows representation; phenomena are not aggre-gated to construct realities. Place is discursive and so we are nowhere, drifting in sensory flow but not in a place. This agnosticism about real-ity leads to a different kind of insecurity. Whereas the principal strat-egy for composing (or decomposing) place in *Garden//Suburbia* co-opts sense experience to many reals through overlaying or stripping away aggregate realities, *Landline* leaves us nowhere, floating in a blank lim-inal space inside the brackets.

Being nowhere or being nowhere in particular is a dominant trope in *Landline*. One way in which the audience is displaced from a specific place is through proposing mutually exclusive alternatives. The narra-tor voice confesses her relationship to the city in which we are walking: "I've always lived in this city because my family has always lived in this city ... Would you think of me differently if I told you this is the third city I've lived in / or / that I just moved here / or / that I'm just visiting and I don't know this place at all?"[105] In just these two sentences we now have three and a half different scenarios. Multiple possible unresolved worlds are spawned just by the word "or." These choices are multiplied again, doubled, if we take into account that my scene partner is hearing this same statement and so the city in question could be either of the current pair. The word "or" also fosters multiplicitous contingency in the actions of the performer-walkers. "Start moving about the city. / Or / You can be still. / Or / You can text "GUIDANCE" to home base for a suggestion."[106] Contingency is implied throughout by the individual wanderings of each participant. This is part of the site-generic quality of *Landline*. The city is (more or less) generic for each iteration of the show[107] and within the fixed framework of one hour, participants in each city trace their own unique lines.

Cellphone technology, which is at the heart of *Landline*, is also characteristically nowhere and everywhere. As opposed to the older technology of telephone landlines which are geospatially fixed, cellphones are "here" everywhere. A cellphone is always here where here is a moving point. "The mobile phone you are holding ... is always sending and receiving signals ... Your phone says: "I'm here. Now I'm here. You can find me here. I'm here. Here."[108] And in being always "here, " the cellphone user is a vector rather than a point, in constant movement from here to here to here, journeying through space unencumbered by geographical attachment. "Try moving through the city without resistance. Instead of choosing, can you allow the journey to choose you? ... It's a form of abdication: relinquishing control. You are vulnerable when you allow the way to become clear – rather than hacking your way through the weeds."[109] Floating without resistance is another ghost image, moving without friction, but also without control. Control has already been consigned to the narrative voice, to the performance recipe. The suggestion here that the audience-percipient yield control and drift aligns the form to the content. Then the reasoning shifts, flipping the argument. "There is the danger that all those potential paths and journeys that you allow to choose you, don't. That the way chooses other yous than you. And then where are YOU left with your go-with-the-flow attitude? / Nowhere."[110] Having given ourselves over to ambient drifting, we are abruptly left hanging. A corollary to being nowhere in our everywhereness is being lost. Being lost, we don't know where we are. There is a double sense here in that we don't know the place – it is foreign, being outside our comprehension or experience – and we cannot locate ourselves securely in space. Kwon takes this one step further, arguing that as global nomads, the security of belonging that we so desire is lost. "One might go so far as to say that this desire for difference, authenticity, and our willingness to pay high prices for it only highlights the degree to which they are already lost to us (thus the power they have over us.)"[111] We are doubly lost.

The conceptual notion of site-specific performance as a haunting, as the ghost of what is brought to the site possesses the host of what is of the site, extends thematically into *Landline* where the audience not only encounters geographically displaced ghosts, but also they themselves become ghosts of the site. Recognizing this potential for self-implication, Cathy Turner asks "who haunts whom?," noting a thematic tendency of site-specific work to raise spectres, giving several examples of narratives about actual ghosts, being told that the performance makes the "buildings come back to life."[112] In the conjunction between what is here now and what was here before that has deposited traces – whether it was a long time ago or just five minutes previous – there are ghosts. The first Field Recording is about footsteps and the ghostliness of being-in-transience. "I just noticed all these footprints. There's, uh ... I saw my own. And then there's just this tiny little set of footprints. It looks like it was running. A large set that's walking up. A happy face that's drawn on the sand."[113] These marks – footprints, drawings, stroller tracks – are literally "landlines" to be deciphered. The lines remain but their makers are now invisible. Later we are asked to "think about all the other people through the years that stood on this very spot."[114] The city is full of ghosts, people who passed this way but are now gone.

Headphones, in addition to generating an internal aural space, also effectively sever me from the external aural space that my body occupies. Headphones make me deaf to the ambient noises of the physical environment. I am a ghost. Isolated from the actual sound, space becomes visual only. This isolation is further solidified by the tag I have pinned to my jacket: "Can't talk. I'm in a show." As part of the rules of the game, audiences are asked to agree not to respond to outside calls or texts for the duration of the performance. Cut off from other people, I am in a bubble. I am silent and the world is silent. "Soundless space feels calm and lifeless despite the visible flow of activity in it, as in watching events through binoculars or on the television screen with the sound turned off, or being in a city muffled in a fresh blanket of snow."[115] Within this ghost world, there are other ghosts to keep me company. In counterpoint to this isolation, *Landline* offers intimacy and connection. First, the voice of the audio guide is a kind of ghost, being audible but not visible or tangible. And yet, there is an (impossible) attempt to break through and to fold ontology and bring these discrete worlds together. At the end of one story, the confession voice asks "Is it ok if I hold your hand? We can stand here for as long as you like. When you're ready to go, just let go of my hand and walk away."[116] Consistent with the ghostly motif that knits presence to invisibility, our aural companion offers physical contact, and in imagination we might accept.

At several junctures in *Landline*, the formal voice of the audio guide yields to a more intimate whispery tone. "Confession: / Some times, at night, I like to turn on the lights and leave the blinds open. / My apartment becomes a light box, visible to my neighbours across the way."[117] She is open to be seen but no one sees her. As she explains, the neighbours are so accustomed to the proximity of the urban high-rise landscape that she is essentially invisible. The train of thought then shifts from the one who is invisible to the one who does not see. "Maybe one day I won't care to see what's outside my window any more. I will look at the other windows stacked across the way as you might look at a tree or a lamp-post outside your house. And the people inside will lead their lives as invisible as the beetles boring into the bark."[118] Attentive looking and noticing is the correlative of being seen; these are two sides of the same coin. As an audience, our work of phenomenological apprehension will bring what was formerly invisible into visibility. One of the things that we almost magically bring into visibility is our distant scene partner. If proximity is a factor of polite urban invisibility, then perhaps the reverse may be possible and visibility or at least presence can be generated by engaged contact over a distance.

This same trope of bringing mutually exclusive positions into contact obtains to the way space is constructed in the play. Musing about how the world is framed and represented, the narrative voice admits: "I can't decide. Is it better to show you the world as it is, or the world as I wish it to be?"[119] It is interesting to note the choice of visual language – "show" – when the world created is audio. Does this person also control my visual world? The voice's follow-up thought emphasizes the divided binary space of *Landline*. "Of course the answer is: a little of both. But considering the binary is so comforting. To think that we only have two choices, what a relief!"[120] Apart from two worlds of what is and what I wish it to be, there are two other worlds that at first glance won't combine as easily. There are two cities, represented one on each side of our circular map with two sides that don't meet. I am a dot moving on one side, my scene partner a dot on the other side of our flat cartographic worlds. Space is compressed to the thickness of a piece of paper and yet meeting is impossible. Where are you? Here I am. I could push a pin through the map and we could move in concert. Meeting is prefigured as impossible and yet we are linked. My scene partner is another me but not here.

The second and most potent ghost of *Landline* is our scene partner. Like the narrator who wants to hold my hand, this ghost is connected to shared intimacy. Progressively, the texts and tasks of *Landline* work to bring the two partners into an affectionate intimate connection. From the beginning, contact between partners is framed as a "rendezvous." "Rendezvous" means an agreed upon prearranged meeting place. It can refer to the place or the event of meeting itself. From the French verb *"rendre"* meaning to present yourself, rendezvous also carries the idea of "to render" in English, meaning to cause to become, to make present.[121] And so these text encounters are also a conjuring. For the first rendezvous, we are instructed "You will need to find a location that reminds you of an old friend."[122] "Old friend" is an emotional trigger, activating feelings of affection and connection in the context of absence, and also possibly temporal absence in the word "old," adding regret and melancholy. "Observe the place you have chosen for your first rendezvous. / Look behind you."[123] Yi-Fu Tuan, writing about the affect of spatial orientation, notes that "behind you" connotes the past, memory, also intimacy or privacy, that which is not public, perhaps also not visible, dark or shadowy.[124] In this context, "look behind you" is not threatening but presents a curious combination of intimacy with invisibility. Turning opens a new vista. Do we half imagine that we will actually see our old friend standing there? Oddly, that feels possible. "Imagine that person you miss." Through a slippage of phrasing "old friend" becomes "person you miss," shifting emphasis from affection to absence, and adding further emotional weight. "Wave to them as if they are walking up to you."[125] "As if" is the actor's method of mimetic realism. So now you are waving to an invisible nobody. "Imagine them waving back at you. / Or / What if I told you there is a person 5,725km away from you right now, and despite all that distance, the two of you are engaged in the same activity. / You are together. / You are both waving."[126] In one more slippery fracture, your text partner becomes the old friend, the person who you miss.

Another task, asking us to lean on a tree or lamp-post, is absurdly affecting, out of proportion with the action, like waving to an invisible person. "Stand so your shoulder barely touches it. / Now ever so slowly, pour your weight into that point of contact. As you might pour sand into a bag. The connection becomes more solid and dense the more your pour in."[127] Like the waving, both partners are doing this, and so we are connected by symmetry. It is almost as if we are touching each other through the tree. "Sometimes we just stand together. Those are the moments that surprise me. When the need is satisfied by proximity.

Because there is always a need."[128] This is another moment of ghostly folding of space. We are satisfied by proximity, but of course we are not proximate. The affection in absence created by the work fills in the space. Also noteworthy in this context is the repeated refrain of *Landline* where we are asked to text STANDING BY to our partners to confirm that we are ready, waiting for the next action. It is also specifically theatrical language, as if we are technicians acknowledging readiness to run the next lighting or sound cue: "Sound standing by." We also "stand by" someone in the sense of offering support and allegiance, readiness to assist.

In texts of several of the *Landline* chats that were shared with me, conversants typically express warm connection to the other one, more than one might expect for a distant acquaintance of mere minutes. "Please come visit me" is a common invitation as participants attempt to transfer their newfound virtual connection to a real physical one. Conversations are marked by expressions of attachment and empathy: "oh me too!" Many declare pleasure in the relationship, and are solicitous of their new friend. "I love the forest. Be there for me. / Wish you were here ... / Thank you ... It would be lovely to meet you / I never thought I would ever say this ... Quite moving."[129] Partners delight at similarities and coincidences: "We have the same weather!" "I ... like the colours gray and aquamarine / I like blue and green (rhymes with yours)" "Ha! We are both in parks more or less / And we are both confused:)" "Knowing that you were doing the exact same thing that I was / It is a strange and warm feeling. Knowing you are mirroring me."[130] In the conversations themselves, the partners share personal details and histories that are strikingly intimate. The audio cues invite this to some extent, asking pairs to share reflections on an old friend, a time when you were lost, a time of profound change. Formal features of invisible connection also ease these admissions.

Warm connection through autobiographical revelation is also a feature of *Garden/ /Suburbia*. Audience members are invited by Melanie and Hartley to play a game that is a variation on Truth or Dare. Melanie says that she used to play this game with her brother: "We'd throw the ball to the other person asking them a question. They had a choice of whether to answer the question or reveal a different secret. The game was meant to be this space of honesty, where we could tell the truth."[131] Under the Mount Pleasant Bridge, the Lawrence Park audience-strollers are invited to toss the ball and exchange personal confidences, which, of course, we do. Eventually, Melanie and Hartley reclaim the game and "the space of honesty," trying to one up the other as the confessions become more discomfiting in their unattractive exposures. In a manner that is not dissimilar to *Winners and Losers*, as the "secret" declarations cut deeper, Melanie and Hartley give voice to the little lies and insecurities of their friendship: "I once cooked dinner for Melanie and I was terrified she wouldn't like it." "One time I hugged you and got concealer on your nice wool coat and I didn't tell you." "I'm jealous of your friendships with other men." "I fear that Melanie will realize that I am a fraud." "I don't think our friendship will last."[132] Candid self-revelation goes hand-in-hand with the spatialized reality-effects of the site to foster a sense of authentic contact; contact with the space but also with our fellow travellers.

Two short confessional anecdotes in *Landline* bridge this thematic line from shared space to personal connection. In the first, the confessional voice recounts the time when "in kindergarten I got into a fight with some boys over Hot Wheels cars or something. To punish us, the teacher made us all sit at a table together without talking for five minutes."[133] After the five minutes had passed, our narrator continues to sit perfectly still, eyes locked on her enemy: "When the time was up, neither of us moved. I wasn't fool enough to turn my back on him. And he knew it."[134] Across silence and anger, and the space between them, these two are connected. Emotion spans the gap. Immediately following, there is another story about emotion over silent distance. "My friend taught me a trick. / It's a trick that she invented with her mother. / Every time my friend sees a full moon, she thinks of her mother and her mother thinks of her."[135]

Running in parallel with formal structures that facilitate the free-flowing transmission of affection over distance, other structures create disruption. Looking at transcripts of the partners' text conversations, as logged in sequence, one can see that the conversation does not proceed in an orderly back and forth like face-to-face communication. Both partners tend to "talk at the same time." Due to the lag of typing and sending, text messages cross and overlap; and the conversation skips and jumps, circling back on itself, non-sequential. Also due to the vagaries of the medium, the texts are riddled with typos, which the participants sometimes try to correct and retype. Sometimes there is a momentary struggle for comprehension. (Not unlike my failures of understanding in *RARE*.) This is not necessarily a fault, but it is a prominent stylistic feature of the form that also speaks to failures of communication even as we strive for seamless interpersonal understanding and relation.

As we make our way back to home base, we are asked to text "SEE YOU SOON" to our partner. This doesn't seem to make sense, but given *Landline*'s affinity for ghosts it doesn't seem too odd. The voice asks us to "rehearse these words and listen acutely to the echoes that arise inside you ... miss you / miss you / miss you."[136] At this point it is not clear to whom "miss you" refers, but it is not inconsistent with the slightly melancholy introspective tone of the work so far. Then we are primed for "one last rendezvous."[137] In the final minute or two, this refrain is repeated and we are again asked to listen in a focused way and know that our scene partner is doing the same: "Miss you / Miss you / Miss you / Hello / Hello / Hello / Goodbye / Goodbye / Goodbye."[138] After returning to our starting location and handing over our audio track iPod, we are ushered into a room with a small screen. There, via video link, is our scene partner (!) and we are able to chat briefly. The affective connection I feel for this stranger – this unexpectedly sudden friend – is bright and it sparkles. It feels real and deep.

But ultimately the feeling is fleeting; it doesn't endure. Keren Zaiontz in her writing about ambulatory site-specific performance considers how the work invites "audiences to reassess how they value objects, relate to strangers, and treat marginalized others ... how their bodily encounters with things and strangers produce binding ethical relationships with the other."[139] This experience of reassessment of value in the positionality of the audience in relation to our surroundings both human and landscape through spatial immersion is central to the action of both *Garden//Suburbia* and *Landline*, and perhaps to all site-specific work. The key word of interest to me in Zaiontz's phrase is "binding." Connection in these plays is potent, but fleeting. Potentially enduring effects that might bind the audience to the encounter are persistently undermined, as I have argued above, by traits of ambience, ghostliness, and ephemerality. Christopher Tilley writes, "To be human is both to create this distance between the self and that which is beyond and to attempt to bridge this distance through a variety of means."[140] It is the attempt to forge that bridge (albeit one that necessarily fails, or succeeds only momentarily) that characterizes these ambulatory site-experiences. Both plays, with their deracinated audiences of global nomads, locate space in an affect of nostalgia. The ontologically fluid site consists of trees standing in water. And we are homesick ghosts. "Indeed the deterritorialization of the site has produced liberating effects, displacing the strictures of place-bound identities with the fluidity of a migratory model, introducing possibilities for the production of multiple identities, allegiances, and meanings, based not on normative conformities but on the nonrational convergences forged by chance encounters and circumstances."[141] Chance encounters may be all we get. Is it enough?

6 Real Bodies Part 1: The Traumatic Real in Immersive Performances of Political Crisis and Insecurity – *Counting Sheep* and *Foreign Radical*

Once upon a time, I joined the revolution. Crouching on the floor, keeping my head down behind a protective shield wall held by my fellow audience members, I clutched in my hand a newspaper-wrapped brick of foam, awaiting the moment to hurl it across the community hall at the makeshift barricade. Elsewhere and in another time, I participated in counterterrorism activities. Prodded by a maniacal gameshow host, my audience group conducted a search of the suitcase of a suspected homegrown terrorist. "What do these objects, possibly innocent, possibly damning – cigarette rolling papers, a silk scarf, notes in a language I can't read – say about a person," we asked ourselves. In both the re-enacted revolution of *Counting Sheep* and the spy-game simulation of *Foreign Radical*, these are worlds of fiction; they are not real. They do not present real stories of autobiographical bodies. They do not recount real testimony. They are not staged in real site-specific locations. These are unabashed fictional environments. Immersive theatre works like these move the border of insecurity, the zone of undecidable ambivalence between fictional and actual, from the stage into the minds and bodies of the synaesthetic audience. Embedded in a full-surround fictional world in which one is a participatory character, audiences experience a dual consciousness, being simultaneously both inside and outside the fictional world. We are actively engaged both in the making of performance and being audience to that performance; a duality that produces a self-conscious meta-awareness of both these tasks. How do we make performance? How do we audience? It is through augmented visceral and sensory awareness that immersive theatre puts pressure on questions of audience ontology. These works are not just physically immersive but also "psychologically absorptive."[1]

Of course, all audience experiences are visceral, experiential, and immersed to some extent; the difference is one of degree. As Adam Alston reminds us, "Once spectatorship is acknowledged as an embodied and potentially affective activity, all theatre and performance is, or at least has the potential to be, an immersive activity."[2] In this context then, site-responsive performances like *Garden/ /Suburbia* and *Landline* are not entirely unconcerned with the physio-affective experience of audiences. Both works situate the audience as immersed in the site and in the world, attentive to embodied experiences of walking and attuned to a heightened sense of looking, but, I would argue, this is not the primary point of aesthetic attention. Their focus is on external spatiality. Attention is still directed outward to the site, rather than inward to the private landscape of audience ontology. Given that we are always immersed, a critical feature of immersive theatre relates to the difference of medium. In *Hamlet on the Holodeck*, Janet Murray astutely writes, "We seek the same feeling from a psychologically immersive experience that we do from a plunge in the ocean or swimming pool: the sensation of being surrounded by a completely other reality, as different as water is from air, that takes over all our attention, our whole perceptual apparatus."[3] She makes an important point. Difference, experienced as unfamiliarity, uncertainty, and possibly creating some anxiety, is part of the experience. We don't want to "drown" in an unaccustomed medium. We are always immersed in air, in the world. The shift to difference makes you more attentive. Defamiliarization makes you mindful but it also introduces an inherent insecurity.

In addition to being submerged in a new and unfamiliar liquid world, audiences of immersive performance are co-opted as co-creators of that world. More than simply drifting spectators, we become necessarily productive participants. Set "loose" in richly detailed but unstructured environments, audiences take up behaviours that have been categorized as both "entrepreneurial," as we seek and strive for the most optimal experiences, to get the most or the best of whatever is available, and as "narcissistic," as our attention is self-oriented; the solo audience self is the locus of sensory and affective stimulation.[4] The values implied by the combined entrepreneurial and narcissistic labour of immersed audiences have sparked a potent critique of the genre as it aligns with the neoliberal ethos that offloads previous social and economic responsibilities of the welfare-state government back to individuals, prizing, as it does, initiative-taking and self-reliance.[5] As Jen Harvie writes, whereas on the one hand, the "socially turned theatre" that we see in relational immersive performances has the potential to offer "many social benefits: extending agency and authority to a greater number and range of non-expert participants; cultivating social engagement and awareness; modelling practices of social collaboration,"[6] on the other hand, when the labour of creating the artwork is outsourced to the audience members themselves, these socially-engaged works arguably replicate neoliberal labour practices, as the audience members are "insecure, deskilled and alienated."[7] Moreover, the focus of the audience at the centre of the work, featuring elements that are made specially for me, or made by me and connecting to a potent contemporary desire for intimate, personal, and authentic experiences, has also been colonized as a marketing tool in the interests of increasing corporate profits. James Gilmore and B. Joseph Pine II, in their books *The Experience Economy* and *Authenticity: What Consumers Really Want,* offer unapologetic practical advice on how to monetize this affective phenomenon. As Maurya Wickstrom documents in *Performing Consumers,* these pervasive strategies proliferating under the umbrella of "experiential marketing" have "turned us into affective, embodied, theatrical laborers on [corporations'] behalf."[8] Although immersive theatre experiences like *Counting Sheep* or *Foreign Radical* are not explicitly experiential marketing tools in the hands of corporate players, aimed at creating brand desire, nevertheless our labour is the performance. Without audience revolutionaries and counterterrorist operatives, there would be no show. It behooves us then, even as we look to the potentially transformational outcomes of engaged citizenship, to likewise be conscious of these built-in inequalities and precarities, and of the lurking external beneficiaries of this kind of immersed endeavour by audiences.

A counterpoint to the pleasures of commodification of the real and the authentic (and it is a pleasure) is Jacques Rancière's concept of dissensus. A running concern of his oeuvre is the contemplation of the political stakes of being an audience. Rancière advocates for art that is political not just in its overt content, but in the enacted structures and contexts of its making and of its presentation. The ideal of the emancipated spectator embodies a key aspect of this theory in action. Famously, he writes, "To be a spectator is to be separated from both the capacity to know and the power to act."[9] The processes of production of theatrical illusion are consciously hidden from us and so we cannot "know," and because we watch we cannot "act." As he continues, Rancière acknowledges that even looking can be active and seeks to unpack the working of a more overtly engaged relationship of the spectator to the work, challenging how audiences can become more equal participants. This is a figure that we might recognize in immersed performance, not simply because immersed audiences are physically active, free of the usual constraints of a seated audience, but because reflexive questions of how audiences know and act are central to the experience of an immersed audience. Dissensus, then, is also about modes of knowing, or perhaps more accurately, what is available to be known. Rancière writes, "Politics consists in reconfiguring the distribution of the sensible which defines the common of a community, to introduce into it new subjects and objects, to render visible what had not been, and to make heard as speakers those who had been perceived as mere noisy animals ... creating dissensus."[10] Significantly, dissensus is not disagreement or conflict. Rather, dissensus points to a gap in the sensible, a rupture in the field of things that can be perceived or felt. In this notion of seeing or sensing the world differently, Andy Lavender recognizes an extended line of thinking from Brecht to Rancière, aligning Brechtian defamiliarization and the redistribution of the sensible as both being politically efficacious strategies of (de)constructing reality.[11] Whereas Brecht makes an appeal for the activation of detached cogitation and the rational seeking of meaning, Rancière's focus on the field of the sensible is oriented more towards affect, sensation, and emotion in the apprehension of phenomenal inputs. Similar to Brecht's *Verfremdungseffekt*, Rancière's notion of dissensus and redistribution of the sensible (*partage du sensible*) speaks to the disruption of an accepted ideological façade, so as to perceive the world afresh. "[Dissensus] means that every situation can be cracked open from the inside, reconfigured in a different regime of perception and signification. To reconfigure the landscape of what can be seen and what can be thought is to alter the field of the possible and the distribution of capacities and incapacities."[12] And it is this reconfiguration of "what is" that may have political effects, as people reimagine "a new topography of the possible,"[13] to propose instead "what might be."

In this chapter, I will argue that immersive theatre as a phenomenologically-oriented genre of the sensible may offer an alternative form of the overt engagement Rancière imagines. Focus on an immersive real may crack open a situation to activate a reorganization of what can be known or felt, but not through mere submersion, nor simply through the physical movements of the audience. Adam Alston points out that what sets immersive theatre apart from more traditional theatre forms in terms of audience activity is that the dominant audience experience is the aestheticization of that experience.

> Because of audience immersion, and where appropriate, participation, aesthetic experience is prone to objectification ... Aesthetic experience in immersive theatre tends to promote introspection, because in the heady heights of immersion and participation it is not art objects that take precedence so much as the affective consequences of an audience's own engagement in seeking, finding, unearthing, touching, liaising, communicating, exchanging, stumbling, meandering, and so on ... [Audiences] are asked to respond not only *to* performance but their role *in* performance.[14]

It is important to note, then, in the context of thinking about what is real in immersive theatre, that it is the real-world audience and their real-world ambivalent awareness of themselves as real that catalyses this focal point.

In *Beyond Immersive Theatre*, Alston draws on performance examples that question the romantic notion of audience productivity, specifically to think about how the aestheticization of experience can be deployed to interrogate the commodification of experience.[15] Self-reflexivity serves to problematize involvement. "Audiences in these performances are encouraged to recognize productive participation as a subject position, unearthing a vitally significant aspect of immersive theatre's politically progressive potential that resists or probes what it means to demand or unquestionably expect rewards attached to productive consumption."[16] Žižek refers to the agon of this dualistic view on audience ontology as the parallax view. The perceptual parallax arises out of "the confrontation of two closely linked perspectives between which no neutral common ground is possible,"[17] residing in the "gap between thought and being."[18] As Peter Boenisch writes in "Theatre of Encounter," "Where reflexive dramaturgies highlight and exploit the parallax of fictional representation and performative presence, of appearing and event, the spectators, as a direct effect, are confronted with their own dislocation and disorientation facing the performance of the text ... Such a constantly shifting spectatorial perspective ultimately prevents any superficial consumption."[19] Caught in this parallax perspective, the self-reflexive, ontologically multiple audience is forced to negotiate between representation and their own presence, enmeshed yet separate from that representation. And it is in that meta-awareness of the terms of negotiation that the processes of how representations (i.e., realities) are constructed are exposed and in that exposure can be reshaped. Laura Levin in her book *Performing Ground* makes visible the ways in which environments of immersion and, by extension, action in those environments are gendered through framing. From the notorious assaults on female performers in *Dionysus in '69* and *Paradise Now* to "free" spaces like Punchdrunk's *Sleep No More* where audience members are encouraged to take license and be bold, Levin observes that this move towards an unmediated unframed environment where interpersonal exchange is unfenced by the usual borders of theatricality can open the way to unwanted expressions of that freedom. Ultimately, Levin argues that in order to avoid this "exploitive ordering of foreground and background, seer and seen, subject and object, past and present,"[20] we cannot simply abandon theatrical framing. Rather, she suggests that we need "to hold onto the frame if we are to make visible the operations of Enframing."[21] Maintaining an active sense of how subjects and objects are enacted by the perceptual workings of the frame encourages critical engagement with how the frame constructs relations within and across that boundary. This attentive reflection on the workings of theatrical framing, on the aestheticization of audience experience shaped by that frame, espoused by Alston and Levin, is central to my analysis of *Counting Sheep* and *Foreign Radical* opening questions about the operations of collective agency and the ethics of engaged yet compromised citizenship.

This reflection on ontological duality is reminiscent of Coleridge's willing suspension of disbelief, which calls for perceptual balance between the provisionally real, fictional world and the actual materials of its construction or Sławomir Świontek's metatheatrical revelation of the two vectors of communication as enunciation oscillates between dialogue that creates the fictional world and dialogue that facilitates comprehension of that world as a theatrical event. However, the significant difference is that rather than locating this reflexive ambivalence around the real-world materiality of the stage illusion, it is found in the circumstances of the event as a whole and in the audience as witness/participant to that event. Lavender speaks to this dichotomy, looking to the interplay between "mise en scène" and what he calls "mise en événement."[22] Whereas mise en scène refers to the representational product of the event, mise en événement refers to the event itself as "an affective *transaction* between its occurrence (or theatrical presentation) and its experiential basis (or theatrical reception and indeed participation),"[23] manifesting in a palpable sense of its ineffable here and nowness. Both elements work in concert. "The spectator experiences the event in its eventness, while enjoying the dramatic mediations ... [The] production of eventual situations that produce experience. These might involve self-interrogation or self-awareness. But they might equally entail heightened experiences of dramatic mediation, indeed engagement with the issues and import that the event stages."[24] Stanton B. Garner Jr writes about the embodied actuality of actor bodies, but the same observations apply to participatory, immersed audience bodies. "A point of independent sentience, the body represents a rootedness in the biological present that always, to some extent, escapes transformation into the virtual realm ... The performing body constitutes the centerpiece of this play of actuality – indeed, it represents a site at which this play is brought to the point of illusionistic crisis."[25] As real bodies and minds in the real world, the audience experiences that crisis, anchored to their phenomenal experience of that world even as they are imaginatively fused to the surrounding fiction. This oscillating dual consciousness that keeps the audience perception divided against itself catalyses a distanced aestheticization of immersive performance and constitutes the locus of realness in the genre.

Janet Murray projects a future where this self-reflexive aestheticization of experience will vanish, arguing that eventually all "successful" storytelling technologies become transparent. When we read, we don't really "see" the print or the page as such, becoming absorbed directly into the imaginative world created there. Likewise for visual media, like film or television, unless the presentation overtly draws self-reflexive attention to itself, the screen as screen is typically invisible to us. Realist drama works in a similar way, erasing, or at least easing, the perceptual work done by the audience to generate theatricality. Of course, this is a fine point of balance; too much "realism" – babies, ticking clocks, running water, or dogs on the stage – and we are back to States's upsurges of the real, which thematize the work of generating theatricality. Murray is writing about digital virtual environments that exist today, like MUDs (originally "multi-user dungeon," later "multi-user dimension" or "multi-user domain,")[26] or that might exist someday, like the *Star Trek* holodeck, and hopes that these genres attain that pinnacle of medial invisibility. "We will no longer concern ourselves with how we are receiving the information. We will only think about what truth it has told us about our lives," she writes.[27] Be that as it may, the invisibility of mediation that generates seamless world creation is not the only (or perhaps not even the most effective) strategy for communicating a core understanding or affect. Indeed even as she hopes for its diminishment, Murray provides a rich example of the potency of our meta-consciousness of how immersive worlds are created and how we, as immersed subjects, are intimately and uncomfortably culpable in that creation to the point where that self-consciousness dooms the worlds to failure. She describes a particular episode of *Star Trek*, in which Captain Janeway rejects her holodeck lover. Despite the superlative fidelity of the simulation, it is impossible to fully immerse in a situation that you know to be a construction, ineffably at odds with your own self-aware reality. It is embarrassing. (Even if no one is watching; you are watching yourself. And that is part of the problem.) Josephine Machon refers to this effect as an "uncanny recognition of audience-participant's own *praesence* within the experience."[28] Indeed, the presence of the real audience-participant in the context of a constructed immersive environment is uncanny. Going back through Sigmund Freud and Masahiro Mori, we can locate that sense of profound unease in the phenomenon of the Uncanny Valley, which marks a specific zone of negative correlation between affinity for an object and its human likeness as it approaches being indistinguishable from a living human. This is the reason for the existential queasiness triggered by zombies, store mannequins, and CGI versions of Tom Hanks in *The Polar Express*. In the case of the *praesence* of the real audience in the context of immersive theatre, the source of self-conscious unease lies in the gap of dissimilar ontology between the inescapably real witness-participant and her world that is uncannily not quite (and can never be) real enough. Personally, I am not convinced that the medium of immersed performance can someday become transparent, no matter how real it appears, because the audience is contiguous with the medium in a way that I am not when reading or watching a video. I know that my self is real and my affect is real. I know that the encompassing world is a construction. Given that knowledge, I am doubtful if it is possible to relinquish the grounded awareness of my own reality that keeps me at a distance ontologically from my virtual companions. Moreover, as this chapter will demonstrate, the lack of transparency, the meta-awareness of the ontological gap in immersive affective experiences, has specific productive value. Full unthinking immersion is not necessarily the gold standard. I don't actually want to get "lost."

Unable to shed this acute sense of uncanny presence, immersive theatre has the potential to turn this persistent self-consciousness, this aestheticization of experience, to transformational ends. It is not an uncommon criticism of immersive theatre to suggest that although it is affectively stimulating as a genre it lacks political backbone.[29] This may be a fair assessment of certain works that prioritize emotional thrills and the electric pleasure of novelty and childish surprise. However, this need not be the case. Michael Billington, who is among those who have expressed reservations about the impact of the form, throws down a challenge: "What I'd like to see in experimental [immersive] theatre is more radical purpose and aesthetic rigour."[30] The two case studies presented here are arguably both radical and rigorous in this way. These are plays that mobilize formal performative features of insecurity through aestheticization of self-presence to meditate on political insecurity. *Counting Sheep* restages the events of the Euromaidan Revolution, which occupied the central square of Kyiv from November 2013 through spring 2014. A popular demonstration against corruption and perceived Russian influence over the Ukraine government of Viktor Yanukovych, the protest also found a unifying cause in demanding closer ties to the European Union. *Counting Sheep* creators, Mark and Marichka Marczyk, met and fell in love in Kyiv in Independence Square during the revolution.[31] After returning together to Canada, where they subsequently married, they brought the idea for a performance about their experiences to Mark's musical group, Lemon Bucket Orkestra, a self-proclaimed "balkan-klezmer-gypsy-party-punk super band."[32] Featuring approximately fifteen members, Lemon Bucket Orkestra is known for its high-energy, chaotic performances, which invariably end with the band and the audience dancing out into the streets. Subtitled *A Guerrilla Folk Opera*, *Counting Sheep* contrapuntally blends traditional Ukrainian folk songs, performed by members of the Orkestra wearing half-face sheep masks with video news footage that traces the course of the months-long protests.[33] The sequence of live scenes in the play mimics that of the videos, following the Maidan Revolution, also known as the Revolution of Dignity, from inciting event, to eating and dancing, to building a barricade, to a wedding, to increasingly violent confrontations with helmeted riot police, to the burning of the barricade, to a funeral, and finally to the Russian military invasion and local defence of the Crimea region. *Counting Sheep* mobilizes immersive theatre as literally a rehearsal for the revolution, paying tribute to the power of ordinary people, past and future, who rise up against autocracy.

Foreign Radical also speaks to the power of ordinary citizens to take responsibility for protecting democracy.[34] A play about surveillance and the collection of online information by government intelligence agencies to create profiles in the interests of protecting Canada from homegrown terrorists, *Foreign Radical* asks, to what extent are we culpable in the actions of our elected government? What price are we willing to pay for safety? Will we exchange personal freedom – rights to travel, rights of privacy, rights of free association – for physical security? The play tells the story of Hesam, an Iranian-Canadian student, who has attracted the attention of Canadian security agencies through his friendship with Jamal, another young Muslim who has become disaffected and radicalized. In parallel with the narrative sketched by Hesam's monologues while in custody, *Foreign Radical* features Milton Lim as a slightly unhinged, somewhat threatening game show host who compels the audience to answer personal questions about our political views, social allegiances, and online behaviours.

Both plays tap into questions of ethical citizenship in contemporary society marked by risk. Ulrich Beck argues that risk characterizes the recent era as never before: "Modern society has become a risk society in the sense that it is increasingly occupied with debating, preventing and managing risks that it itself has produced."[35] Alston glosses Beck's vision of risk, observing that "Terrorist attacks, the menace of malicious computer viruses for national security, misplaced laptops holding the data of countless citizens and identity theft, are just a few examples that produce a commonplace and toxic brew of paranoia, scaremongering, and potential catastrophe that threatens to shatter the optimist's rose-tinted spectacles."[36] Critically, as Beck points out, risk does not entail catastrophe: "risk means the *anticipation* of catastrophe."[37] Whether or not from an objective standpoint we live in the safest decades in history, our *perception* of risk is unprecedented. Beck attributes this to three factors: one, de-localization – risk is not limited geographically; it is omnipresent; two, incalculability – the consequences are impossible to fathom; we simply cannot know what we do not know; and three, non-compensability – the outcomes of certain risks (like attacks with weapons of mass destruction or climate change) are irreversible and potentially world-ending.[38] In the context of the insecurity of risk, terrorism is the quintessential unknown – a "not-yet" crime where intelligence agencies attempt to prevent a future act by profiling people likely to commit such acts. Basically, this is an impossible task. Likewise, popular protest also carries that sense of the uncertain future in the spontaneous uprising of collective civil disobedience. What pushes people to the brink? What future awaits them on the other side? Is the risk worth the outcome? Questioning the balance between freedom and security, both plays direct attention to how citizens negotiate power and risk within democracies. When government is by the people for the people, we ourselves are both responsible for and subject to the actions of that government. *Counting Sheep* and *Foreign Radical* – in different ways – invite reflection on how we perform ethical citizenship, how we live according to our beliefs, practising collective decision making in the context of radical insecurity. What actions should we take to render governments accountable to the people? How are we accountable to each other?

Examining the ways that *Counting Sheep* and *Foreign Radical* as collective immersed performances about political insecurity manage the interplay of different kinds of realness, this chapter argues that each of these works functions as "trauma-tragedy" according to the model outlined by Patrick Duggan in his book of the same name. Breaks in the plays' respective mimetic fields create an uncomfortable indecidability that is related to the experience of trauma. It is through these breaks or puncta that the audience encounters the return of the real. Displacing one kind of real through a failure of mimesis, we break out into another yet more real real. Writing about the attacks of 11 September 2001, Slavoj Žižek writes, "The Real which returns has the status of a(nother) semblance precisely because it is real, that is, on account of its traumatic/excessive character, we are unable to integrate it into (what we experience as) our reality."[39] Hal Foster, in his book *The Return of the Real*, collects examples of contemporary visual art under the descriptor "traumatic realism"[40] to show how the unavoidable imperfections and shocks of near-photographic realism operate to create a punctum or error that "rips" the screen so as to show the screen and reveal the truth of their constructedness, and so return to reality. Reflecting on the genealogical trajectory of these works through the twentieth century, he writes, "the angel with whom we wrestled was Marcel Duchamp by way of Andy Warhol, more than Picasso by way of Pollock."[41] Drawing on Lacan's formulation of the Real, Foster argues that Warhol's reiterative photographic works, like *White Burning Car III*, both reproduce traumatic effects and produce them. "Somehow in these repetitions, then, several contradictory things occur at the same time: a warding away of traumatic significance *and* an opening out to it, a defending against traumatic effect *and* a producing of it."[42] Lacan defines the traumatic as a missed encounter with the real. Therefore, it cannot be represented, it can only be repeated. Repetition as an aesthetic strategy, then, both screens the real and points to it, where at that pinpoint of deictic contact, it ruptures the screen; Lacan calls this the "*tuché*," similar to Barthes's *punctum*.[43] Locating this puncture effect in the, at times, galling indifference to violence in repetition or the blurred and streaked evidence of the silkscreen replication process, Foster notes that Warhol's "pops" serve as visual equivalents of our missed encounters with the real. And it is "through these pokes or pops we seem almost to touch the real."[44]

A central feature of trauma, as described by Foster in this analysis, is a confusion about the location of the rupture, "a confusion of subject and world, inside and outside."[45] This ontological ambiguity connects the effects of traumatic realism described by Foster to the aestheticization of presence experienced in immersive environments. That metatheatrical folding of a Moebius strip of worlds, located inside the immersed audience, fills the same function, and may be taken as another instance of a tear in the mediating screen that both shields us from reality and at the same time reveals it through that puncture. Foster's citation of the painting *Las Meninas* by Diego Velasquez supports this extension from photographic repetition and hyperrealism into other styles that also raise the screen or frame to view, simultaneously hiding and exposing it through manipulations of form. *Las Meninas* presents an enigmatic arrangement of inside and outside, of real and fictional space. The painting, which depicts the young Infanta of Spain with her ladies and other members of the court, also presents a self-portrait of the painter as part of the scene of a portrait sitting in progress, the back of the canvas visible to the viewer. The Infanta meets our gaze, as does Velasquez. Ostensibly, the subjects of the painting of the painting are the king and queen, visible at the far back of the room, reflected in a mirror. From this we can extrapolate that they are standing exactly where the real-world viewer is standing, impossibly outside the frame of the picture, invisible and yet palpably and unnervingly present. "The pivotal content of the painting is not communicated in its visible part, but located in this dis-location of the two frames, in the gap that separates them."[46] To add another layer of ontological frisson, that same spot co-occupied by the king and queen as subject of the primary painting, and the viewer – both subject of one painting and viewer of another – must also have been occupied at the time of the creation of this secondary painting by Velasquez himself, even as his fictional double is inside the frame. Through these ontologically complex manipulations manifested spatially, the work self-reflexively draws attention to its own "screen," rendering the aesthetic experience of these manipulations central to the work's meaning. "Herein lies the fundamental ambiguity of the image in postmodernism: it is a kind of barrier enabling the subject to maintain distance from the real, protecting him or her against its irruption, yet its very obtrusive 'hyperrealism' evokes the nausea of the real."[47]

Meditating on the notion of immersion in immersive theatre, Gareth White addresses this confusion of being both in and out, to ask, "What are we 'in' exactly?" White establishes a metaphorical link using the image schema of a bounded container to describe artwork (e.g., "getting into a role," references to frames and the fourth wall) and combining it with another schema that depicts experience as a body of water ("sink or swim," "go with the flow") to derive the higher-order metaphor "Art is immersive."[48] We are in something and it surrounds us, but even in this intimate situation we are separate from the encompassing medium. The boundary is not merely skin or the limits of identity but, as Erin Hurley notes, "It is our senses ... that tell us that we are distinct from the world; they define and patrol our physical perimeter by registering the effects of the world on our selves. We live then with near-constant reminders that we are separate from our surroundings; they may encompass us, but they are not of us."[49] But, White continues, this is not the whole story: What if performance does not just surround us – we are in it – but it is in us? White imagines a mutual "interpenetration of works of performance into the body of the audience member."[50] Considering specific examples of immersive performance experiences (*Masque of the Red Death* and *Tunnel 228*, both produced by Punchdrunk), White connects the formal metaphor of being immersed with an audience desire to be "in," a desire that manifests thematically in these works by solving a core mystery, or gaining access to private interior spaces, either physically by exploring hidden or closed rooms or affectively in an exclusive one-to-one scene. Sometimes this interiority manifests as the inside of the drama – its secret narrative heart – or as the inside of the production – access to a backstage world. Ultimately, White turns to Heidegger's assertion that "Art is an event of truth ... [that] centres on the 'uncon-cealment' of things in their essence,"[51] to offer another account of what is revealed when we reach the inside. What is unconcealed in immersive works? It is the insight that "the world worlds" – i.e., worlds are created in acts of self-generation – and "the shocking realization of the space that remains between the two realms."[52] This territory between fictional worlds and the conditions of their creation constitutes the fertile landscape of metatheatrical awareness.

The embodied audience perception located ambiguously both "inside" and "outside" the fictional space of immersive environments renders that fiction fragile. Not sure where to stand or where to look, Sophie Nield recounts her discomfort inside immersed environments. She too is concerned about the "fragility of the surface." Perhaps it is stronger than she supposes, but perhaps this sense of fragility is a key quality of the genre. She writes, "But perhaps the tension and melancholy of it comes from the fact that we all know that if one of us tells [the actor] to fuck off, we break some kind of spell, and the whole experience suffers. So we feel the thinness of his performance, not the thinness of our civility."[53] Conventions are needed to sustain this fragile theatricality. Somehow the fourth-wall boundary or its equivalent must be shored up against collapse, defended against the intrusion of the too-real audience. "When we enter the enchanted world as our actual selves, we risk draining it of it delicious otherness,"[54] worries Janet Murray. Counterintuitively, one way to strengthen the boundary against ourselves, against our own destructive knowing, is to explicitly acknowledge the space we occupy in our physical and self-reflexive intervention. Murray gives the dual examples of the famously "meta," ostensibly autobiographical novel *Tristram Shandy* about a man who is writing a novel and a Daffy Duck cartoon where Daffy is at war with a malevolent cartoonist. In both cases, overtly displaying the way the "world worlds" allows the characters to be divorced from the means of representation. Through this metatheatrical trickery, they become free of it and are perceived (impossibly) to be superior to the medium of their own creation.[55] Ultimately the effect is to deepen rather than disrupt the power of world-construction. It is this in-between space of metatheatrical play that also characterizes trauma, the nausea of the real, latent in the inevitable gap between the event and the experience of that event.

Patrick Duggan, in his book *Trauma-Tragedy*, forges a rich link between trauma manifesting in the return of the real and the interplay between representation and differing levels of reality. To articulate this relation, he coins the term "mimetic shimmering." Instead of the more traditional binary relation between fictional and actual, between representation and a singular real, Duggan proposes a multivalent oscillation between three poles – the materiality of a thing, its representation, and the real-world thing to which it refers. The first two poles are familiar components of theatrical mimesis: actual-world things that are on stage (people as actors, or the physical material of sets or props) and the mimetic representation ventriloquized by that material (characters, fictional settings). It is the third element that is novel, coming into view when "that which is on stage imputes the presence/reality of that which is represented, itself evoked by the real of the performance (in other words, the 'out there, in the real world' referent is not a mimetic illusion but becomes present through the agency of the reality of the performers/performance)."[56] Basically what Duggan is doing is separating actual-world stuff (what I think of as world^a material) into two kinds; both the things on the stage (world^{a1}) and the "out there" reality to which the fiction points (world^{a2}) share the same ontology. If we apply this model to "ordinary" artistic transposition, nothing very interesting happens: Paint and canvas (world^{a1} objects) become mimetically a "fictional" bowl of fruit (world^b) which comes to impute the existence of bowls of fruit as a generic entity in the actual world (world^{a2} objects). Both paint and canvas and fruit and bowls are real things. Things get interesting when, following States, the material is so specific as to be iconic. In this special case, the initial material object (^{a1}) is identical to, i.e., it IS, the object imputed (^{a2}). Autobiographical performance works this way, where the actor-subject present on stage (self^{a1}) is the same person as the protagonist of the performed self-story (self^{a2}). These selves may be somewhat separated by time in the immediate moment of performance, but they re-cohere afterwards in the future as a temporally continuous persona. A significant phenomenal aspect of this iconic realness is that the material real resists becoming "neutral," departing from its usual silent passivity standing by to be ventriloquized; instead it speaks as itself and it is loud. The value of Duggan's separation of the actual elements of theatricality into real "inputs" and "outputs" (my terminology) is that he draws pointed attention to the process by which realness is manipulated. In *Shattering Hamlet's Mirror*, Marvin Carlson outlines the stakes for such a move:

> The concern is rather to demonstrate that the real and the represented are not a set binary, but are the products of human consciousness and ways of seeing and encoding ... [The tripartite model of mimetic shimmering has the potential to change our perspective] suggesting not an either or of the real and the mimetic, but a constantly shifting awareness of the construction and deconstruction of the "real" world around us.[57]

How does this connect to trauma? Conventional thinking suggests that traumas are "experienced too soon, too unexpectedly, to be fully known and [are] therefore not available to consciousness until [they impose themselves] again, repeatedly, in the nightmares and repetitive actions of the survivors."[58] Traumas are failures of representation. Trauma manifests in the return of the real. Duggan agrees that "there can be no denying the relationship between trauma and mimesis, for to remember the trauma-event as part of the trauma-symptom is to recreate/restage that event imaginatively."[59] Yet, he contests any naturalistically limited conceptualization of that mimesis. Representation may include verisimilar mimetic copying, but also stylized distortions arising in nightmares and hallucinations. Also, according to my view, the re-embodied simming of immersive theatre, which is representational but not realistic, being full of gaps, can also open experience to trauma. The performance is "acutely related to and imitative of the original,"[60] and yet the gaps are obvious and undeniable. Drawing on Michael Taussig's *Mimesis and Alterity*, Duggan points out that mimesis holds and grants power over the thing portrayed – a kind of shamanism – but it need not be an accurate copy to still have mimetic power. Mimesis spins "sticky webs of copy *and* contact, image *and* bodily involvement of the perceiver in the image."[61] The tricky thing about representation is that it is always already both the copy and the thing itself – image and body.[62] Effects of mimetic shimmering in theatres of the real that attach to iconic objects (like autobiographical bodies, testimony, and specific sites) dwell on this sticky mimetic power, where realness is both divided and blended between the actual material object co-opted to produce its own representation, and its virtually-identical self, imputed to an elsewhere real-world existence. In immersive theatre, that frisson of iconicity is located within the audience body. It is the ontology of the audience that shimmers. And in that destabilizing self-conscious shimmer, we witness the "collapse and layering of the mimetic order [that] creates an unease which is cognate with the experience of traumatic reoccurrence."[63]

Duggan's stated goal is to "identify dramatic modes or forms which are engaged in shortening the gap between traumatic event and its re-witnessing and also the gap between traumatic expression and the discovery of the structure of feeling."[64] This is achieved by "experiencing the world in more cathected ways than normally made available in everyday life."[65] Duggan's examples range from live art created by Franko B to the plays of Sarah Kane, and includes practitioners such as Forced Entertainment and Socìetas Raffaello Sanzio as they stage the realness of real things. To his list I propose to add fictional immersive performances, locating the traumatic gap, not on the far side of the

fourth wall, but intimately near, in the ontologically unstable reflexivity of the aestheticization of the audience experience. As an innately
cathected form where we feel more alive through unfamiliar embodiment in a novel medium, immersive theatre performances like *Counting
Sheep* and *Foreign Radical* generate effects of mimetic shimmering that
open gaps between the material real, and the world to which it refers,
via vertiginous or failed representation. The move towards an indecidable authenticity punctures the "screen" of theatricality and "signals
a new tragic mode."[66] "Socially and aesthetically, the trauma-tragic
mode is concerned with embodying an experience that shortens the
gap between event and experience and so helps us to rehearse, contemplate or indeed (re)experience our own (psychic) trauma by creating the
effect of cathected presence."[67] In these specific examples, it is through
locating uncertain affects of realness in the aesthetic reflection on audience as audience that these works activate mimetic shimmering, and
attempt to bear witness to trauma.

Counting Sheep

In the centre of the community hall where *Counting Sheep* is performed,
there is a long table covered by a red and white striped cloth with
benches and room for at least thirty people seated along its length.
More people occupy more benches behind both sides of the table, facing
the centre of the room. Surrounding the head of the table, suspended
from the ceiling are three large screens. From start to finish, the screens
(each showing the same images) broadcast the unfolding history of the
Maidan Revolution. Lifted predominantly from news broadcasts, these
images constitute a kind of testimony, a visual documentary parallel to
Annabel Soutar's first-person interviews used to create *Seeds*. Here the
selected videos also shape the performance, acting as a kind of script for
our gestural verbatim. As events appear on the screens, they are acted
out by the Orkestra ensemble and the audience. Via our re-enactment
of these historical events, mediated by the video script, *Counting
Sheep* is, in Scott Magelssen's terms, a "sim." Describing "a simulated,
immersive, performance environment,"[68] sims, or the act of simming,
can be scripted or improvised and feature a high degree of interactivity
between the immersed audience and that environment "in order to gain
or produce understandings of a situation and its context."[69] Magelssen
lays out the ways in which simming promises "a different kind of effi-
cacy and social change than other media through affective, embodied

practice."[70] *Counting Sheep* is predominantly a backward-looking simulation, bringing history into the present, and admitting contemporary audience bodies into a historical role-play. Among the different functions of simming listed by Magelssen,[71] *Counting Sheep*, as a past sim, can thus be categorized as a sim of witness, marking our empathy and solidarity for the Maidan protesters that we re-animate, but also as a sim of reification, confirming and endorsing the values of the revolution. That said, *Counting Sheep* creates a conduit for connecting the past to the present, but also extends that temporal bridge into the future as audiences think with their bodies about what they might do in the future, as a kind of rehearsal for the revolution.[72]

In the wake of the 9/11 attacks on New York's World Trade Center buildings and the subsequent imprinting on our collective consciousness of the literally incredible video footage of the second plane crashing into the South Tower, Žižek marked this confluence of the lived event and the consumption of its mediatized image as the most potent recent return of the real. In his essay "Welcome to the Desert of the Real" (a phrase aptly borrowed from the film *The Matrix*), Žižek perceptively accounts for the sense that the images of the catastrophe seem somewhat familiar – and they are, from numerous blockbuster movies depicting similar explosive spectacles. What is shocking to us, but should not be, is that the "screen fantasmatic apparition entered our reality. It is not that reality entered our image: the images entered and shattered our reality."[73] In this moment of irruption, "the distance between event and its representation became almost indistinguishable as the filmed images came to stand in for and define the events."[74] This profoundly destabilizing merging of the event and its image is deployed in *Counting Sheep* through the continual rebroadcast of Kyiv news video of the Maidan protests and the subsequent guerilla war in Crimea. The variable reality status of these images and their relationship to the likewise variable reality of the live action re-enactment constitute a central dilemma for *Counting Sheep*: Where does the real lie? First, these images are framed as "live." Featuring television news channel logos and text "crawl" along the bottom, they carry connotations of direct access to a historical real. As Philip Auslander notes, television as a medium is characterized by two essential properties – immediacy and intimacy.[75] Despite its potential for being pre-recorded, television exudes liveness. A window on events happening when and as they happen, television feels like a front-row seat. In this sense, images of the revolution are a window on the revolution. In contrast with this immediacy, television, broadcast like other documentary texts, manifests its situation as collected, framed, recorded, and edited both for original broadcast and secondarily for inclusion in the performance. The same overlaid screen text that communicates liveness also renders the intermedial screen visible. There is clearly something between us and the image.

Second, these images lead the action of the performance, prefiguring it as a script. Audience actions are subject to the usual theatrical duality, being both real bodies in the here and now and a representation that uses those bodies to point to a real world that is elsewhere and not now. Thus the videos are one kind of representation of history, and the performance is another, reflecting one another. Uncannily, both audience re-enactors and videoed Kyiv protesters are ambiguously real and representational. Occasionally this creates vertigo as the two mirrors fold into one another, sometimes seeming to co-occupy time and space as we become extras in their world, or they in ours, the crowd of bodies extending up and through the screen or conversely out and into the hall. Is the Lemon Bucket Orkestra playing the music they are dancing to in Kyiv? How is it that we are all now eating perogies and borscht? Further complicating this ontological feedback loop, *Counting Sheep* features the constant presence of a TV cameraman-sheep who is filming it all. With a large professional-grade camera strapped to his chest with a harness and military-style metal helmet that says "TV," he moves through the action. Significantly, we never get "live" footage of the audience in the hall. The link is purely imaginary between us and what we see on the screens; and yet we think, "It could be us. Is it us?"

At other points, emphasis is placed on the differences, the incomplete or imperfect verisimilitude of enactment. In one corner of the hall is a large cone-shaped wooden scaffold, at least fifteen feet tall. I can see it here and I can see it on the video. It is a Christmas tree in Independence Square. As protesters climb it to hang banners, Ukrainian and European Union flags, actor-protesters do the same here. I can look from one to the other to compare them. It is live both there and here, same and not same. In scene four, the play restages a specific episode from the video news where some young protesters commandeered a bulldozer with the intention of driving it through a line of riot police. As they approached the cordon, other protesters linked arms in front of the police and persuaded their compatriots to reverse course and maintain the up-to-now peaceful tenor of their protest. In the hall, the bulldozer is replicated with a scoop-like snow shovel, and a cluster of

6.1 In *Counting Sheep*, members of the Lemon Bucket Orkestra represent a bulldozer commandeered by the protesters with news footage of the actual bulldozer on the screen behind them. Photo credit: Nechepurenko Dmytro.

Orkestra-sheep playing trombone, saxophone, and a white sousaphone painted with lemons in its bell. Clearly it is not a bulldozer, and yet as it lurches noisily (and musically) forward towards the doubled lines of peacenik-sheep, and riot police-sheep with helmets and shields, the stakes are clear. The most moving of these disjunctions comes when the barricade is set on fire. Against the backdrop of live footage of the conflagration, red ribbons, many metres long, fly down from above and behind us in the dark flame-lit hall, unfurling as they fall on our replica barricade. Throughout the performance, the now-live and the then-live play in parallel. We dance and they dance. Riot police bang their shields, here and there, now and before. Multiplied and amplified, what is here and now in the hall is both more and less real. It is obviously imperfect as mimesis but it is through the aestheticization of that gap that the real returns.

Talking about the Wooster Group's 2004 reenactment of a section of the archival film of Jerzy Grotowski's landmark production of *Akropolis*, Rebecca Schneider locates a kind of traumatic access to that third pole of imputed elsewhere reality through mimetic failures. Schneider writes, "The effort at gestic cloning both succeeds ... and completely fails as the problem of unruly details (call it gender difference, bodily difference, language difference, anachronism, or any other number of inevitable errors) takes the stage with a palpable force in direct proportion to the technical accomplishment of reiterating the affects of the 'master's piece' faithfully."[76] This is exactly the kind of gestic cloning (or what I called previously, in relation to the iterated choreography of *300 TAPES*, "gestural verbatim") at work in *Counting Sheep* as the audience both reflects the historical video record, successfully bringing it to life in the community hall through our re-embodiment, and also inevitably fails at that task by our mere presence, different in all the ways Schneider lists. Yet, it is in those gaps that we access realness. Schneider continues,

> Paradoxically, perhaps, it is the errors, the cracks in the effort, the almost but not quite, that give us some access to sincerity, to fidelity, to a kind of *touch* across time David Romàn has termed 'archival drag.' [It is in these mistakes of the 'not-quite' that we] feel a leak of affective engagement ... that brings time travel, as it were, into the fold of experience: shimmering on an edge, caught between the possible and the impossible, touching the interval itself.[77]

Errors of replication are one way that the real returns; another is through the mimetic failure triggered by the alchemical reaction between hyperrealism and excessive stylization. Duggan, in one of his examples, describes the performance of an abstractly stylized assault that, despite its superficial unreality, nevertheless was deeply disturbing. [The] "embodied sense of the beating as real even as that 'reality' is being undone by the disjunction between readable theatricality and a sense of reality, and so a circulation begins."[78] Activation of the affect of indecidability need not be tied exclusively to the hyperrealism of appropriation art. There are other ways to unsettle representation so as to aestheticize the experience of the "how" of representation and touch the traumatic real through that puncture. As noted at the outset, immersive theatre is not realistic in the way a documentary snapshot is. These are unquestionably fictions. When the real irrupts, it is not because the fiction fails to cover up its makings and materials, as in traditional metatheatre, but because the fiction doesn't stabilize in the first place. Representation fails as it "refuses to settle into a comfortable sense of illusion."[79] When it no longer is believable as a representation, it becomes real – the thing itself. The semiotic pathway skips directly from the iconic signifier to its self-same signified. Duggan gives an example of the baby on stage (*pace* States's dog on the stage). What is disruptively real about it is not its materiality, he suggests. The locus of interest is not in its current state as theatrical materiality (pole^{a1}), "thing it was before," but what its reality is beyond (pole^{a2}), "the reality of the referent of which [the baby] is a sign," the mimetic (pole^{b}) flares weakly or is omitted entirely.[80] Similar to his example of excessive blood on the stage, the baby is real first and mimetic second, reversing the usual pattern of metatheatrical upheaval. Rather than the real bubbling up to disrupt a formerly sturdy mimetic illusion, mimesis irrupts into the real. Like an unstable isotope, the mimetic effect flickers, resisting coming into focus.

Counting Sheep triggers this same effect in the failure of representation through the presentation of overtly stylized elements in the hyperrealistic context of the participatory audience. Whereas on the one hand, *Counting Sheep* presents a strong naturalism via its use of documentary techniques (the continual video feed, and its verbatim re-enactment), on the other hand, *Counting Sheep* is a fable, performed by anthropomorphic sheep, and steeped in Ukrainian folk wisdom. From the outset, the performance is bracketed by projected title cards, with white font on a black background framed with a curlicue border reminiscent of the silent film era, that announce: "Lemon Bucket Orkestra presents / Counting Sheep: A Guerrilla Folk Opera" and "based on a true story." This title frame concretizes the work as an artistic representation of reality, an "opera" with a maker. But the tag line "based on a true story" links that representation back to the imputed reality of a past world. Moreover, *Counting Sheep* invokes that imputed historical real in at least two ways, via the video footage to the recent past of the Maidan and via the music to a mythic popular folk past. The music and lyrics of *Counting Sheep* that form almost the whole of its text are composed exclusively of traditional Ukrainian songs which in this new context have new things to say. In a scene titled "7. Whose side are you on?," which depicts the defection of a member of the riot police to the side of the protesters, the projected lyrics read: "In our master's yard / In his yard, in his vineyard / There was a tall, thin birch /

Tall and thin, with wide leaves / The path to that birch was ruffled / Who ruffled the path?" Allusive and elevated, the lyrics evoke a non-specific rural world long-gone that only glancingly refers to the current action, adding yet another reality to the mix. The sheep masks create a similar kind of ontological displacement. Not only is the audience engaged in present/*praesence* interactive co-production with actors, blurring fourth-wall ontology, these actors are sheep (and they only speak Ukrainian). Consciousness of this disjunction prevents the audience from sinking comfortably into the illusion of the fiction. Caught in a liminal space between fiction and varying levels of reality, we bear witness to the struggle of the real and the mimetic, unable to commit fully to perceptual balance. It is that meta-reflection on reflection, the act of witness to the impossibility of our easy theatrical making, that then becomes the primary subject of audience experience.

Indecidability located within the audience body reduces the gap between event and experience and thereby generates perception in the trauma-tragic mode. It is in three particular moments or aspects of *Counting Sheep* that effects of uncertain realness trigger a self-reflexive aestheticization of the audience experience. And in these moments of mimetic shimmering of ambivalent audience ontology, the work attempts to bear witness to trauma. The first and most pervasive strategy for locating this indecidability in the audience body is through movement, simple at first and gradually increasing in complexity and performative commitment. Audiences to *Counting Sheep* are initially seated in rows, a not unfamiliar position for theatregoing. It begins in the first scenes gently with clapping and stamping our feet to the music. Audiences pass food along the line, handing out and receiving plates. We eat. This kind of behaviour is already scripted as mundane social niceties. Then, audience members are plucked out of their seats to dance with the masked sheep, and when the sheep spin away, you find yourself partnered with another random audience member. Waltzing in pairs and dancing in concentric circles, as well as the communal serving and eating of food, constitute formulaic festival behaviour that eases participation. This is a repertoire that we already possess. Audience action progresses from passing food to passing benches and tires as we are conscripted shoulder to shoulder to build the barricades. And in the process all the seats disappear, absorbed into our makeshift defences. Gareth White (*Audience Participation in the Theatre*) focuses on the moment of invitation to participation. He notes, "participatory theatre ... presents special opportunities for embarrassment, for mis-performance, and reputational damage, such that the maintenance of control and the assertion of agency that protect this decorum is important ... especially at the moment of invitation."[81] This is a critical juncture of insecurity as conventional expectations slip away and audiences are stranded in a public situation unsure what is being asked of them. Being part of a crowd can allay some of the unpleasantness of this uncertainty. Likewise the gradual progression from familiar social scripts to novel and autonomous acts serves to extend the audience's comfort zone or what White calls "horizon of risk" and makes us braver. Citing research into how the body shapes the mind, White considers sites of intersections of body and environment where the specific way that the environment or objects in the environment are formed subtly coach the body to particular adaptive reactions.[82] Objects like "teacups, computer keys, and door handles, have motor senses or meanings ... 'affordances' which elicit appropriate actions. Things in the world bring forth suitable intentional actions and motor projects from the subject."[83] Similarly, communal festive behaviours – eating or dancing – constitute social affordances, somewhat reducing performative uncertainty.

Beyond specific accommodative affordances, real body movements shape emotions and understanding as "kinesthetic experience ... places pressure on the conditioning a body receives, encouraging variations in performance that account for larger innovations in cultural practice."[84] If gesture and movement are culturally shaped, they can be reshaped. "These variations can accumulate and cascade into forms of innovation and, yes, resistance that produce profound effects on behaviour, effects that can spread out and radiate into realms of conscious decision-making and other, supposedly more mindful areas of cultural and political practice."[85] In the renewed body actions of the *Counting Sheep* audience-protesters, re-enactment of past events collides with rehearsal for the future. The actions of throwing bricks and building barricades put revolution into our bodies. This is one way that "rather than looking back at a historical moment of trauma, trauma-tragedy is attempting to bridge or reduce the gap between the historical moment, its witness and (that) experience."[86] In addition to action as renovative rehearsal, at a more basic level these actions "get my blood moving" and remind me that indeed I have a body. I am a body. Not merely a cognitive eye/I, I experience theatrical immersion on different planes as adrenaline, as choreography, as an obstructed view, as tired feet. Food is really real and it is really entering my body. And like dancing, or throwing bricks, it is a real thing that I am doing. These real actions intersect uncertainly with more patently fiction elements of the performance. "Foucault reminds us how the body is constitutively unstable, always foreign to itself – an open process of continuous self-estrangement where the most fundamental physiological and sensorial functions endure ongoing oscillations, adjustments, breaks, dysfunctions and optimizations."[87] Alison Griffiths, writing about immersivity in cinemas, museums, and cathedrals, remarks on the specific quality of interstitiality in being immersed: We are "neither fully lost in the experience, nor completely in the here and now ... We are never fully 'there' because our bodies can never fully leave the 'here.'"[88] In our physicality and in our consciousness, our immersed presence works against immersion. "Audiences guarantee the failure of a perfect totally immersive environment."[89] We can see audience bodies, both ourselves and others, that do not fit in the sim, bodies wearing inappropriate clothes, speaking the wrong language. Sophie Nield, witness to an immersive performance about the doomed love of Abelard and Heloise, and hyperconscious of her modern clothes and demeanour, wonders absurdly "Who on earth is this monk supposed to think I am?"[90] She continues, "For how else is this theatre dreaming us? If its time and space are 'real' to it, if it is immersed in its own cohesion, then who are we; some ghosts, some transient presences? Imagined before we ever arrived, how else can it cope with our difference? It doesn't know who we are."[91] This inescapable feature, being caught in an interstitial layer that is neither quite inside nor outside the fictive environment, is the foundational experience of the immersed audience. It is a different kind of postdramatic indecidability than that described by Lehmann. It is not that I cannot ascertain whether I myself am actual or fictional; it is that I am simultaneously both (or in Duggan's model all three). I shimmer in my awareness of myself as the material actor in the creation of the work, improvising my way through an unknown script; in my mimetic role as a protester performing for myself and also as part of the scenographic field of others; and finally I am aware of myself as "imputed to my real-world existence," occupied by concerns that are not performative but are spectatorial. Even as a spectator I remain off-balance "preoccupied with staying safe/invisible/out of the way/on top of the story, and ... using the headspace [I] would normally be using to analyse and engage with the signs onstage to work out the logistics of just spectating."[92]

Apart from the generalized situation of the immersed audience that activates mimetic shimmering through the reflexive aestheticization of audience experience, two other specific moments in *Counting Sheep* create the same effect of insecure ontology to open gaps in representation where we can touch the real beyond and bear witness to trauma. While audience members hurl fake-bricks at the police barricade, black paper airplanes zoom back in our direction. Simultaneously harmless and ominous, it is clear that these are bullets fired into the crowd of protesters. Several sheep are shot and killed. As one sheep lies prone on the floor, a cellphone rings. It is the standard factory-setting "Opening (Default)" ringtone, sounding like jaunty marimbas. The first reaction is a kind of subdued panic accompanied by the patting of pockets as audience members search for the culprit, worrying that it might be theirs. Once I have determined that it is not my phone, the second phase of my reaction and evidently that of others in the group is anger and (again subdued) annoyance at the profound rudeness of other people, marked by shuffling, sighing, and looking around pointedly at audience fellows. These first two reactions are decidedly grounded in the world as they speak to contraventions of the etiquette of the event as theatre. Then we identify the source of the sound. The cellphone is in the pocket of one of the dead sheep-protesters. Words are inadequate to describe the electricity of the revelation and magnitude of the perceptual recalibration that shakes the audience. As in Duggan's model, the mimetic penetrates the real, triggering that effect of reverse mimesis, and making a profound connection between the material of theatrical creation (pole^{a1}) and the world at large (pole^{a2}). This is what happens when young people die unexpectedly by violence. Their cellphones ring unanswered. Flowing in the opposite direction from usual metatheatrical irruptions, the shimmering of mimesis across Duggan's three poles rends the representational fabric to access the traumatic real.

Another example of mimetic shimmering appears in the archival video of *Counting Sheep* recorded during its run in Edinburgh in August 2016. After we re-enact the street funeral of the protesters, a slogan is shouted over and over by crowds of thousands in the video and by the sheep around us: "*Geroyam Slava!*" ("Glory to the Heroes!"). Gradually the chorus fades, and one sheep alone continues the chant. After two or three solo repetitions, he is joined responsively by an audience member – a young man in a white t-shirt kneeling near the front of an audience group. They shout at each other and the young man stands and grips the shoulders of the sheep. The sheep clutches him into a hug and dissolves sobbing. While the sheep sobs loudly and almost musically, the young man squeezes his eyes with his hand. When they part, they acknowledge each other again with *"Geroyam Slava!"* more softly, one to the other, and the young man sinks back to his place on the floor. As the action continues, he can be seen in the periphery of the video wiping his eyes.[93] Who is this young man? It is my belief that he is a member of the audience. (Certainly he is performatively marked as such through his lack of sheep mask/eye makeup and spatial context among the audience-watchers.) He is clearly someone for whom this re-enactment of the revolution is deeply meaningful. Again, we witness a moment of reverse mimesis where something real becomes ambivalently mimetic and in so doing scalds representation as a traumatic conduit of iconicity from the present material real to the event in the world. Autobiographical iconicity folds the three poles – the young man as the material of performance (pole^{a1}), the young man as representation ontologically equivalent to the sheep-protester he is hugging (pole^{b}), and the young man in the world containing his experience before, and also now (pole^{a2}) – into almost singularity and the gaps shimmer.

Foreign Radical

Foreign Radical also features a young man who is phenomenologically marked as ambivalently real. At the beginning of the show, the audience of about twenty people is ushered into a darkened space, a curtained square perhaps six or seven metres on each side. Ever-so-Canadian, we well-trained audience members take up positions equidistant from each other around the edges and as far as possible from the naked man in the centre of the room. Lit by a spotlight, he is leaning forward with both hands on a table. He does not speak or move. And he and we remain silent and motionless for several self-conscious minutes. From the outset of the play, we are uncertain. Being unsure of the scenario is the natural situation of any audience member once the curtain rises or the stage lights first come on. But here not only are we uncertain of the scenario, we are uncertain what the "game" is. What is being asked of us? What is the ontology of this figure? Most likely, he is a fictional character – a world^{b} person; however his realness as a world^{a} body is phenomenally present; nakedness is another of those markers of en soi to be added to States's dog, running water, and fire. The body remains stubbornly actual, hovering on the cusp of theatrical transposition, and shimmering between the material real co-opted to theatrical creation and the imputed real of the world elsewhere. As is the audience, but we don't know that yet.

Like *Counting Sheep, Foreign Radical* is a kind of sim. But whereas *Counting Sheep* is a historically-oriented sim of witness and reification of values of the revolution, *Foreign Radical* is a "sandbox" sim, testing ideas for future application. Instead of an invocation of the past, the performance as simulation is a "potential space"[94] that may offer hope for an imagined future through the reversal of an unsatisfactory status quo. As Magelssen says, "sandbox sims are largely pragmatic in nature and can be high in attention to detail and low on emotional or affective sincerity."[95] This is a fairly accurate description of the *Foreign Radical* sim, which combines concrete real-world issues with the aesthetic of an over-the-top, hyperactive TV game show. In the second scene, after we are directed into another curtained square away from the naked man, but before we meet the game show host, audiences watch a short video. The video recounts the publication on the website *The Intercept* by journalists Glen Greenwald and Laura Poitras of the United States Watchlisting Guidance – a leaked document used by government agencies specifying the protocols for designating someone as a terrorist. From this exposition, we are to understand that our sandbox sim has been designed to test through interactive play the application of these security guidelines against the audience's values and beliefs concerning the judicial sacrifice of rights like privacy, mobility, liberty under habeas corpus, and freedom of association to the interests of security priorities. Having pointed to the Watchlisting Guidance as the manual for labelling a terrorist, the voiceover declares, "These are the rules of the game." Overlapping the word "game," the game show host in a white suit, frilled shirt, and hot pink bowtie bursts in dancing and shouting, accompanied by colourful flashing lights and upbeat TV music. "Did someone say 'game'? Let's play the game! We're going to fucking play a fucking game! Goddamn play the goddamn game!"[96] That semantic crossover in the repeated word "game," effectively mixes the rules for governmental identification of terrorists with the rules of *Foreign Radical* the theatre event with the rules for the game that we are "going to fucking play" – Are we going to identify terrorists? Really? – thereby situating the audience in uncertain territory. What is our ontology in relation to these different games?

What does it mean in this context to play a game? The central defining characteristic that separates a game from not-a-game is not dissimilar to that which separates the representational from the real.[97] Despite their external similarity, to the point of being indistinguishable, play-fighting is not fighting, for example. Games are framed as part of their essence as ontologically distinct from the world outside the game. What happens inside the game-world is enacted with a firm understanding that these events are not quite real; they don't "count" insofar as they are not expected to have real-world consequences. I might learn something from a game, acquiring knowledge or skills. Or I might experience real-world material gains or losses from winning or losing a game, but the internal actions of the game, moving a token down a path, collecting cards, or putting a ball in a net, are arbitrary actions whose meaning only accrues within the game world. Just like drama. Located inside the game frame, audience members of *Foreign Radical* are therefore somewhat distanced from their real-world selves. This alternate version of myself is not differentiated by mimesis; the difference is not one of theatrical representation but nevertheless the distinction is activated by the perceptual framing of a role. Who are we inside the game? Where do we fit in ontologically? Are we in world[a] or in world[b]? In *Counting Sheep*, for example, it is clear that we are not in the same world as the musician-sheep. Principally, unlike them, we are not masked; the masks serve as an external indication that while we participate in some of the actions of the revolution we are not fully fictionalized. We remain to some extent, partially outside the frame, self-consciously straddling world[a] and world[b]. In *Foreign Radical*, although we may not fully adopt roles – even a generic role like "Kyiv protester" as in *Counting Sheep* – we still experience an ontological shift; we are "players." As players of a game, our goals and attitudes are also slightly different. We are ourselves, but also not; the qualities that impel game-playing shape our behaviour.

Immersive audience-players are frequently cast as seekers.[98] In dispersed environments of autonomous action there is a built-in drive to maximize experience. Elinor Fuchs was one of the first to identify this audience attitude in early proto-immersive events like the dinner-theatre phenomenon of *Tony and Tina's Wedding* and Canadian playwright John Krizanc's groundbreaking choose-your-own-adventure *Tamara*, both of which she saw in New York in the late 1980s. Fuchs coins the term "shopping theater," cottoning on to the key characteristics of consumption and the act of "trying on" as acquisition of objects and experiences contribute to the creation of a richer extended self for the audience-seeker. Fuchs notes that her "trained responses as a theatre shopper made [her] quickly alert to the nature of this experience, the immediate ambition to see and hear as much as possible, the scanning for the best place to stand, the being confronted at every moment with the choice between lingering in a room, or hurrying on to the next."[99] This is the root of the critique that immersive theatre is susceptible to co-optation by neoliberal market ideals of entrepreneurial DIY. All game players are self-oriented seekers to the extent that we look out for our own interests (or the interests of our team) in efforts to "win" the game. The active pursuit of "points" or strategic advantages drive the game narrative. In this fundamental way, simply by being a player, the player-self persona has a different priority and impetus for action than my non-player self. Beyond "trying to win," another distinction in player behaviour relates to the non-seriousness of games. We are "just" playing and so this opens the door to non-seriousness/non-realness in my engagement with the sandbox scenario. In this specific case, the game frame creates an ethically-rich disjunction between the morally weighty content of *Foreign Radical* – Do I endorse practices of holding potential terrorists in judicial custody without a warrant? – and the more playfully callous motivation of how my answer to that question affects my status in game.

There is also a self-reflexive public aspect to being players that shapes the player persona in that we constitute the active scenography of the game for other members of the audience, performing roles in the gameplay as viewed from their perspective. Likewise, even as we are self-consciously monitoring our own performance as secondary audience, like Captain Janeway in the holodeck, we are also watching others. Being asked if I shop online or sign petitions against the government seems innocent enough in my performance of this particular public self. But in being asked if I support Sharia law in Canada or if I think Israel is committing genocide in Gaza, the stakes go up. Who is looking at me and judging my responses? And which of my fellow players has expressed views that I might find repugnant? In a play about surveillance and the use of surveillance to make judgments about our trust in others as potential security threats, these questions efficiently move these issues out of the realm of the purely conjectural. Adding another layer, relating to the question, "Which game am I playing now?" how we answer particular questions also encourages others to judge me not only as a potential security threat but also as a possible threat to the game of *Foreign Radical* itself, to the mise en événement. Am I a cooperative co-player? Do I take up too much oxygen, being a dominant participant? Or am I too passive? Is my passivity shyness or active resistance? If I object to a question or refuse a task, will I "break" the game? Like group social dancing and sharing food in *Counting Sheep*, the genre of game-playing is another social cue that we understand. Patterns of call and response, obedient answering of questions, following the rules – no matter how arbitrary they may be – are part of our social repertoire. However, in *Foreign Radical* that easy adherence to this repertoire is troubled as the meaning of the various games come into conflict. In the intersection of all these performative features, how we play the game, whichever game that might be, is cast in an ethical context. Playing the game "well" may be at odds with my personal beliefs in what is right. What political positions am I endorsing by my actions within the game? – actions that might be aligned with my true beliefs, or aligned with a desire to "win," or with a desire to enact what Erving Goffman calls a "cynical performance" where I maintain a superficially agreeable performance "for the greater good of the community."[100]

In one such troubled collision, ethical culpability is stacked against entrepreneurial desire and responsibility to move the event forward. Selected audience members who have "won" a previous challenge are sent into another room and tasked with searching through a suitcase to collect intelligence and determine if the suitcase's owner should be placed on the terrorist watchlist. The act of searching is positively charged insofar as it is a pleasure of the game, an experience we are granted. Also, willing participation and following instructions serve the mise en événement of the show. And yet, there is something perhaps uncomfortable about rummaging through another person's personal effects without permission. (Who gave us permission? The Host? What's his authority in the game or in the real world beyond the game, to the reality imputed by this sandbox?) Some audience members dig avidly, pulling out clothes, flipping through books, searching pockets, even unwrapping gifts. Some stand back; perhaps they are unsure how they feel about this invasion of privacy or perhaps they are just reluctant game-players who prefer to observe. How shall we read their nonparticipation? Those who are not selected for the suitcase search task are not completely absolved, as they watch their companions from a different curtained quadrant; the actions of the searchers broadcast on the wall as surveillance video footage. For my own part, the remnants of the disembowelled suitcase, its contents tossed willy-nilly, chills me somehow; nevertheless I do assist. Caught in that liminal ontology between the fictional and the actual, my real body performs real actions in a fictional (?) context that confuse my mind attempting to discern the stakes of these actions. As Patrick Duggan notes in relation to other examples of trauma-tragedy, "this very duplicity of the experience of the event holds the audience up to it as both victim-witnesses and as possible complicit perpetrators or conspirators. We are not allowed to ignore the reality of what is happening, nor are we able to deny the pictorial/painterly aesthetic we are presented with."[101] This is fun that is not fun. *Foreign Radical* fosters what Daniel Oliver calls "critical paranoia," a condition that is "suspicious of participation, identifying a heightened self-awareness of not participating in an environment that seems to invite participation."[102] Ultimately this insecurity is productive insofar as *Foreign Radical* mobilizes that uncertainty of action, giving it an ethical slant, compelling us to act while simultaneously accusing the participatory audience of complicity (whether active or passive) in the surveillance and mistreatment of others even as we ourselves are being subjected to scrutiny.

Compared with other immersive seeker-environments, *Foreign Radical* is not dominantly a consumption-acquisition environment. In fact, in many ways it is just the opposite. To play the game, you need to share or reveal personal information and views. Neoliberal performance-creation labour is constituted here by giving away your autobiography. This is your currency – not unlike online "likes" or card swipes of customer loyalty programs, which are a by-product cost of shopping. The first thing to notice is that this playing-as-giving is coercive. Choosing not to respond is not a viable option. People are looking at me and when we "vote" with our feet, moving to positions that represent our views – unlike *100% Vancouver* – there is no neutral or ambivalent zone in the middle. The *Foreign Radical* audience is not free-roaming through an environment. In fact, just the opposite: we are tightly controlled. The strict limitation on audience action is a dominant attitude of many scenes of the play. Action is restricted physically, as, for example, we are asked to stand in particular quadrants that have been taped out on the floor, sorting ourselves into these various boxes according to how we respond to certain questions. At another point, we are instructed to stand in a line, shoulder to shoulder, and to take steps forward corresponding, again, with how we answer the Host's questions. "Please take one baby-to-medium step forward if you answer YES to any of the following statements. I hate airports. I love airports. I have spent more than an hour in a lineup at the border or airport security."[103] The questions progress along these lines, becoming more serious as we move ahead. "I have been refused entry when trying to cross a border. I have been detained for more than 24 hours while trying to cross a border. I have crossed a border illegally."[104] We are Alice-in-looking-glass-land chess pawns, moving or being moved across the board. In addition to spatial restriction, audience-players are also restricted in terms of our responses. Answers are limited to yes or no, agree or disagree. It is an experience that is reminiscent of bureaucratic processing, especially the interminable and stressful switchback queues in airports. We are literally boxed in, contained in quadrants, by lines on the floor; we process and we are being "processed." Moreover, when confronted with more complicated questions, like, "Security agencies need more powers to prevent terrorist attacks" or "I understand why people become jihadists,"[105] and asked to respond in seconds, these simplistic binary answers are woefully insufficient. And we are shamed by that insufficiency. With regard to the compulsion of the invitation, Alston notes, "Audiences are faced with at least the threat of being condemned to participate. It is in this sense that participation may be seen to be extorted. Being inescapably implicated within a situation, together with the demand to do something, even if that something is simply to negotiate how and where to spectate."[106]

Sandbox sims, like *Foreign Radical*, are pedagogical or oriented towards social change, providing opportunities to rehearse for real-life situations or to bear witness to experiences of others who do live it in real life.[107] Within the sim, participants learn by making choices within the constrained parameters of the scenario and also from the consequences of those choices.[108] A common critique of interactive immersive performances is that although it may seem that audiences are being given a wide scope of participatory agency, the reality is that options are strictly limited. It is rare for audience action to change the outcome of the work. As Richard Schechner notes in *Environmental Theatre*, "participation is just one more ornamental, illusionistic device: a treachery perpetrated on the audience while disguised as being on behalf of the audience."[109] Responding to similar criticism from W.B. Worthen's analysis of *Sleep No More*, Gareth White sidesteps the question noting that "the feeling of making choices within immersive works can be important to their overall sensation, but the question whether any apparent agency in participatory performance is real or significant is not part of my agenda here."[110] In *Foreign Radical*, the conditions of choosing are so limited and pressurized at times that the takeaway rests not so much in the outcomes of those choices, but in an experience of the complexity and burden of making choices in the first place. Within the constructed environments of immersive work, perhaps agency is more interesting not as agency itself, where actual power to make change which may be indeed illusory, subsumed to perpetuating the integrity of the mise en événement, but instead resides on a meta level where the central issue is how we deal with the choices we get. What we think about and what we might do (but don't). This formal conundrum of the ostensibly free immersed audience under control of the event is thematized in *Foreign Radical*. Subject to bureaucratic constraint and forced to answer questions, audiences are invited to consider how this applies in the world. What information am I willing to sacrifice in order to be free? Will I trade privacy and the freedom to associate with whomever I choose for the freedom to fly? This central question that balances freedom against security also invokes the larger question of what I am called to do as a democratic citizen, as a surrogate of my government, in endorsing or opposing these restrictions on other people.

As a corollary to the tension between freedom and security that impels us to make choices in this balance, these choices themselves are cast as profoundly uncertain. Not only are options limited so as to direct attention to the challenges of choosing, the outcomes of those choices are obscured. A key element of the Watchlisting Guidance, we are told, is that suspects are subject to a "secret process that requires neither 'concrete facts' nor 'irrefutable evidence' to designate an American or a foreigner as a terrorist."[111] This Watchlisting Guidance formed the basis for Canada's controversial security law, the 2015 Anti-Terrorism Act (also known as Bill C-51 before it passed into law). Without solid parameters for this designation, we are down the rabbit hole, as it were. New identities, new world realities in miniature – that is, "terrorist" – can be created arbitrarily. This kind of contingent world construction where worlds come into being through collective internally self-affirming acceptance without evidence or facts is the marker of a post-truth world.

Foreign Radical's questioning and sorting mechanisms subject the audience-players to exactly this kind of arbitrary determination. Questions are asked where we are uncertain as to how our responses are being evaluated. For example, we are asked, "Are you an atheist?" If we answer yes, are we more or less likely to be labelled a terrorist? And consequently what are the effects of this answer in life and also within the confines of the game. According to the game protocols, if you answer yes to "Who has purchased something online using a credit card in the past week?" and yes to "Who here has looked at porn in the past 24 hours?," nothing happens to you. (Apart from possibly mild embarrassment for admitting private predilections in public.) But if you answer yes to the next set of questions: "You regularly change online passwords for security" and "You have used a pseudonym or alias online to remain anonymous," you get sent away from the group, alone into another curtained-off section.[112] None of this can be fathomed from the questions asked. In an early version of *Foreign Radical*, the audience-players are divided into two groups. The host then flips a coin, announcing, "A very important question for you – heads or tails?" The result of this random choice groups are assigned to opposite sides of a debate: "Should we assign Hesam to the watchlist?" Two elements contribute to our sense of the insecure foundation of this game world in which we find ourselves at this point. First, we are being asked to choose – heads or tails – without knowing what we are flipping for, only that it is "important." Second, these two yes/no questions are established as equivalently important; the outcome of a life reduced to no more than the outcome of a coin toss. Arbitrariness combined with the opacity and flippancy of judgment of these questions is disconcerting. The in-game benefits of certain answers are neither clear nor appropriately meaningful. No matter what you do, no matter how active you are, you still might get sidelined into a less "interesting" role or path. The real-world analogy is clear: whatever information we mine and whatever decision we make in efforts to ensure security, we might still be wrong. Worse, no matter what you do, you might still be relegated to the Watchlist.

Language, which is usually a source of comprehension and community because it opens conduits of communication between individuals, plays the opposite role in *Foreign Radical*, creating insecurity through selective failures of understanding that flag our differences. In *Counting Sheep*, the lyrics and spoken text are dominantly in Ukrainian. But even as a non-Ukrainian speaker, I am not alienated or lost. The effect is one of distancing, yes, but the distancing is comparable to that of a fairy tale, events that perhaps have happened elsewhere and a long time ago. Significantly, my lack of comprehension is non-threatening. It doesn't seem to matter. By contrast, in *Foreign Radical*, non-English text feels hostile to monolingual anglophones. At one point, after a series of questions in English, two questions are projected on the wall, one in Farsi: "Do you know anyone who has been unfairly treated by the authorities due to their race, religion, or ethnic background?" and one in Arabic: "Do you know anyone who has been unfairly judged due to the actions of friends or family members?" The Host then instructs us "If your answer is yes, go to this side. If your answer is no, or if you can't read either Farsi or

Arabic, go to this side."[113] Translations of the Farsi and Arabic questions are never provided. Anglophone audience-players are left in the dark being asked to answer questions they can't even understand. On the one hand, this experience mimics an additional Kafka-esque stress of bureaucratic processing when we can't comprehend what we are being asked. But on the other hand, not knowing Arabic or Farsi casts players in a certain political light; paradoxically, linguistic ignorance is aligned here with privilege, with not experiencing discrimination by security authorities. The inverse is the profiling that if you do speak Farsi or Arabic you are a potential threat.[114]

While on one track, the ontologically ambiguous audience is subjected to the threatening contingencies of arbitrary questioning, on another track we are the instruments of that authority tasked with the question of whether or not we should assign Hesam to the Watchlist. Hesam Rahmani is a twenty-eight-year-old Iranian-born Canadian citizen, and a graduate student in Middle Eastern history at Laval University. Hesam is also a fictional character, played by Aryo Khakpour. We first encounter Hesam/Aryo as the naked man in the very first scene. Subsequent scenes feature monologues by Hesam concerning his relation to his childhood friend Jamal whose anger reached a breaking point, who has been posting provocative material online – an image from Abu Ghraib beside an image of Canadian soldier Corporal Nathan Cirillo shot across from Parliament Hill with the comment 1+1 = 1 – and who has consequently been nominated to the Watchlist. Lying partially clothed on the floor, having been perhaps himself subject to torture, Hesam laments the loss of his friend, the loss of their soccer-playing joy, and his need to sacrifice association with his friend to protect himself. These traditionally structured scenes with the audience solidly in world^a bearing theatrical witness to Hesam's story in world^b are complicated when we are instructed to collect information on Hesam, and then through public debate to determine his fate. At first, only Hesam's things come through the frame, tangibly present in our world. When certain audience members are sent into the second room with keys to three locked boxes, this is the first inkling we have of another relation to Hesam. In the boxes, we find a map, a journal, a voice recorder, and, in the innermost box, photos. In those photos, we recognize Hesam as the naked man in the earlier scene. It is Hesam's suitcase that we are instructed to search. In the end, the game frames of *Foreign Radical* are given another twist, and Hesam confronts us as an ontological equal.

For the final scene, one audience member is selected at random to sit in a spotlit chair. She is handed a microphone. When the curtain in front of her is pulled aside to open the space into another quadrant, Hesam is there, standing on a table. Around his feet are the scattered remains of his disembowelled suitcase, evidence of our culpable searching. Now he is really here with us; no longer on the other side of the fourth wall. What happened to him, what we made happen to him, happened in the same world that we now occupy. The shock of that revealed connection is moving. The ontologically unstable aestheticization of our audience experience distributed among disparate and conflicted game contexts sets up this *coup de théâtre* moment. Hesam as a materially real (naked) actor body collides with Hesam the fictional torture victim and potential terrorist collides with the man who stands before us. Our ethical disorientation parallels the mimetic shimmering that arises out of the insecure vertiginous status of Hesam's representation; Hesam fails to remain safely fictional. Here is another example of reverse mimesis where the fictional will not stabilize and become comfortable. And in this shimmering oscillation, we bear witness to trauma; we are able for a brief moment to touch the traumatic-real in that gap. Standing above us atop the table, as if on a stage or on the block at Abu Ghraib, Hesam throws a cascade of the red and yellow cards that we had used in a previous scene to express our votes on political cartoons – red for most offensive; yellow for funniest. These cards, the same as those used by soccer referees to dispense penalties, raining down singly flicked across the space, express, I think, his disdain or repressed anger for our casual judgment. When he comes down off the table, he takes a chair some distance from the seated player. He also has a microphone. The use of the microphones combined with the spacing of the chairs about three metres apart makes this encounter formal and awkward. Calmly and in a detached, cold tone, Hesam begins to ask the audience-player personal questions: "When was the first time you flew? What was your favourite trip? Is life a game? Is life a fight? What is your biggest victory?" Audience respondents were candid but shy. Hesam pressed the interviewee asking for details and drawing out increasingly intimate revelations. I'm not sure I can adequately describe the tension and profundity of this encounter. Those of us who bore silent witness to the interview were riveted. The reality-effect of the introduction of our fellow audience members as "experts of the everyday" catapults us back to acute awareness of our real-world selves, dragging the fictional Hesam and the concerns of *Foreign Radical* with it. We touch the real through that

6.2 (l–r): Aryo Khakpour (Hesam) and Milton Lim (The Host) interrogate an audience member in *Foreign Radical*. Photo courtesy of Tim Carlson.

gap created by this displacement. In this moment of mimetic shimmering, we experience that nausea of the real in the overlap. It is not trauma as violent upheaval, but as an unspeakable encounter through a rent in the fabric of constructed reality with something beyond representation. The play ends with a looping projection of a first-person view of travelling on a twisting, desolate, desert road in an unspecified country. As the stage directions note, it *"could be shot from a car on the highway – or a drone."*[115] Again it is unclear if we are the surveillers or the surveilled, game-players or rule-makers.

In her survey of immersive performance Josephine Machon quotes David Jubb, who suggests that a strong appeal of this genre is a desire for "conviviality and congregation."[116] Eschewing the formality of traditional theatre architecture, physically by removing the proscenium and its concomitant rows of fixed seats, but also perceptually by loosening the strictures of the enframing function of the proscenium, immersive theatre feels more like a club, a concert, or a gallery opening. Machon lists *communitas* as a core feature of immersive experiences along with risk-taking, empowerment, and sensual engagement.[117] This sense of *communitas* is central to *Counting Sheep* and *Foreign Radical*, where the audience is figured as a collective. Asked about the meaning of the title of *Counting Sheep*, Mark Marczyk says "Everybody is a sheep of one kind or another. Everyone wears a mask. It's human nature to join a herd."[118] He continues, "People are stronger together than they are apart – and that works on both sides of the coin. The flip side of that is that sometimes it leads to a loss of individuality or identity, much in the same way that it could lead to togetherness."[119] To fulfill the expectations of engaged democratic citizenship, we are adjured "not to be sheep," not to be passive followers of the status quo. Sometimes this means protesting corrupt and authoritarian rule, sometimes it means not being a bystander in the face of government wrongdoing. We may be sheep but we must stand up and be counted. Undeniably, *Counting Sheep* has a strong singular political slant. It says, "There is value in joining the group; there is value in participation." Audience members are not individuated; we are not overtly set in competition with each other neither explicitly in our story-roles, nor in our seeking for immersive "Easter eggs." Collective participation in accordance with this view is valued. It is in that collective, powered by the fictional mise en scène of the revolution but also powered by the collective enactment of the mise en événement, that sheep are figured as possessing agency. And simultaneously the autonomy of that agency is compromised by those same forces. Choices are limited. At the same time that the narrative compels us to join the Ukrainian protester-sheep (not the police-sheep), the event as event also restricts our choices to join the collective action if we want the event to continue to proceed.

The audience of *Foreign Radical* is likewise cast as a collective where compromised agency is the shaping force of our experience. *Foreign Radical* actively explores the tension between the group and the individuals who comprise the group. For example, from the outset we are not allowed to remain anonymous. When asked by the Host, everyone gives their names. At approximately twenty participants, the group is small enough that everyone quickly becomes recognizable and memorable. In our interactions, the Host calls out people by name whenever possible. At each juncture or scene, the group is constantly being pushed together or teased apart only to be recombined again later. Often when people are isolated from the group and sent away, the Host co-opts the rest of the group in making that decision. As part of the "Threat-Level Assessment," the Host looks to send one person away. Who should he pick? "Is it Jen, the one who made a mistake earlier?" "Is it Alex, who looks at porno?" The group picks "the one who makes mistakes" and sends Jen out. Even without names, the Host categorizes people, "the tall one" or "the short one." The blocking of the game is all about being sorted into groups and staring at who is in your group (organized in circles) and who is opposite (divided into quadrants and line-ups). The debate section is confrontational, but also intimate, an intimacy fostered by forced physical proximity and an incipient social proximity through the revelation of personal details. We are not anonymous strangers – not quite, anymore. And, like *Counting Sheep*, these formations rehearse citizenship behaviours where democracy depends on resolving this tension between self and society. In his analysis of the work of Punchdrunk and its manifestation of neoliberal ethos of individual action, Alston concludes by suggesting that in order to address the built in exclusivity and exclusion that are tied to entrepreneurial values, immersive performances might handle audiences differently to create a different spectrum of political implications. He doesn't specifically discuss a shift from the audience configured as lone wolf to the collective audience, but this might be one approach to addressing this concern.

Contrasting participatory performances in the 1960s with that of the first decades of the twenty-first century, Jessica Santone writes, "Earlier modes of participation in performance art connoted allegiance with coalitional identity politics, activist sensibilities or poststructuralist liberation from authoritative narratives ... 'participation' is differently charged today."[120] I agree that critical concerns about the implications of neoliberal values on labour and audience prosumer behaviours are unavoidable in the current context. Nevertheless *Counting Sheep* and *Foreign Radical* work to sideline solitary seeking role-behaviours not only by shaping the performance through collective action but also by actively questioning the source and composition of that collectivity. This is not to say that features that co-opt audience desire for high-quality authentic experiences, conscripting audience leisure as labour to create the work of art, are not in play but that what audiences are doing inside these environments is oriented towards collectivity in ways that are important.

Rancière writes, "Human beings are tied together by a certain sensory fabric, a certain distribution of the sensible, which defines their way of being together; and politics is about the transformation of the sensory fabric of 'being together.'"[121] In this construction, politics is attached to how communities collectively experience, compose, and engage their sensory fabric, i.e., the way they have world-ed their world. Žižek says something similar about the Lacanian Real. In this understanding, the Real is the material that is worked on by the Symbolic, through semiotic representation. The Real is also the excess that remains, that which cannot be captured by the Symbolic, and as such manifests as a failure or void in the Symbolic.[122] Žižek points out that if the Real and the Symbolic were perfectly aligned with nothing left over, humans would cease to be subjects. The thing that makes us human is "the signifying chain and the decisions we make"[123] in negotiating the symbolization of the Real. That is, what makes us human subjects is how we craft reality. In a political context, the core act of engaged citizenship is performative creation. Thus, it is imperative to the effective workings of democratic citizenship that we are sensitive to the mechanisms of enframing, to how the world worlds, so that we can make worlds that express our collective values, worlds that we can all live in.

7 Real Bodies Part 2: Narcissistic Spectatorship in Theatrical "Haunted Houses" of Solo Immersive Performance – *Everyman*

Occupying a central position in our affective desire for contact with the real is authenticity. Although not quite a synonym, authenticity speaks to an understanding of a thing or experience as being "the real thing," that is, not only not fake or unmediated in terms of representation; it transcends or resists any kind of manipulation. It is pure somehow. A uniquely modern phenomenon, the desire for authenticity can be traced back to the late eighteenth century where it comes into our lexicon as a by-product of Romanticism. The ideal of exercising the capability and honesty to live in accordance with one's own inner truths took root in artists and philosophers of the era. "This young cabal prioritized the virtues of intuition, imagination and feeling over reason and method, replacing the notion *I think, therefore I am* with a philosophy more akin to *I feel, therefore I am*."[1] In *The Ethics of Authenticity*, Charles Taylor contends that "the residue of these aesthetic standards has diffused into the contemporary social milieu, manifesting as a cultural preoccupation with self-realization predicated on the belief that human beings are imbued with moral codes that must be explored and clarified in order to actualize their intrinsic potentialities."[2] We live in "a culture of authenticity."[3] More than a spiritual philosophy, authenticity is also being consumed in the early twenty-first century as a lifestyle. David Boyle, in his book *Authenticity: Brands, Fakes, Spin and the Lust for Real Life*, notes the value assigned to goods and experiences that are "natural," "honest," "unspun," and "rooted in the local." We can see this influence driving the yen for backyard chickens, midwives and doulas, DIY everything, vintage clothing, freecycling, store greeters, microbreweries, and so on. "Half a century ago, this attitude would have been dismissed as quaint or downright

Luddite."[4] Although authenticity is always framed as morally good, being straightforward and without guile, its application is not always entirely benign. This same impulse to authenticity is a key pillar of fascism, expressed in fascism's nostalgia for a lost purity or unity that is to be restored through violent social upheaval as so-called polluting elements are cast out. Whether deployed in the consumer interests of social grooming and lifestyle improvement or more aggressively as a cleansing of the body politic, authenticity connects to security. Security in this context relates to the transparent equivalence between what a thing seems to be and what it is. When outer appearance is identical with inner ontology, then I can feel secure. This person, thing, or experience has no tricks for me. This is why many of the features of contemporary consumption of authenticity point specifically to the provenance of a product. Things originate "here" (or nearby) or I made/grew it myself. As a corollary, the person, thing, or experience is also as unprocessed as possible. The journey from raw material to the consumable is short, direct, and again, critically, transparent.

Another facet of authenticity links the above characteristics of immediacy – understood in the dual sense of being both unmediated and here/now – to singularity or uniqueness. Contemporary manifestations of authenticity position its pursuit as the path to self-actualization. Getting out from under the pervasive and popular evils of mass culture means being as much "me" as possible. "When it comes to personal fulfillment, many of us subscribe to the idea that the self is an act of artistic creation, and living a meaningful, creative life is impossible within the confines of the modern world."[5] Seeking authenticity, then, is an antidote to modernity itself marked by "spiritual disenchantment, political liberalism, and growth of the market economy."[6] The security offered by authenticity suggests a panacea for the contemporary condition of being free but lost. Crafting my most authentic self is a recognizable (and privileged) project manifesting, for example, in buying fruit, vegetables, and honey at the local farmers' market, listening to my unique music stream moulded by algorithms tracking my likes and dislikes, designing a custom cellphone case, or sourcing vintage or handcrafted one-of-a-kind clothing and jewellery. The attitude that these things are "good," being worth premiums of time, money, and effort, is not unfamiliar. Andrew Potter (*The Authenticity Hoax*) argues, however, that this is all nonsense. Like "the real," designating anything as actually authentic is an impossibility in a poststructuralist, performative world. It is a prelapsarian ideal. Moreover, Potter continues, the conditions of modernity that authenticity seeks to heal are not actually a problem. Collectively, we have never been freer, more peaceful, safer, healthier, or better educated, and we have more leisure time than in any previous era. Nevertheless, possible or not, problem or not, like real-ish-ness, authenticity is something my twenty-first-century, secular, liberal, globalized self wants. That authenticity "has become part of the moral slang of our day points to the peculiar nature of our fallen condition, our anxiety over the credibility of existence and of individual existences."[7] In this search for meaning, authenticity becomes narcissistic. Not only am I the physical focal point of authenticity's immediacy, but that inward-looking orientation locates authenticity as selfish, being not just near me but "in" me, specifically as it pertains to me, my possession of it, or my experience of it as a central characteristic.

Those who wish to sell me the authenticity I crave have conceptualized this strategy as "experiential marketing."[8] Beyond purchasing a free-run, organic egg because it is somehow actually quantifiably better (which it may well be) than a mass-produced, battery-farmed one, I am also gaining an emotional experience of how I feel about the egg and about my specialness as its consumer. Whereas traditional marketing assumes that customers are rational decision makers who weigh benefits, and thus can be approached with advertising methods that are analytical, quantitative, and verbal,[9] experiential marketing recognizes that customers' decisions are also shaped by emotional responses to a product or experience. The focus of experiential marketing, then, is to conceptualize and craft valuable experiences that bring the customer into an affective relationship with the product. The five pillars of experiential marketing are the "appeal to sense," which directs sensory attention to my own body to foster attachment through a pleasant awareness of intimate contact in personal stimulus; the "appeal to feel," which usually triggers emotions like comfort, happiness, and security; the "appeal to think," which activates creative thinking and the pleasures of problem solving often through surprise or intrigue; the "appeal to act," which targets behavioural outcomes or lifestyles using role models or positive norms; and the "appeal to relate," which taps into the desire to belong and aligns this with brand desire.[10] Examples of experiential marketing techniques involve richly designed, themed restaurants like the Rainforest Café[11] or the "classic" (but franchised) "Firkin" Irish pubs,[12] weekend rally gatherings for the owners of specific car brands like Jeep or Subaru, interactive store elements like the two-storey rock climbing wall at Mountain Equipment Co-op, or the ability to customize your own American Girl doll to look exactly like you.[13] In each of these cases, experience is crafted in support of a tangible product, be it a meal, a car, climbing paraphernalia, or a doll. Experience, which is always figured in this context as pleasurable, generates a positive ambience around the product that fosters customer loyalty to the brand.

Immersive theatre is another such commodity that sits squarely in the centre of this confluence of desire for authenticity and narcissistic experience. In fact, in immersive performance environments, experience is not a by-product; it is its raison d'être. "Experiences offer something that goods cannot; visceral sense-engagement in and across time. In an era that privileges presence and immediacy, they locate us in the affective non-moment. In an era of individual agency, they provide the authentic guarantee of personal involvement."[14] What are the common markers of this experience that is being sold in an immersive performance? Elinor Fuchs, bearing witness to early manifestations of immersive theatre, dubs this "shopping theatre." Fuchs makes the connection not only between audience behaviour in immersive realms in terms of making choices but also in terms of how those choices reflect or perform my vision of myself. Considering her participation in *Tamara*, she writes, "There is no mediating space between my body and the world of entitlement this environment (part real, part fiction) exudes. I am flattered into feeling not Tamara but *myself* the subject of a living movie. While chuckling at the absurdity of such a response, I see in myself and in my fellow 'guests' subtle changes in voice and gait, and a heightened decorum to meet an expanded sense of privilege."[15] Accompanying the augmented sensory stimulation of immersive experience ("appeal to sense") is a heightened sense of myself. The foundation for this alteration is a change in the relation of the audience to the dramatic world. As Fuchs observes, this puffed-up feeling is a response to my special role in the fiction. But also I have an increased role in the production of the event itself. I have been invited into the game. This feeling becomes even more self-important and exclusive in the shift from group immersive to solo immersive.[16] Now not only am I being tasked with filling a dramatic role and assuming increased importance in the production of the event, the entire event has been created for me, and only me. I am its centre. In this way, immersive theatre attains the pinnacle of the experiential marketing ethos. The show is not only completely for you, it is completely about you. You are the show.

As discussed in the previous chapter, the characteristic audience ontology of immersive theatre that situates the audience in that self-conscious liminal space between the dramatic world that surrounds us and the inescapable awareness of the event as event and ourselves as real-world people foregrounds the aestheticization of that audience self as its main feature. Under these conditions, Alston asserts that "Attention tends to be turned inwards, toward the experiencing self, accompanied by a persistent reaching towards a maximization of experience, underscoring the potentially indulgent meaningfulness of that 'special complicity.'"[17] Unpacking this audience function of "reaching towards a maximization of experience," Keren Zaiontz connects the self-attentive orientation of immersive performance to entrepreneurial acquisitiveness. In answer to her question why spectators want to engage in participatory performances where they in fact have very little agency over the conditions or effects of their participation, she suggests that "narcissistic spectatorship encourages the viewer to fully engross herself in an artistic production in a way that highlights her own singular relationship to the piece."[18] So, in Zaiontz's construction, participation is reflexive. "Spectators adopt the experiencer position as a badge of individual acuity."[19] Pleasure accrues to how well I participate. Pride in acuity is linked to competitive acquisitiveness, thus marrying the entrepreneurial spectator to narcissism. In the two productions Zaiontz describes, narcissism manifests in comparative assessments (sometimes projected in the imagination) of the quality and quantity of individual experience she is collecting to that of other experiencers. As she observes, "this spectre of uniqueness generates its own set of demands ... whereby spectators may not author the event, but feel entitled to privileged access to it."[20] In this context, the experience of self is oriented to the event and to maximizing my privilege within it. This feature of immersive performance environments as affective playgrounds of acquisitive specialness pervades the genre. But this need not be an end in itself. One question that presents itself is: "To what dramatic purpose might this experiential characteristic of the form be effectively employed?"

Enter *Everyman*. Produced in Kingston, Ontario in January of 2007 in a church basement by the non-professional Single Thread Theatre Company,[21] *Everyman*, my selected case study, offers one perspective on how this experiential quality of narcissistic spectatorship may be brought to bear in support of the play's thematic understanding. Consistent with its origins as a medieval Christian morality play, this contemporary adaptation of *Everyman* presents a blunt and unwavering didactic lesson. The clever immersive twist on the conventionally presentational, historical text of *Everyman* is that the solo audience member is now cast as Everyman and his journey becomes ours, as the character is compelled to confront a lifetime of ethical failings and make amends before being summoned to God's judgment. The Single Thread version of the play is structured as a maze-like, haunted house where the solo audience member travels (or is pushed) linearly forward from room to room, and from episode to episode. This analysis will demonstrate how formal elements of immersive theatre experience contribute not only to the communication of *Everyman*'s narrative content, but also to its transformative metaphysical aims. In a general sense, *Everyman* mobilizes the affective power of sensory immersion to catalyse spiritual insight and recalibration. The emotional "overwhelm" of the immersive haunted house – characterized here principally by fear – combined with self-reflexive aestheticization of yourself as the performance, renders the audience-experiencer susceptible to this personal renewal. In specific terms, the devotional lesson of *Everyman*, which exhorts the audience to set aside undue attachment to worldly possessions and relationships in favour of good works that can transcend the terrestrial realm, aligns with, and productively complicates, the key characteristic of prideful or self-aggrandizing acuity in acquisitiveness that defines narcissistic spectatorship. Ultimately what the immersive sermon of *Everyman* is "selling" its audience is an opportunity for serious soul-searching with the aim of fostering a renewed ethical engagement with the world. In a dominantly secular contemporary theatrical context, this seems presumptuously out of proportion in its ambition; however, it is entirely consistent with the goals of medieval morality plays. And in my personal experience, quite successful.

Although solo immersive performances commonly operate to leverage the intimacy of encounter towards affects of care, there is no reason why this need be necessarily so. Slavoj Žižek notes that while an audience is "supposed to enjoy traditional art, [which] is expected to generate aesthetic pleasure, in contrast to modern art which causes displeasure – [...] modern art, by definition, *hurts*."[22] Žižek makes the connection from affects of displeasure in art to the phenomenon of young women who cut themselves to feel more alive. He writes, "Take the phenomenon of 'cutters'; this is strictly parallel to the virtualization of our environment: it represents a desperate strategy to return to the Real of the body ... Far from indicating a desire for self-annihilation, cutting is a radical attempt to (re)gain a hold on reality or (another aspect of the same phenomenon) to ground the ego firmly in bodily reality, against the unbearable anxiety of perceiving oneself as nonexistent."[23] Pain, in this construction, is an anchor, binding the realness of affect to one's existential reality in and of the world. This radical strategy for asserting and experiencing realness through potent affect shares common ground with the workings of affects in immersive theatre. In the triggering of potent affects in the immersed limbic systems of the audience-experiencers, it becomes clear that this is not a theatre of pleasure necessarily. It is a theatre of feeling more realness. It is a theatre of feeling more alive. Gareth White points out that "actors may be immersed in something, but they are not in a literal sense inside the story of the play."[24] The same applies to immersed audience-participants. We are not inside the fictional world of the play, rather we are, as Martin Welton says, inside the "affective ecology" of the performance.[25] Fear, I believe, is endemic to immersive theatre. Even when affects of care and comfort are foregrounded as central outcomes, I am still afraid.

As cited in the previous chapter, UK reviewer Michael Billington critiques immersive theatre on the grounds that it lacks "radical purpose and [should] challenge the status quo."[26] He goes on to situate his assessment of the form's superficiality in fear: "I've noticed that much of what passes for experimental theatre relies on infantile scare tactics ... My main grievance is that, at the moment, we are confronted either by a heavily commercialized international avant garde or – with some striking exceptions – by a domestic penchant for playground scarification."[27] Scarification in immersive theatre, in what are essentially theatrical haunted houses, comes from at least four distinct sources – fearful anxiety arising from suspense about what happens next, fear of simply being alone and feeling vulnerable, fear of being lost, and fear of embarrassment associated with performing (specifically in being looked at). First, suspense and surprise. Although audiences, even in traditional situations, always face the unknown as the narrative unfolds, in immersive experiences those narrative actions are intimately close and will have a direct impact on my body, so my adrenaline is elevated as I prepare for the unexpected. Pure leap-out-of-the-closet shock is a standard feature of haunted houses. Even if this is not likely to happen in any given performance work, my body is primed for this tensed flight reaction by virtue of my proximate immersion in an unknown scenario. Listing features of the emotional landscape of online games, along with fear of abandonment and fear of loss of self in the undifferentiated mass, Murray includes fear of lurking attackers.[28] Online attackers in the form of digital orcs and goblins are scary enough, and there are no vicious orcs and goblins to be concerned about in solo immersive experiences (usually), and yet this fear still factors into my thoughts. For women particularly, this fear cannot be ignored; it rises unbidden in the experience of simply being alone in one-to-one encounters with male performers who are strangers or journeying through unfamiliar environments, especially at night. Even without specific danger cues, the theatrical frame, in my experience, is not strong enough to assuage these concerns.[29] This is the second source. The third source pertains to fear of being lost. The path of the audience-experiencer through the performance narrative is a journey, sometimes literally so. There are pleasures of navigation and exploration, but there is also uncertainty and anxiety. It is necessary to strike a balance of tension between the boring security of a single secure path and the anxious enervation of an undetermined rhizomatic network. Again Murray, writing about online games, notes the need to find this ideal point between game scenarios that are sufficiently goal driven to guide navigation but flexible enough to allow free exploration, finding balance between arousing and regulating anxiety.[30] Sometimes I literally don't want to get lost. But beyond this, I don't want to lose the thread of the game. Anxiety surfaces when I am uncertain that I am participating correctly. This is the classic actor's nightmare, being thrust onstage unprepared. I don't know what to do (or where to go) and I don't want to break the world. The fourth source of fear also relates to my role in the performance as event, specifically in my position as a reluctant actor. Being looked at by the other personages in this immersed world is embarrassing. As Nicholas Ridout asserts with regard to more traditional punctures of the usual safety of the fourth wall via direct address, being spoken to and being seen in this way creates complicity between the actor-speaker and the audience-addressee by reminding us that we are both actual-world people. "Being looked at ... tends [...] to make us more acutely conscious than usual of the real flesh-and-blood actor behind whom the represented character presumably stands."[31] Garner describes the effect this way: "The reverse-gaze catches me in the act of looking, challenging ... the *ecstasis* by which I 'surpass' my corporeal boundaries through the outer-directedness of vision. In so doing the reverse-gaze returns me to myself, forcing a corporeal self-consciousness that registers itself in a physical discomfort and in the tingling of embarrassment on my face."[32] Beyond simply being seen and returning a direct gaze, audience-participants to immersive theatre have an added fear of being judged. Any kind of choosing or sharing in this environment reveals one's private self. "To expose unconsidered thoughts or emotions in a semi-public space is risky, just as it is to display incompetence, inappropriate enthusiasm, neediness, distress or a loss of poise ... The 'economy' of self-presentation in any social milieu ... will shape the horizons of those who inhabit it."[33] Fear, then, as demonstrated, is a pervasive and potent affect generated by innate formal elements of immersive theatre, that co-mingles with (if not overrides) other emotions produced by the work.

From the first chapters of this book, the locus of attention has shifted slightly and insecurity in this kind of work is not an intellectual puzzle about epistemology arising from ambiguity between what is fiction and what is real. Fear is what insecurity feels like. Fear is the raw emotion. It is interesting to note that for Billington in his critique of experimental immersive theatre, the experience of heightened emotion seems to stand in opposition or is an obstacle to the laudatory potential for radical purpose. Erin Hurley notes a similar devaluation of affect, pointing out that "profitable" forms of theatre, that is, those that are intellectually stimulating, are granted superior artistic and social value than forms that are simply pleasurable.[34] She uses the example of melodrama which "may be usefully understood as a kind of feeling-producing machine, formally engineered to elicit emotional response."[35] Dissecting the feeling-technologies of melodrama, Hurley locates its emotional core in its predictability and familiar moral patterns that evoke pleasure. Arguably, immersive theatre is also principally a feeling-producing machine, but rather than pleasure in familiarity, that emotion is fear in insecurity and the unknown. "To feel – that is, to be physiologically responsive to your environment (affect), to experience ambient mood, and to interpret your body's physiological signals as emotions – is to be human in the most flattering sense of the term."[36] It is in this replete feeling of humanity that the work shifts our engagement with its narrative, pulling us in deeply to reflect on that human condition. It is perhaps not a coincidence that, like melodramas, *Everyman* is also aligned to a certain moral view of the universe in which being human is its full expression.

White also notes the potential results of potent affect to deliver a narrative message: "the heightening of the senses through a little fear might make people more than usually susceptible to the multisensory signals of the space."[37] Mobilization of fear in the service of profound self-transformation is precisely the method at the heart of *Everyman*. What is at risk, then, in this experience, is the self; your pure self as soul. Fear drives Everyman – fear of death, fear of leaving the world he knows, fear of undertaking this journey alone, fear of the encounter with God – fear of being judged insufficient and being sent to Hell (although the script does not say that specifically). In the auto-ethnographic description of my experience of the performance below and the analysis that follows, it is my aim to present a potent example of immersive work where the formal characteristics of the genre, notably the machinery of affect and the self-reflexive acquisitiveness of narcissistic spectatorship, are employed in support of a specific and moving understanding.

In its opening scene, *Everyman* recognizes its traditional theatrical roots. Having been divested of my coat, bag, and boots, I am invited to sit in a single red velvet-covered theatre seat, the kind with wooden armrests and a flip up seat cushion. Alone in this antechamber I sit facing a door which slowly opens a crack, light from the other side leaking into my darkened private auditorium. The invitation is clear. I am being asked to step through the door, to go through the proscenium and enter a world beyond the fourth wall. This second room is much larger, and much brighter. In the far corner is a puppet stage. Using puppets of God, Death, and Everyman, the core thesis of the play is made clear. The play in miniature begins with a Messenger puppet who delivers the framing moral: "I pray you all give your audience / And hear this matter with reverence / By figure a moral play / The Summoning of Everyman called it is, / ... For ye shall hear how our Heaven-King / Calleth Everyman to a general reckoning. / Give audience and hear what he doth say."[38] It is here that audience members, if they are not already familiar with the plot of the morality play, come to understand both the magnitude of Death's imperative summons and also Everyman's panicked resistance and his unreadiness. After failing to bribe Death, "a thousand pound shalt thou have / and defer this matter till another day,"[39] the Everyman puppet declares its intention to seek a companion for this journey to the grave. "The day passeth and is almost agone / I wot not well what to do. / To whom were I best my complaint to make?"[40] Also watching this mise en abyme-*Everyman* are members of the ensemble, dressed all in white, as well as God and Death in human form. At this point, God and Death begin the play again. "Go thou to Everyman / And show him in My Name / A pilgrimage he must on him take / Which he in no wise may escape / And that he bring with him a sure reckoning / Without delay or any tarrying."[41] In this moment, the meta-theatrical layers dilate to encompass the audience member in this new world. Situated as fellow audience members to the inset play-within, there is no frame separating me from them, and I am now in the same ontological world as the allegorical figures of God and Death. So when

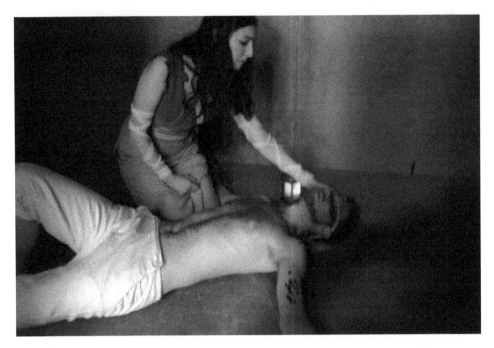

7.1 Joanne Williams and Scott Dermody as the allegorical figures of Knowledge and Good Deeds confront the audience member in the role of Everyman with their sins and failings. Photo credit: Matthew Daubaras.

Death replies "Lo, yonder I see Everyman,"[42] he turns to look directly at me. And as we lock our gaze, my heart drops and my adrenaline spikes. The white-clad members of the ensemble are suddenly afraid and scramble to the corners of the room to get as far away from me as they can. My fear has a double source – performative fear about these sudden obligations in the role of Everyman and spiritual fear for my life as Everyman who is going to die. The actor's nightmare collides with the classic existential nightmare. One by one Death kills the white-clad innocents. My arm is grabbed by an alarmed young woman, the last one still alive, who pulls me towards the door on the far side of the room. Grappling to successfully open the door, she drags me through and we are safe for the moment. Death is unable to cross the threshold and from that distance vows that he will return for me. Heart pounding, I cling to my saviour's hand.

After being sent on my way alone, the play unfolds as per the medieval script and Everyman journeys from Fellowship to Kindred and Cousin to Goods – each of whom refuses to accompany him – and finally to Good Deeds. A "gated" series of one-to-one performance scenes pushes the audience-Everyman from encounter to encounter through a warren of small rooms, some barely bigger than a closet. At one point, Death appears in a doorway in the middle of the Fellowship scene. I scream. This series of encounters ended with Goods pushing me out of his room into a pitch black corridor where I feel my way along with my hands in front of my face. Finally I find a dim hand lantern and the allegorical figure of my Good Deeds lying "cold in the ground / ... so weak / That [he] can neither go nor speak."[43] Under the guidance of Knowledge in a white gown, I come to understand that I have too much valued worldly Goods and neglected my immortal Good Deeds. Knowledge leads me to Confession, a woman in a blue dress, at whose feet I kneel and confess my too-common sins of materialism. I am given a text to read asking for redemption, my heart full of contrition, but I am also moved to improvise promising to give more attention to good deeds, specifically in doing more charitable works and making donations. Good Deeds returns to my side, walking "whole and sound / Going upright upon the ground."[44] No longer alone, I am surrounded by the ensemble now as allegorical representations of my Strength, my Beauty, my Five-Wits, and my Discretion. All these are aspects of myself so I suppose on a spiritual level I am actually still alone. Each one promises in verse never to abandon me and yet as we approach the bed that will serve as my grave, they quail. One by one they depart and the sense of my aging decline is very affecting. Finally without strength, beauty, my senses, and my intellect, I am assisted by Good Deeds to lie down on a kind of bed on wheels. After a final benediction, my soul commended into the hands of God, Death appears again and this time I am not afraid. I die. "Now hath he made ending / Methinketh that I hear angels sing / And make great joy and melody / Where Everyman's soul received shall be."[45] With Death at my head and Good Deeds at my feet, the coffin-gurney is wheeled into a dark tunnel (a disused brick-lined coal chute only about four feet high), where I lie peaceably for several minutes until a light grows somewhere near my feet. I take this as a prompt to action and I climb off the gurney and walk towards it. I emerge in a kind of theatre lobby area where I am greeted by the house manager with my coat, bag, and boots. I am the only audience member in the space. I exit up several steps and out through a pair of angled storm cellar doors.

Since this is Canada in January, I come up out of the ground, up from under the church at the corner of Union and Arch Streets, into a thick snowfall. Snow is swirling through the night air, caught by the street-light overhead. I feel a kind of transcendent spiritual joy in simply being alive. (Even writing about this ten years later I get goosebumps and my eyes feel an emotional pressure.)

Fintan Walsh situates this kind of participatory experience of emotional labour in a larger tradition of "neo-Aristotelian notions of catharsis,"[46] tracing strategies of "confession, physical and emotional intimacy, and rich affectivity within its structures."[47] Walsh, like a number of other critics,[48] recognizes the economy of affective or immaterial labour done by the audience-participants. "If we do not engage in this labor, the performance won't happen. We fail the performance, we fail [the performer.]"[49] Intimacy is not so much a gift as it is an exchange. The work pivots on "dual notions of transaction and transformation, with exchange anchored in the dialogic: the oral/aural, the spoken and the heard [...] exchange that asks for a committed and at times vulnerable sort of spectatorship."[50] We are paying for intimacy. In a series of first-hand accounts, Deirdre Heddon, Helen Iball, and Rachel Zerihan collect and collate their experiences of intimacy and confess their fears and failings. Zerihan confesses that she faked her enjoyment of being fed strawberries, even though she hates strawberries. "My role as a dutiful spectator ... was led by my desire to please."[51] Built into performances of intimacy and self-revelation is a limiting factor whereby we are compelled to operate in "a (danger) zone where the practitioner's assumptions meet the participant's desire to 'give good audience.'"[52] In another entry, Heddon and Iball dissect their internal cogitations while tucked separately into bed with a solo performer. Iball overthinks the performance of seduction. "Did she want me? I wanted her to think well of me. I wanted to appear collected, unfazed. Game to participate but sending clear signals about the performance of all this."[53] Heddon is sick. "I am hot and feverish – though not with desire but raging tonsillitis. It is true, I want to be in bed, but I don't think this is the bed I want to be in."[54] All three accounts capture in detail the multilayered complexities of reactive participation in performances of care and intimacy and the near impossible challenge of escaping the mood-killing hyperawareness of the transactional nature of that work when the audience is not ever a passive blank slate.

What distinguishes *Everyman* in terms of this critique pertaining to some of these other works where affective experience is an end in itself, and where these affects become curdled in our awkward consciousness of the mise en événement as neoliberal exchange, is that *Everyman* is a play *about* transactional exchange, about the right and the wrong way to effect exchange between material and spiritual or affective economies. First, it is significant that Everyman is not simply anybody. Unlike other medieval morality plays featuring characters like Mankind and *Humanus Genus*, who are generic representations of humanity, Everyman is a part of a relatively new social class whose business is money. His wealth is not inherited; he is not an aristocrat. He is a profit-seeker. He thinks in the language of commerce. Connecting to a common trope of the time, God's judgment is figured as a reckoning; Everyman must present an account of himself. The image of Christ the Redeemer also occupies this imagistic intersection between material and spiritual transaction. The soul with its fleshly attributes of Strength, Beauty, Five-Wits, and Discretion is merely on loan from God, and is to be redeemed (with a profit) at the end of one's life. In this quasicontractual language, the purpose of life is to generate return on investment back to God. When Death first comes to him, Everyman offers him a bribe to go away and come back later. This clearly is the wrong way to turn material goods to spiritual advantage. Likewise Everyman's attempt to bring Goods with him to the final reckoning also demonstrates this misguided thinking. The reason why Everyman's heavenly judgment before God is at risk is because he has invested too much value in his worldly possessions and not enough in doing good deeds, specifically giving charity. The lesson of the play advocates for the Christian notion that giving alms is the correct method for applying material wealth in the service of spiritual profits.

This idea that material things gain value when they are exchanged for spiritual outcomes, that is, for affective experiences, resonates with the central action of immersive theatre. For critics like Heddon, Iball, Zerihan, Ridout, and Alston, the exposure of this transactional exchange spoils the authentic creation of an affect of care in the experiences they describe. Experiences of intimacy in one-to-one immersive performances are irreconcilably at odds with the consciousness that these intimate acts are purchased as commodities and also that our reciprocal affective labour in this relational exchange is also actively solicited and manufactured. Alston makes the argument that there is a "third party" in the room in one-to-one performances: "a financial transaction."[55] Ridout also locates the inescapable embarrassment inherent in being an audience in commerce, "I have paid to have this man look at me, and he is paid to look. Our intimacy is always alienated."[56] For *Everyman*, that relational transaction is not a barrier but instead centrally constitutes its thematic message aligning the audience's formal experience with the play's moral content. In teaching the audience to not only eschew excessive attachment to material possessions, but also to give away those goods in support of charitable works, which accrue spiritual value to the giver, *Everyman* replicates the affective transaction of immersive audiencing. The takeaway message is that good deeds do endure; their effects can leave this world (both the fictional world of the dramatic event and this earthly world). Experience as good deeds bifurcates such that it is not purely self-indulgent. Being principally directed at others, its positive value returns to the doer only indirectly. In this way, *Everyman* mobilizes immersive theatre's innate narcissism in ways that are both self*ish* in my active concern for the state of my immortal soul and self*less* as that state is dependent on how I redirect my resources, both physical and emotional, towards the good of others.

Beyond simply confronting the neoliberal problem of performative labour through its thematizing of transactional exchange of material value for affective or spiritual value, *Everyman* redirects neoliberal pathways of behaviour through its central action of loss. *Everyman* is not about accumulation. It is not about winning, but as mentioned above it is about redemption, literally about "cashing out." In his article about his experience of a performance titled *Half Cut*, Alston considers the political value of risk and "how this commitment might encourage reflection on the socio-economic anchors of affective responses such as embarrassment and awkwardness."[57] Building on Ulrich Beck's notion of a risk society, Alston suggests that in addition to the main two broad categories of risk – future-oriented predictions of possible occurrences and those that are radically unpredictable, what Nassim Nicholas Taleb calls "Black Swans" – there is a third category where risk is neither predictable nor unpredictable in the future but is present now and certain as a deliberate choice.[58]

> This is a kind of risk that makes little sense when phrased in terms of potential gain, because loss is pitched as a positive attribute – loss of self-esteem, loss of dignity, and loss of self-assuredness. Loss is referred to here as a politically effective tool in the risk society, if what is lost is lost as a product of choice ... This is risk at odds with Enlightenment rationalism and the act of insuring against loss; loss might be approached profitably as the very thing to be invested in."[59]

This idea of being good at losing and choosing to be unsettled reso-nates with the earlier discussion of the dubious value of winning in *Winners and Losers*. At every turn, the audience as Everyman confronts loss; first being rejected by worldly companions to be left bare and desolate, and second having the very elements of the material hous-ing of the self – strength, beauty, sensory reception, and finally mind itself – stripped away until only the soul remains. The endgame of life in these terms is an experience of loss. The question is not "Shall we lose?" but how to exert our limited choices until we do lose. *Everyman* enjoins us to be thoughtful about how we dispose of the resources we are given. Alston's observation about *Half Cut*'s generic characteristics may also apply to *Everyman*. He writes, "instilling a political aware-ness of our capacity to manipulate circumstances, grounded in a sense of personal responsibility for our actions, consequently presents itself as an admirable motivation for participating in one-on-one theatre in the twenty-first century."[60] "In *Half Cut* – a mix [of the trivial and the challenging] which I [Alston] claimed was typical of one-on-one theatre generally – renders the triadic relationship between risk, agency, and responsibility uncomfortably strong."[61] In that work, as in *Everyman*, the audience-participant is not overwhelmed by lack of agency; we are not confronted with a problem too big to solve. Responsibility rests squarely with the subject and cannot be passed off to circumstances or to risk that has been passed on from others. Alston gives the example of the circulation of toxic loans, arguing that "what emerges as significant is a sense of *accountability*."[62] Literally in *Everyman*, this is what happens as you are compelled to offer an account of yourself. Alston concludes:

> In this sense, committing to risk scenarios in one-on-one theatre produces pockets of resistance that expose the breaks in agency and responsibility operating elsewhere in the risk society. The political ramifications of the seemingly trivial ... seems to raise the stakes of a politics of engagement in one-on-one theatre and an aesthetics of risk forged through theatre form. One instance of a pragmatically radical engagement with risk might begin on the personal level of committing to an existential queasiness in one-on-one theatre.[63]

8 Coda: Theatres of the Real in the Age of Post-Reality

We are free and yet we are lost. In the early decades of the twenty-first century, we – mostly urban-dwelling citizens of socially liberal, capitalist, technologically-sophisticated democracies – have never been so safe and at the same time we have never felt so profoundly insecure. A brief survey of the zeitgeist: "Relativity, abstract art, Heisenberg's uncertainty principle, indeterminacy, Wittgenstein's failure to find a firm foundation for meaning in language, ... huge migrations and cultural exchanges, [civil rights movements that have] overturn[ed] centuries of social practices, ... chaos theory – all of these have brought into doubt assumptions that once were beyond question."[1] Postmodernism has pulled down the grand macro-narratives that gave structure to a façade of homogenous reality. Intellectual traditions have been systematically rejected. Experts have lost their former authority. Methodological conventions have been undermined. "As a result it is no longer possible to be sure what anything is, whether it is made of plastic, whether we or our food have been irradiated, whether images have been electronically reprocessed, or whether strawberries, carrots, and sheep have been genetically modified."[2] This morass of uncertainty manifests in academic circles as poststructuralist scepticism, which denies access to the real, insisting that there can only be representation. That our "realities" are contingent performative constructions dependent on conventions of citationality for their felicitous uptake is taken as doctrine.

Without a single objective real, these performative realities proliferate. On the positive side, performative deconstruction has been a potent feminist political tool, furnishing the means to shatter monolithic conservative ideology, mobilized as a tool against patriarchy, against conventionality, against strict norms – used to create space for otherness, for feminism, for LGBTQ identities. To take just one example, in her article "Mimesis, Mimicry, and the 'True-Real,'" Elin Diamond asks, Can there be a feminist mimesis? Seeking to crack open the normative façade of conventional realism, Diamond sees a potential counter-strategy in multiplying playful distortions and replications of representation. As she writes, "While Irigarayan mimicry dismantles the Truth – patriarchal mimesis – through endless repetitions and reflections, the hysteric's true-real dismantles Truth by referring to yet refusing to symbolize its meaning."[3] The power of performativity is that if I can say it, perform it, embody it, then it can be real. (Insofar as anything is real.) This is real political power and in the civil rights movements of the second half of the twentieth century we have witnessed its impact.

When I first read Diamond, I felt the uplifting potential of this kind of multiplicity. Now I read her and I feel profoundly unsettled. It is one thing to leverage multiple performative realities against oppression and the status quo to create space for previously excluded selves and perspectives. It is something else when that same impulse says, "Who cares?" "There is no Truth." It is something else when the idea that all realities are equally admissible is leveraged in the interests of the racist alt-right, in the interests of climate change deniers, in the interests of undermining faith in democratic processes by an American president who insists, based on zero evidence, that millions of undocumented immigrants voted illegally in the 2016 election, and in the interests of chaos in general. It is something else when alternate realities (previously known as lies) espoused by said president of the United States and his surrogates are consumed without question by significant portions of the electorate. Oxford Dictionaries declared "post-truth" to be 2016's word of the year. This moment brought home to me the realization (which should have been obvious) that my beloved theory of performative social realities is ethically neutral and that the same idea that facilitated progressive liberal ideologies (especially around identity) also enables the primacy of feelings over facts, the burgeoning of fake news, and the legitimation of conspiracy theory thinking.

So when I woke up to this new awareness, not only was I concerned that my political world had been unmoored, I had a bit of a panic that my research into theatres of the real was likewise unmoored; suddenly rendered artistically irrelevant and also possibly ethically suspect. As Baz Kershaw writes in *The Radical in Performance*,

> So long as we accept the full force of the postmodern paradigm and allow that Barthes has finally done for the intentional fallacy by murdering the

author, Foucault has incontrovertibly shown that power is everywhere, Derrida has uncoupled the signifier from the signified forever, Lyotard has raised incredulity about master narratives to a new order of intensity, Butler has demonstrated that even gender is a cultural construct, and Baudrillard has possibly capped it all by banishing the real, we will be plagued by an acute indecision about the politics of theatre and performance in the contemporary world.[4]

Although the inauguration of Donald Trump may have been the watershed moment that brought this idea to the forefront of my attention, and indeed he may be the poster-boy for this phenomenon, post-reality has been a feature of global reality creation through politics and the media for a number of years, and shows no signs of diminishing. Part of a longer trend, post-reality characterizes an overarching disposition to the dissemination and consumption of information in these early decades of the third millennium, relentlessly shaping and fracturing our world view. Thus my question: Whither theatres of the real in an age of post-reality?

One prevalent counterstrategy, when faced with alternative facts, has been to endorse aggressive fact-checking, calling out lies point by point and countering with corrections. This seems to be a laudable idea. And one endorsed strongly by the mainstream media. After all, that is the business of journalists, who arguably are in the business of seeking and publishing facts. The new slogan of the *Washington Post* is "Democracy dies in darkness." Reality-based theatre draws inspiration from a similar source, tapping into a contemporary zeitgeist for authenticity. This determination to stage realness is at the heart of the theatre of the real genre. Consider some of my case studies: *Winners and Losers* uses confessional autobiography to offer intimate access to the lives of protagonists Jamie and Marcus. *RARE, Polyglotte*, and *100% Vancouver*, which bring ordinary people, framed as nonfictional, as non-actors, to the stage, do so with the broad intent of facilitating an encounter between these strangers and the audience. Verbatim plays like Annabel Soutar's *Seeds* likewise promise a faithful correlation between the testimony collected by Soutar as a kind of researcher and the delivery of those words in the play. Affirmation of a secure conduit through which something real passes from the world to the stage is central to theatres of the real. This is the bread and butter of the genre.

In the context of politics, this appeal to facts as a defence against alternate realities runs aground on at least three points. The first is that crumbling deference to authority – to experts and institutions of all kinds – promulgated by postmodernism, invites questioning as to the source of those facts. Another problem is the "oversupply of facts." There are too many disparate facts. Too many experts. Too much information to process. The problems are too complicated. Finally, facts are no match for feelings. William Davies, in his article "The Age of Post-Truth Politics," distinguishes between facts and data. Facts we can agree on (maybe); data, especially big data, can mine and quantify sentiment. It now becomes possible to get a sense of how lots of people are feeling about something. In trying to persuade people of the reality of something, the appeal to emotion – to what feels real – may be more persuasive that an appeal to reason. It is possible to live in a world with no facts, only data. "Conspiracy theories prosper under such conditions. And while we will have far greater means of knowing how many people believe those theories, we will have far fewer means of persuading them to abandon them."[5] In a theatrical context, another potent counter to claims of realness lies, of course, in the theatrical frame. The frame exerts a strong perceptual pull, fictionalizing everything contained within. Presentation is inescapably transformed to representation. The closest we can get to an objective real is an affect of real-ish-ness, replacing fact with feeling. Simply demanding aggressive fact-checking and trying to assert a return to "capital T" Truth will not work. The poststructuralist genie is out of the bottle and will not go back in. Or even if it would, I think we would not like that. Hello 1950. Hashtag MAGA.

Taking the opposite tack, a multiplicity of realities is equally problematic as recourse to a singular monolithic truth. Post-reality with its disregard for fixed truths does not actually embrace multiplicity so much as lay the groundwork for a single authoritarian arbitrary truth: 'There is only one truth, what I say.' At a veterans' convention in July 2018, as part of a rant against the "fake news" media, US president Donald Trump instructed the crowd, "And just remember, what you're seeing and what you are reading is not what's happening."[6] In a recent article in *The Economist*, "The Art of the Lie," the writer notes, "the deeper worry is for countries like Russia and Turkey, where autocrats use the techniques of post-truth to silence opponents. Cast adrift on an ocean of lies, the people there will have nothing to cling to. For them the novelty of post-truth may lead back to old-fashioned oppression."[7] Indeed, as Peter Pomerantsev writes in *The Atlantic*, "The new Russia doesn't just deal in the petty disinformation, forgeries, lies, leaks, and cyber-sabotage usually associated with information warfare. It reinvents reality, creating mass hallucinations that then translate into political action."[8] He cites the example of the renaming of the contested Donetsk region of southeastern Ukraine as Novorossiya (a tsarist-era name long out of use). Novorossiya is being restored as an entity to maps, its history inserted into textbooks. It even has a flag.[9] The fecundity of proliferating realities also sets the stage for gas-lighting. A term engendered by Patrick Hamilton's 1938 play *Gaslight*, in which a husband psychologically terrorizes his wife, consistently presenting lies as truth in order to make her doubt her sanity, for his own nefarious purposes. Gas-lighting in this context involves presenting statements that are obviously false but with such conviction that the recipient is disoriented. The general risk in a multiplicity of relativistic equivalent realities is that this leads to anomie and lack of direction. When any reality is as good as any other, there is a wearying, paralytic sense that it doesn't matter which one you choose.

The plays that I am working with consistently conclude that nothing can be known. In fact, this is the core thesis. And this was another facet of my awoken panic. Plays that revel in insecurity, plays that produce insecurity for our pleasure, suddenly feel a lot less fun. Epistemological insecurity, epitomized in a cynical, millennial shrug and consumed with your single-origin hipster coffee, is no longer a harmless philosophical position. Liz Tomlin, in her book *Acts and Apparitions: Discourses on the Real in Performance Practice and Theory*, articulates the problem this way. How can we re-engage with the world and take up direct political engagement through reality-based performance? She says we need "an alternative mode of poststructuralist resistance which seeks to reconfigure contemporary notions of reality rather than merely highlighting the simulated nature of all representation of the real."[10] After several months and many long walks, I have evolved my thinking and I can see that there is more to this beyond simply getting stuck. Theatres of the real, which on the surface offer authenticity and epistemological certainty in their attachment to an extra-theatrical reality but in fact persistently show that promise to be empty, producing instead contingency and insecurity, are not the end of the story. If we embrace insecurity, we can care about reality (even contingent reality) and still be in doubt.

Insecurity is difficult. It is uncomfortable. Absolutely. Sometimes it is outright dangerous. And people will seek to avoid that feeling. We might ask what the connection is between epistemological uncertainty arising from poststructuralism and recent faux-nostalgic desire for security, as manifested by the Trump campaign slogan "Make America

Great Again" and the Brexit Leave campaign slogan "Take Back Control." I would argue that this is not so much about economic hardship but about insecurity pertaining to identity as people wonder "Where do I fit?" in the face of globalization, mass migration, social fluidity, transience of traditions and conventional value systems. Miwon Kwon writes, "How do we account, for instance, for the sense of soaring exhilaration and the anxious dread engendered by the new fluidities and continuities of space and time, on the one hand, and their ruptures and disconnections on the other?"[11] Kwon is thinking specifically about geography in her work on site-specific art: "This persistent, perhaps secret adherence to the actuality of place may not be a lack of theoretical sophistication but a means of survival."[12] Conversely, too much attachment is also a bad thing; "a compensatory fantasy in response to the intensification of fragmentation and alienation wrought by a mobilized market economy."[13] This is a classic strategy for managing anxiety. Suffering from anxiety, I start to eliminate things that make me feel anxious. I restrict my circle of experience, progressively shrinking my world to only those things that feel safe. I build border walls, restrict immigration, and raise import tariffs. And my world gets smaller and smaller as I am able to manage less and less. And no surprise that anxiety abounds. As Ulrich Beck argues, we live in a "risk society" with lots of unknowns, and uncontrollable, unpredictable problems, often of our own making.

Central to the argument espoused here has been the concept of "productive insecurity." Coined by Ulrike Garde and Meg Mumford, "productive insecurity" arises in postdramatic works that feature ontological ambiguity where the audience is not certain whether they are witnessing something actual or something fictional. In their initial conceptualization, Garde and Mumford draw their examples from works that feature verbatim testimony, but in my book I apply the principle widely to works across the genre. They describe the "productive" aspect of insecurity as a challenge to established ways to knowing, exhorting us to be humbly aware of our limitations in the face of complex problems. I extend this argument to suggest that the affects of insecurity are not just something to be endured but to be embraced and fostered. And that theatres of the real do this. From that viewpoint, we can acknowledge not only that we can only ever partially know the world; but also that we are surrounded by hybrids and multiplicity creating more rather than fewer worlds. Breaking away from the rigidity of binary views – real/not-real; red!/blue! – we are actually better off with more worlds.

In moving the positive embrace of multiple unsecured realities from theory into practice, two more concepts bear looking at as potential catalysts: the felicity of community and strategies of double mediation. In Lily Tomlin's one-woman play *The Search for Signs of Intelligent Life in the Universe*, written by Jane Wagner, the character of Trudy the bag lady says, "After all, what is reality anyway? Nothin' but a collective hunch."[14] I want to put the focus here on the word "collective." In order to have reality, we need to have community. The power of performativity to create new worlds with words is delimited by community. As J.L. Austin asserts, a performative is only "felicitous" if there is "uptake;" that is, performative utterances can only be valid if other people agree that they are. Aligned with Derrida's citationality, Wittgenstein counters in his *Philosophical Investigations* that there can be no private language. Certainly, the need for uptake enacts normative drag on the creation of new performative worlds, restricting innovation to what people can agree to; but conversely it also requires that we listen to each other en route to crafting a larger territory of shared perspective. In *The Sublime Object of Ideology*, Žižek tells a joke about a man who thinks he is a kernel of corn. After some time in hospital he is cured and knows that he is not a kernel of corn but is a man. But immediately upon his release, he comes running back. Having met a hen, he is terrified that the hen will eat him. The doctors say, "You have nothing to fear, you are not a kernel of corn. You are a man." The man replies, "I know that but does the hen?"[15] Žižek uses this anecdote to illustrate the concept of symbolic efficiency. Symbolic efficiency describes the means whereby in order for a fact to become true it is not sufficient for one person to know, or even for a small group; it must be known by "the big Other," that is, by that collective of social understanding that underpins customs, laws, beliefs, and social mores. In the face of the postmodern disintegration of the big Other (which Žižek argues was always dead but we didn't know it), we have no mechanism to communicate with the hen, as it were, to ensure its corroboration of a particular reality. Žižek concludes, "When symbolic efficiency is suspended, the Imaginary falls into the Real."[16] Perhaps part of a response to post-reality and the radical unmooring of reality from evidence and experience is to rebuild these social connections, using a relational sensibility, so that more people can agree together on what constitutes reality.

For performatives to be successful, for new realities to come into existence, we don't actually need to agree about content but about process. There needs to be common concord about what constitutes a felicitous performative. Critical attention needs to be focused not on whether or not this world is objectively valid as true but on how that reality is constituted as true. So rather than pressing for an impossible absolute singularity, theatres of the real model the uncertain embrace of multiplicity. Not unmediation, but double mediation, mediation on mediation, to provide an alternate approach to the proliferation of unmoored realities. I am borrowing this term double mediation from Kenneth Frampton's essay on critical regionalism. Frampton is writing about an architecture of resistance under postmodernity. Miwon Kwon takes up his idea to think about the innate tension in site-specificity between freedom and fixity, projecting works and worlds that are "neither a simulacral pacifier nor a wilful invention."[17] Beyond the double negation of being neither this nor that, mediation of some kind is inescapable. Double mediation is about approaching the real through reflexivity about mediation. To doubt is to question appearances; to doubt is to contemplate and weigh. It is an essential part of critical description; not to dismiss surface but to see hidden structures. Doubt forms the foundation of meta-representation, of double mediation, impelling us to engage insecurity through questioning how the representation was made. It invites the creation of a "poetics of the ways in which witnessable coherence is continually produced."[18] Lehmann hints at something similar when he suggests that postdrama has the potential to direct focus away from the mimetic binary of here and there, inside and outside, and instead "move the *mutual implication of actors and spectators in the theatrical production of images* into the centre and thus make visible the broken thread between personal experience and perception."[19] When conspiracy theories flourish and alternate facts are indifferently accepted, the thread between lived experience and our cartography of that world is indeed broken. Returning to first principles of how these two positions are mutually implicated and how reals come to be is a necessary first step.

In the end, I come to the conclusion that post-reality is not a threat to theatres of the real. As my case study analyses demonstrate, theatres of the real are not principally about presenting authenticity, truth, the real, or what have you. Yes, the genre is reality-based, drawing from documentary sources to stage reality-effects and affects of real-ish-ness. But in terms of content, this realness is always doomed to failure, being radically contingent under poststructuralism. What theatres of the real are producing instead of reality is insecurity. It is through insecurity that we are impelled to move past simply noting the proliferation of free-floating realities and ask how realities are constructed. I don't think I am overstating the case by saying that this critical work is central to the grassroots exercise of democratic citizenship. How did these realities come to be? Do they represent my local experience? Does my experience of reality align with that of other people? Are these the realities that we want? Instead of being fearful, insecurity makes me hopeful.

Notes

Chapter 1

1 Produced by Punchdrunk from the UK, *Sleep No More* is an immersive promenade theatre experience that retells Shakespeare's *Macbeth* through the stylings of a film noir lens ("*Sleep No More*"; McKittrickHotel.com). Audiences are given masks and encouraged to explore the multi-floor venue, following whichever scenes they wish. The show was first presented in London in 2003, but has been running continuously in New York since March 2011. It is probably the best known international exemplar of the immersive theatre genre.

2 Created in 2004, by Kate Morgan and Morgan Lloyd, *You Me Bum Bum Train* is an immersive journey for a single audience member or "passenger." Producers are secretive about the events, suggesting a richer experience the less you know in advance, but the overall gist is that passengers are thrust sequentially from one surreal participatory scenario into another where in each situation you are the central character. The show has run off and on since 2012, with the most recent run closing in April 2016 ("*You Me Bum Bum Train*," Wikipedia, 17 June 2018.).

3 David Shields, *Reality Hunger*, 3.

4 William Shakespeare, *Hamlet*, 3.2.20–4.

5 The word "real" is used throughout the book with the clear appreciation that this is a contested word, referring not to an absolute real but to the so-called real. With this understanding in mind, and in the interests of a clean reading style, I have elected not to use scare quotes throughout.

6 Josette Féral, "Theatricality," 97.

7 Ibid., 97.

8 Carol Martin, *Theatre of the Real*, 5.

9 Ibid., 4.

10 Ibid., 5.

11 Ibid., 14.

12 Andy Lavender, *Performance in the Twenty-First Century*, 31.

13 Slavoj Žižek, "Welcome to the Desert of the Real"; Lavender, *Performance in the Twenty-First Century*.

14 Lavender, *Performance in the Twenty-First Century*; Liz Tomlin, *Acts and Apparitions*.

15 Lavender, *Performance*, 12.

16 Tomlin, *Acts and Apparitions*, 5.

17 Zygmunt Bauman, *Culture in a Liquid Modern World*, 11.

18 Bauman, *Culture*, 13.

19 Peggy Phelan, "Marina Abramović: Witnessing Shadows," 577.

20 Lavender, *Performance*, 19.

21 Josephine Machon, *Immersive Theatres*, 23.

22 Ibid., 26.

23 Alan Filewod, *Collective Encounters*; Martin, *Theatre of the Real*; Derek Paget, "The 'Broken' Tradition"; G.F. Dawson, *Documentary Theatre in the United States*.

24 Hans-Thies Lehmann, *Postdramatic Theatre*, 100.

25 Ibid., 100.

26 Ibid.

27 Samuel Taylor Coleridge, "Biographia Literaria," 3.365.

28 Coleridge, "Progress of the Drama," 4.37.

29 Ibid.

30 Bert O. States, *Great Reckonings in Little Rooms*, 34.

31 Ibid., 29.

32 Jenn Stephenson, "Portrait of the Artist as Artist."

33 Stephenson, "Singular Impressions."

34 States, *Great Reckonings in Little Rooms*, 40; original emphasis.

35 Lehmann, *Postdramatic Theatre*, 100; original emphasis.

36 Ibid.

37 Ibid., 103.

38 Catherine Belsey, *Culture and the Real*, 3–4.

39 Jim Baggott, *A Beginner's Guide to Reality*, 28.

40 Belsey, *Culture and the Real*, 4.

41 Ibid., 18.

42 Ibid., 41–2.

43 Jacques Lacan, *Freud's Papers on Technique 1953–1954 (Seminar 1)*, 262.

44 Ibid., 66.

45 Belsey, *Culture and the Real*, 14.
46 Ulrike Garde and Meg Mumford, "Postdramatic Reality Theatre."
47 Ibid., 164.
48 Helena Grehan, *Performance, Ethics and Spectatorship in a Global Age*, 22.
49 Zygmunt Bauman, "The World Inhospitable to Levinas," 159
50 Grehan, *Performance, Ethics and Spectatorship*, 20.
51 Ibid., 22.
52 Ibid., 23.
53 Ibid., 35.
54 Sara Jane Bailes, *Performance Theatre and the Poetics of Failure*, 2.
55 Belsey, *Culture and the Real*, 10.

Chapter 2

1 Kevin Reid, "MagNorth2013 – Winners and Losers"; original emphasis.
2 Created and performed by James Long and Marcus Youssef, *Winners and Losers* was directed by Chris Abraham. The play is co-produced by Theatre Replacement and Neworld Theatre in association with Crow's Theatre.
3 Paula Citron, "*Winners and Losers*: Virtuoso Word Play Gives Way to Nasty Verbal Sparring in this Tour de Force."
4 Charles Isherwood, "Friendship Frays, a Topic at a Time."
5 Elisabeth Vincentelli, "A Parlor Game has Serious Consequences in Soho Rep's '*Winners and Losers*.'"
6 Liz Nicholls, "Citadel's *Winners and Losers* Insightful, Unsettling."
7 After premiering at the Gateway Theatre, Studio B, in Surrey, British Columbia, Canada 22 November–1 December 2012, and 30 January–2 February 2013 at Vancouver's PuSh International Arts Festival, *Winners and Losers* embarked on an international tour. Performance sites include Brighton, UK (May 2013); Montreal, Canada (May 2013); Ottawa, Canada (June 2013); Groningen, Netherlands (August 2013); Reykjavik, Iceland (August 2013); Aarhus, Denmark (September 2013); Terni, Italy (September 2013); Toronto, Canada (November–December 2013); Seattle, USA (April 2014); Berlin, Germany (June 2014); New York, USA (January–February 2015), Edmonton, Canada (April 2015), Washington, DC, USA (October–November 2015), Vancouver, Canada (February 2016), Calgary, Canada (January 2017), Portland, USA (March 2017).
8 Martin, *Theatre of the Real*, 13; original emphasis.
9 Judith Butler, *Gender Trouble*; Jacques Derrida, *Limited Inc.*; Erving Goffman, *Presentation of Self in Everyday Life*.
10 Jacques Derrida, *Of Grammatology*, 158.

11 Jean Baudrillard, *Simulacra and Simulation*, 1.

12 Ibid., 5–6.

13 Guy Debord, *Society of the Spectacle*.

14 Tomlin, *Acts and Apparitions*, 29.

15 Garde and Mumford, "Postdramatic Reality Theatre."

16 Philippe Lejeune, "The Autobiographical Pact," 5.

17 Susanna Egan, *Burdens of Proof*, 86.

18 Ibid., 3.

19 Ibid., 6.

20 Shields, *Reality Hunger*, 133.

21 Ibid., 132.

22 Jenn Stephenson, *Performing Autobiography: Contemporary Canadian Drama*, 4.

23 John Keats, *The Complete Poetical Works and Letters of John Keats*, 277.

24 The production I am describing here is the one that I witnessed during the premiere run at the Gateway Theatre in Surrey, BC. I saw the play three times during its initial run – once on 30 November and twice on 1 December 2012.

25 James Long and Marcus Youssef, *Winners and Losers*, 15–16.

26 Ibid., 32–3.

27 Ibid., 5.

28 This is a system of notation that I have developed for describing the relative and equivalent ontology of metatheatrical frames. World[a] refers to the actual world, the so-called real world inhabited by audience members and actors and the play as an event. World[b], accordingly, is the first constructed fictional world. This is the world occupied by the characters of the play. Additional subsequent inset worlds can be denoted by world[c], world[d], and so on.

29 Long and Youssef, *Winners and Losers*, 13.

30 Cormac Power, *Presence in Play*, 3.

31 Ibid., 47.

32 Stephenson, "Portrait of the Artist as Artist."

33 Long and Youssef, *Winners and Losers*, 16; original emphasis.

34 Ibid., 9.

35 The third remaining strategy described by Power, making-present: the fictional mode of presence, is substantially different from the other two in that it is not about the (attempted) unmediated staging of real-world persons or objects, but rather is concerned with engendering a perception of presence (or realness) in patently fictional worlds. Power considers the workings of nineteenth-century naturalism in this context.

36 Power, *Presence in Play*, 95.

37 Ibid., 103; original emphasis.
38 Peter Boenisch, "Towards a Theatre of Encounter and Experience," 171.
39 Garde and Mumford, "Postdramatic Reality Theatre," 149; original emphasis.
40 Erika Fischer-Lichte, "Reality and Fiction in Contemporary Theatre," 95.
41 Lehmann, *Postdramatic Theatre*, 102; original emphasis.
42 Tomlin, *Acts and Apparitions*, 10.
43 Anton Piatigorsky, *Eternal Hydra*, 86.
44 Long and Youssef, *Winners and Losers*, 10–11.
45 The principal tenets of Enlightenment liberalism value self-determination of the individual, endorsement of privacy, and control of one's personal environment. English philosopher John Locke (1632–1704) "formulated the classic expression of liberalism, which was instrumental in the great revolutions of 1776 and 1789," familiar in the phrase "life, liberty and the pursuit of happiness." (Graham, A.J. Rogers, "John Locke," *Encyclopedia Britannica Online*, 14 December 2015.)
46 Long and Youssef, *Winners and Losers*, 34.
47 Ibid., 25.
48 Ibid., 50–51.
49 Ibid., 50.
50 Citron, *"Winners and Losers."*
51 *"Winners and Losers," Theatre Replacement*, 2016.
52 J. Kelly Nestruck, "The Year in Theatre: The Stage Tackled Topics to Drop Your Jaw."
53 Long and Youssef, *Winners and Losers*, 31.
54 Ibid., 46.
55 Ibid., 40.
56 Ibid., 41; original emphasis.
57 Ibid., 42.
58 Ibid.
59 Ibid., 52.
60 Ibid., 54.
61 Ibid., 63.
62 Ibid., 55.
63 Ibid., 64.
64 Ibid., 65.
65 Garde and Mumford, "Postdramatic Reality Theatre," 158.
66 Ibid., 152.
67 Lehmann, *Postdramatic Theatre*, 185–6; original emphasis.
68 Jenn Stephenson, "Uncertainty: A User's Guide," xv.

Chapter 3

1 Judith Thompson and ensemble, *RARE (Toronto)*, 26.
2 It is conventional in autobiographical performance criticism to refer to the eponymous character by first name only and to the performer by their full first and last name.
3 Thompson, *RARE (Toronto)*, 26.
4 Stephenson, *Performing Autobiography*.
5 Paul John Eakin, *Fictions in Autobiography*; Susanna Egan, *Mirror Talk*; Deirdre Heddon, *Autobiography and Performance*; G. Thomas Couser, *Vulnerable Subjects*; Susan Bennett, "3-D A/B"; Ric Knowles, "Documemory, Autobiology, and the Utopian Performative."
6 Heddon, *Autobiography and Performance*, 157.
7 Ibid., 157.
8 Meg Mumford, "Rimini Protokoll's Reality Theatre and Intercultural Encounter," 153.
9 Rosemarie Garland-Thomson, *Freakery*; Michael Chemers, *Staging Stigma*.
10 Nicholas Ridout, *Stage Fright, Animals, and Other Theatrical Problems*, 4.
11 Jacqueline Lo and Helen Gilbert, "Toward a Topography of Cross-Cultural Theatre Praxis," 47.
12 Sara Ahmed, *Strange Encounters*, 21.
13 Ibid., 6.
14 Ibid., 145.
15 Ibid., 157.
16 Ibid., 145.
17 Ibid., 144.
18 Ibid., 148.
19 Kelsey Jacobson, "Through the Ficitve to the Real(ish)."
20 States, *Great Reckonings in Little Rooms*.
21 Michael Kirby, "On Acting and Not-Acting," 3–15.
22 Ibid., 3, 6.
23 Willmar Sauter, "Playing Is Not Pretending," 67.
24 Ibid., 77.
25 Henri Schoenmakers, "'Being Oneself on Stage,'" 226.
26 Lehmann, *Postdramatic Theatre*, 135.
27 Florian Malzacher, "Dramaturgies of Care and Insecurity."
28 Mumford, "Rimini Protokoll's Reality Theatre and Intercultural Encounter," 153.
29 Garde and Mumford, "Postdramatic Reality Theatre," 151.
30 Ibid.

31 Ibid., 148.

32 Shannon Jackson, *Social Works*, 168.

33 PuSh Festival website.

34 *100% Vancouver* was performed three times on 21 and 22 January 2011. Jointly produced by Theatre Replacement and PuSh International Performing Arts Festival, *100% Vancouver* premiered at the Goldcorp Centre for the Arts, SFU Woodwards, Fei and Milton Wong Experimental Theatre. The production was directed by Amiel Gladstone. Tim Carlson was casting director and dramaturge. Donna Soares, Sara Bynoe and Xanthe Faulkner were casting assistants.

35 Casting graphs depicting the desired demographical composition for *100% Vancouver* were published in the program for the show.

36 Keren Zaiontz, "Care and Capital in 100% Vancouver," 114.

37 Ibid., 109.

38 George Pendle, "Colour by Numbers."

39 *100% Vancouver*, 16.

40 The *100% Vancouver* production schedule for 15–22 January 2011 indicates a total of three rehearsals of three hours before the first show on 21 January.

41 Ariana Colenbrander, "100% Vancouver's Tim Carlson."

42 Bailes, *Performance Theatre and the Poetics of Failure*, 2.

43 Michelle Reid, "100% Vancouver."

44 Jeff Khonsary and Kristina Lee Podesva, "Vital Stats: (an afterword)."

45 *100% Vancouver*, 13.

46 The premiere of *RARE* at the Toronto Fringe Festival in July 2012 occurred in the Tarragon Theatre Mainspace, directed by Judith Thompson, with Sarah Carney, Dylan Harman, James Hazlett, Nick Herd, Suzanne Love, Mike Liu, Nada Mayla, Krystal Nausbaum, and Andreas Prinz in the cast. The production was then remounted at the Young Centre for the Performing Arts from 28 January to 7 February 2013 as part of the Soulpepper Theatre Company's season. In November and December 2014, an adaptation of the script with a new cast and creative team was produced in Kingston, Ontario at THE BOX, a studio space associated with H'art Centre. This production was directed by Kathryn MacKay, and performed by Jacob Ballantyne, Kevin Beauregard, Erin Bennett, Natasha Daw, Ashaya Garrett, Anna Gervais, and Nathan Sikkema.

47 Thompson, *RARE-Toronto*, 5.

48 Ibid., 11.

49 I use the word "normate" here following Rosemarie Garland-Thomson's coinage of the term to reference the play's ostensible interpellation of its audience as uniformly able-bodied, and ignorant of Down syndrome

culture (*Extraordinary* 8). However, when I saw *RARE* performed in Kingston in an adaptation by a local cast, the audience was notably not all as imagined, as the members of the original Toronto cast of *RARE* were present that afternoon, along with their families and supporters. Moreover, in Kingston, *RARE* was performed in the physical space, and under the auspices, of the H'art Centre studio. The H'art Centre is a charitable-arts hub with a mission "to offer high quality opportunities for people with disabilities and those facing barriers to create, study, and produce works in the arts" ("Welcome to H'art Centre").

50 Ric Knowles, *Theatre & Interculturalism*, 29.

51 David Patterson, "Molecular Genetic Analysis of Down Syndrome," 195.

52 Among parents who are offered genetic testing for Down syndrome, 70 per cent accept the testing (Morris and Alberman). Rates for those with positive results who elect to terminate the pregnancy vary, with 67 to 85 per cent of women opting for abortion in the United States (Natoli et al.), a figure that rises to 92 per cent in the United Kingdom (Morris and Alberman).[1] In the US, babies with Down syndrome represent 1 in 691 live births (Parker et al.). The rate in Canada is slightly lower: babies with Down syndrome represent 1 in 740 live births (Public Health Agency of Canada). In the UK, that number is closer to 1 in 1000 (Morris and Alberman). In Ireland, prior to the legalization of abortion in May 2018 that number was 1 in 550, nearly double that of the UK ("Down Syndrome" HSE).

53 Morris and Alberman conclude that "the number of antenatal and postnatal diagnoses of Down syndrome has increased by 71% (from 1075 in 1989/90 to 1843 in 2007/08. However numbers of live births . . . fell by 1% (752 to 743; 1.10 to 1.08 per 1000 births) because of antenatal screening and subsequent terminations. In the absence of such screening, the numbers of Down syndrome births would have increased by 48% (from 959 to 1422) since couples are starting families at an older age."

54 Thompson, *RARE-Toronto*, 24.

55 Ibid.

56 Tobin Siebers, *Disability Aesthetics*, 24–5.

57 Ibid., 25.

58 Keiron Smith, *The Politics of Down Syndrome*, 49–50.

59 Ibid., 52.

60 Harlan Hahn, "The Politics of Physical Differences: Disability and Discrimination."

61 Sara Ahmed, *The Cultural Politics of Emotion*, 64.

62 Ibid.

63 Catherine E. Chamberlain and Robin M. Strode, *The Source for Down Syndrome*; JoAnn Simons, *The Down Syndrome Transition Handbook: Charting Your Child's Course to Adulthood.*

64 Thompson, *RARE-Toronto*, 4.

65 Ibid., 14.

66 Ibid., 6.

67 Ibid.

68 Ibid., 19.

69 Robert Cushman, "Judith Thompson's RARE makes the familiar strange."

70 Ahmed, *Strange Encounters*, 12.

71 Mumford, "Rimini Protokoll's Reality Theatre and Intercultural Encounter," 154.

72 Thompson, *RARE-Toronto*, 23.

73 Stephenson, "Portrait of the Artist as Artist."

74 Marvin Carlson surveys this phenomenon specifically considering nudity, but also bodily injury and taboo public acts like urination. (*Shattering Hamlet's Mirror*, 50–4).

75 Fischer-Lichte, "Reality and Fiction in Contemporary Theatre," 85.

76 Carrie Sandahl, "The Tyranny of the Neutral," 262.

77 Jens Roselt, "Making an Appearance," 47.

78 Two of the actors in *RARE* boast professional acting credits. Krystal Nausbaum appeared in the Emmy-nominated TV movie *The Memory Keeper's Daughter* and Dylan Harmann Livaja performed in *The Rainbow Kid*, which premiered at TIFF in 2015. Training and professional performance opportunities for disabled actors are notoriously difficult to access. Madeleine Greey, Krystal's mother, produced *RARE*, "partly, she admits 'so Krystal could work'" (Timson).

79 Bailes, *Performance Theatre and the Poetics of Failure*, 22.

80 Ibid., 13.

81 Malzacher, "Dramaturgies of Care and Insecurity," 40.

82 The popular high-school musical drama *Glee*, created by Ryan Murphy, Brad Falchuk, and Ian Brennan, features character Becky Jackson, who has Down syndrome. Becky is co-captain of the Cheerios cheerleading team and minion of villainous Sue Sylvester, the cheerleading coach. Becky Jackson is played by actor Lauren Potter.

83 Written and edited by Olivier Choinière and co-directed by Choinière and Alexia Bürger, *Polyglotte* premiered in Montreal at Théâtre aux Écuries under the auspices of Festival TransAmériques from 31 May to 4 June 2015. The play was remounted 15 September through 3 October 2015 in the same venue with the same cast. The performers were

German Barragan, Tatiana Burtin, Mondiana François, Samira Ghorbani, Mahmoud Shawky Hamed Ali, Pamela Robertson, Somnath Shinde, Mireille Tawfik, Farlene Thelisdort, Edward Wong, and Jorge Suarez.

84 Citizenship and Immigration Canada, 3, 6.

85 Choinière, *Polyglotte*, 4.

86 Ibid., 6.

87 Ibid., 3.

88 Ibid., 18.

89 Ibid., 19.

90 Ibid.

91 Ibid., 21.

92 Ibid.

93 Ibid., 31.

94 Ibid., 31–2. Thomas Mulcair is known for his long distance swimming. He boasted in an interview with *The Ottawa Citizen* of swimming 5 kilometres in just over two hours. This determined distance swimming characterizes his steady tortoise-like persona. (Kennedy, Mark. "The Making of Mulcair: How the NDP Leader Became a Contender," *The Ottawa Citizen*, 24 July 2015.) Pierre Karl Péladeau is a multimillionaire businessman and president of the Quebecor media empire. Péladeau was the leader of the opposition in the Quebec National Assembly from his election in May 2015 until his resignation one year later. He has a reputation of being tough on unions and concerns were raised about conflict of interest when he did not divest himself of his media holdings upon his election to public office. Jacques Parizeau was premier of Quebec during the contentious sovereignty referendum of 1995. When the "Yes" side, of which he was one of the leaders, was narrowly defeated, Parizeau vented his frustration in public and infamously blamed the outcome on "money and the ethnic vote." So in this context it is an understatement to say "He is bitterly disappointed."

95 I saw *Polyglotte* for the first time on 3 June 2015, just two days after the death of Jacques Parizeau on 1 June. When his face appeared, a woman spoke up clearly in the silence and named him as "Monsieur Parizeau." The honorific "Monsieur" was both respectful and also an expression of a particular cultural knowledge. As noted in his CBC obituary, "his bourgeois background, penchant for three-piece suits and proper style of speaking all contributed to his nickname, 'Monsieur.'" ("Jacques Parizeau, Former Quebec Premier, Dead at 84," *CBC News*, 2 June 2015.)

96 Choinière, *Polyglotte*, 26.

97 Printemps érable (Maple Spring – a verbal pun on Arab Spring that works better in French "Printemps arabe") refers to the Quebec student protests in the spring of 2012 against proposed tuition increases. ("2012 Quebec Student Protests," *Wikipedia*, 30 August 2018.)

98 Elaine Normandeau, Personal email.

99 The Charter of Values was a proposed bill in the province of Quebec asserting government secularity and neutrality. Contentiously the Charter would have limited the wearing of conspicuous religious symbols and garments by public sector workers and included the requirement to uncover one's face when providing or receiving government services. ("Quebec Charter of Values," Wikipedia, 14 August 2018.)

100 Choinière, *Polyglotte*, 34, 37.

101 Ibid., 17–18.

102 Ibid., 18.

103 Ibid., 15.

104 Ibid., 23–4.

105 Citoyenneté et Immigration Canada, *Decouvrir le Canada: Les droits et responsabilités lies à la citoyenneté*, 2012, 10.

106 Choinière, *Polyglotte*, 24.

107 Ibid., 39.

108 Collection du Musée national des beaux-arts du Québec

109 Choinière, *Polyglotte*, 39.

110 Bailes, *Performance Theatre and the Poetics of Failure*, 3.

111 Ahmed, *Strange Encounters*, 72.

Chapter 4

1 Paget, "The 'Broken' Tradition of Documentary Theatre," 235–6.

2 Tomlin, *Acts and Apparitions*, 115.

3 Carol Martin, "Living Simulations," 88.

4 Garde and Mumford, "Postdramatic Reality Theatre."

5 *Seeds* was directed by Chris Abraham and premiered in English in February 2012 at the Young Centre for Performing Arts in Toronto. Set and costume design by Julie Fox, lighting design by Ana Cappelluto, original music and sound design by Richard Feren, and video design by Elysha Poirier. The cast featured Bruce Dinsmore, Mariah Inger, Alex Ivanovici, Tanja Jacobs, Eric Peterson, Cary Lawrence, and Liisa Repo-Martell.

6 Developed in residency at the Theatre Centre in Toronto, *300 TAPES* premiered there on 1 December 2010. The play was performed from 15 February through 6 March in Calgary at Alberta Theatre Projects. The

performance was co-created by Ame Henderson and Bobby Theodore, with performers Joe Cobden, Frank Cox-O'Connell, and Brendan Gall with Anna Friz as the sound artist. Trevor Schwellnus was the scenographer, and Bojana Stancic designed the costumes. Vicki Stroich was the dramaturge.

7 It is interesting to note in this context that canola is itself a manufactured bioproduct developed at the University of Manitoba in the 1970s by Keith Downey and Baldur R. Stefansson. Developed through conventional breeding from rapeseed, canola has a different nutritional profile and contains less uric acid. The name canola, derived from Can (Canada) + ola (oleum/oil), was initially a trademark, but is now the common name for this plant. (Wikipedia: "canola")

8 Annabel Soutar, *Seeds*, 71.

9 Program for *300 TAPES*.

10 Bobby Theodore quoted in Kaplan.

11 Tomlin, *Acts and Apparitions*, 122.

12 Walter Benjamin, "The Work of Art in the Age of Mechanical Reproduction," 220.

13 Plato, "The Republic, Book II," 21.

14 Ibid.

15 Elin Diamond, "Mimesis, Mimicry, and the 'True-Real,'" 62.

16 Gilmore, James H., and B. Joseph Pine II, *Authenticity: What Consumers Want*.

17 Roberta Levitow, "Some Words about the Theatre Today," 26.

18 Benjamin, "The Work of Art in the Age of Mechanical Reproduction," 222.

19 Robin Soans, "Robin Soans," 17.

20 Benjamin, "The Work of Art in the Age of Mechanical Reproduction," 225.

21 Ibid., 222.

22 Mariah Horner and Grahame Renyk, "Matter Matters: Performing a Stone in the Woods," 60.

23 Benjamin, "The Work of Art in the Age of Mechanical Reproduction," 222–23.

24 Ibid., 223.

25 Ibid., 223, 225.

26 Philip Auslander, *Liveness*, 28.

27 Kirby, "On Acting and Not-Acting," 5.

28 Steve Wurtzler, "The Live, the Recorded and the Subject of Representation," 92.

29 Auslander, *Liveness*, 53.

30 Ibid., 31.

31 Tomlin, *Acts and Apparitions*, 97.
32 J.F. Gubrium and J.A. Holstein, *The Self We Live By*, 67.
33 Anna Friz's sound cues created from the tapes include "tape hiss," snippets of stories, "ominous osculations," "room tone," and a collage of "ums."
34 Soutar, *Seeds*, 56.
35 Power, *Presence in Play*, 178.
36 Andy Lavender, "The Moment of Realized Actuality," 189.
37 Power, *Presence in Play*, 8.
38 Ibid., 14.
39 Diamond, "Mimesis, Mimicry, and the 'True-Real,'" 68.
40 Soutar, *Seeds*, 2.
41 Ibid.
42 Ibid., 127–8.
43 Ibid., 24.
44 Tomlin, *Acts and Apparitions*, 92.
45 J. Kelly Nestruck, "300 TAPES: Memories from Before Everything Became Digitized."
46 *300 TAPES*, "Halloween."
47 Ibid.
48 Ibid.
49 *300 TAPES*, "Daisy."
50 *300 TAPES*, "Halloween."
51 *300 TAPES*, "Getting Dumped."
52 *300 TAPES*, "My Little Ole Baby."
53 *300 TAPES*, "Halloween."
54 Brendan Gall recorded 45 tapes; Frank Cox-O'Connell recorded 35 tapes; Joe Cobden recorded 49 tapes = only 129 original tapes + versions + generations.
55 *300 TAPES*, "Dilly Dally."
56 Jay David Bolter and Richard Grusin, *Remediation: Understanding New Media*.
57 Roman Ingarden, *The Literary Work of Art*.
58 Soutar, *Seeds*, 127.
59 Tomlin, *Acts and Apparitions*, 116.
60 Josette Féral, "Performance and Theatricality," 176.
61 Bolter and Grusin, *Remediation*, 53.
62 Lawrence Grossberg, "The Media Economy of Rock Culture," 206.
63 Ibid.,175.
64 Auslander, *Liveness*, 72.
65 Andrew Goodwin, *Dancing in the Distraction Factory*, 77.
66 Tomlin, *Acts and Apparitions*, 95.

67 Derrida, *Limited Inc.*, 49–51.
68 Elinor Fuchs, *The Death of Character: Perspectives on Theater after Modernism*, 75.
69 Bailes, *Performance Theatre and the Poetics of Failure*.
70 Diamond, 66. footnote 37; Luce Irigaray. "The Power of Discourse" *This Sex Which is Not One*. Translated by Catherine Parte and Carolyn Burke. Ithaca: Cornell UP, 1985. 76.
71 Diamond, 66.
72 Ibid., 67.
73 *300 TAPES*, "Elvis."
74 *300 TAPES*, "Getting Dumped."
75 *300 TAPES*, "Daisy."
76 *300 TAPES*, "Halloween."
77 *300 TAPES*, "3 Flights."
78 Soutar, *Seeds*, 71.
79 Benjamin, "The Work of Art in the Age of Mechanical Reproduction," 238.
80 Soutar, *Seeds*, 127.
81 *300 TAPES*, "Dilly Dally."
82 *300 TAPES* program
83 Power, *Presence in Play*, 174.
84 Baudrillard, *Simulacra and Simulation*, 1.
85 Ibid., 2.

Chapter 5

1 Melanie Bennett, Hartley Jafine, and Aaron Collier, *Garden//Suburbia*, 8.
2 Ibid., 9.
3 Dustin Harvey and Adrienne Wong, *Landline*, 74.
4 Miwon Kwon, *One Place After Another*, 11.
5 Ibid.
6 Ibid.
7 Michael Fried, *Art and Objecthood*, 163.
8 Mike Pearson and Michael Shanks, *Theatre/Archaeology*, 23.
9 Nick Kaye, "Introduction: Site-Specifics," 11.
10 Pearson, "Site-Specificity and the Narratives of History," 70.
11 Cathy Turner, "Finding a Vocabulary for Site-Specific Performance," 374.
12 Ibid., 377.
13 Ibid., 374.
14 Kwon, *One Place After Another*, 29.
15 Lucy R. Lippard, *The Lure of the Local*, 33.
16 Ibid., 9.

17 Ibid.
18 Kwon, *One Place After Another*, 160.
19 Ibid., 8.
20 Brandon LaBelle, *Background Noise*, x.
21 Ross Brown, *Sound*, 1.
22 LaBelle, *Background Noise*, xv.
23 Salomé Voegelin, *Listening to Noise and Silence*, xii.
24 Ibid., ix.
25 Ibid., x.
26 Seth Kim-Cohen, *In the Blink of an Ear*, 46.
27 Carolyn Christov-Bakargiev, *Janet Cardiff*, 16.
28 Ian Watt, *The Rise of the Novel*, 11.
29 Roland Barthes, *S/Z*, 156.
30 Émile Zola, "Naturalism on the Stage," 143.
31 Ibid., 152.
32 Marvin Carlson, *Shattering Hamlet's Mirror*, 60.
33 Ibid., 60.
34 Victor Hugo, "Preface to *Cromwell*," 55.
35 Carlson, *Shattering Hamlet's Mirror*, 67.
36 Ibid., 80.
37 Stanton B. Garner Jr, "Sensing Realism," 116.
38 Ibid., 117.
39 August Strindberg, "Preface to *Miss Julie*," 572–3.
40 Garner, "Sensing Realism," 118.
41 Ibid., 119.
42 Misha Meyers, "Situations for Living," 173.
43 Heddon, *Autobiography and Performance*, 88.
44 *Garden//Suburbia: Mapping the Non-Aristocratic in Lawrence Park* premiered in June 2010 as part of Performance Studies International 16. Melanie Bennett and Hartley Jafine were the autobiographical performers and guides. Andy Houston was the director. Aaron Collier designed the soundtrack.
45 Kirk Williams, "Anti-theatricality and the Limits of Naturalism," 97–98.
46 J. Hillis Miller, "The Fiction of Realism," 125.
47 Bennett et al., *Garden//Suburbia*, 10.
48 Eric Auerbach, *Mimesis*, 413.
49 The neighbourhood of Lawrence Park is bounded by Lawrence Avenue on the north, Bayview Avenue on the east, Yonge Street on the west, and the Blythwood Ravine to the south. Mount Pleasant Road runs north–south and is the main thoroughfare of the community. According to

Barbara Myrvold and Lynda Moon, "The beginnings of Lawrence Park go back to 1907 when Wilfrid Servington Dinnick, the young, English-born president of a Toronto loan and mortgage company, convinced the board of directors to purchase two farm properties near Yonge Street and Lawrence Avenue East. His intention was to create a garden suburb – one of the first in Canada – for the city's middle classes" (*Historical Walking Tour*).

50 John Barber, "We know something the fearmongers don't" quoted in Micallef and Zuber.

51 Shawn Micallef and Marlena Zuber, *Stroll: Psychogeographic Walking Tours of Toronto*, 52.

52 Laura Levin, "Can the City Speak? Site-Specific Art After Poststructuralism," 250.

53 Williams, "Anti-theatricality and the Limits of Naturalism," 101.

54 It is important throughout this discussion, as with any treatment of autobiographical work, to keep in mind that "Hartley" and "Melanie" are fictional correlatives of their real-world counterparts. Although they certainly share a physical body and likely share a significant portion of their life experiences, these two distinct ontological personae must not be conflated carelessly. I will use "Bennett" and "Jafine" to refer to the world[a] creators of the work and "Melanie" and "Hartley" to refer to their world[b] characters.

55 Bennett et al., *Garden//Suburbia*, 1.

56 The "Lawrence Park Survival Kits" consisted of shopping bags blazoned with the names and logos of local upscale shops. They were filled with a water bottle, a field guide featuring "facts" about Lawrence Park, and a map of the route. Also included were two contrasting postcards of 79 Dawlish Avenue: one showed a photograph of the house with a sold sign and the other showed a child's drawing of the house as an idealized place to have Christmas morning. Audience members were invited to choose their own favourite house along the route, write a message on one of the postcards (completing the phrase "This is a nice house to BLANK in"), and leave it in the mailbox. The survival kit also included baggies for collecting souvenirs along the way (pine cones, rocks, etc.), and little Canadian flags to hold during the singing of Alexander Muir's "Maple Leaf Forever" song.

57 Bennett et al., *Garden//Suburbia*, 1.

58 Ibid.

59 Ibid., 2.

60 Ibid., 4.

61 Ibid.
62 BVG is Bayview Glen Day Camp. UCC is Upper Canada College. In the play, Hartley never explains what BVG is and so the reference remains impenetrable to those who are not in the know, further reinforcing the division between Lawrence Park insiders and outsiders.
63 Bennett et al., *Garden//Suburbia*, 1, 2.
64 Ibid., 2.
65 Ibid.
66 Ibid.
67 Ibid., 12.
68 Ibid., 12–13.
69 Ibid., 3.
70 Ibid.
71 Ibid.
72 Ibid.
73 A prototype of *Landline* was live tested in September 2013 between Vancouver and Halifax. The first full production ran in August 2014 partnering Ottawa with Dartmouth. Subsequent productions include Halifax-Cardiff (November 2014), Reykjavik-Edinburgh (August 2015), Vancouver-Kitchener (September 2015), Mashteuiatsh-Montreal-Wendake (June 2016), Whitehorse-Ottawa (June 2016), and Calgary-St. John's (January 2017).
74 Bennett et al., *Garden//Suburbia*, 6.
75 Ibid., 12.
76 Ibid., 6.
77 Harvey and Wong, *Landline*, 71.
78 Ibid., 70.
79 Ibid., 70.
80 George Lakoff and Mark Johnson, *Metaphors We Live By*, 3.
81 Ibid., 30–32.
82 Don Ihde, "Parmenidean Meditations," 73.
83 Peter Salvatore Petralia, "Headspace: Architectural Space in the Brain," 97.
84 Keren Zaiontz, "Ambulatory Audiences and Animate Sites," 176.
85 Harvey and Wong, *Landline*, 73.
86 Petralia, "Headspace: Architectural Space in the Brain," 102.
87 Harvey and Wong, *Landline*, 70.
88 Ibid.
89 Petralia, "Headspace: Architectural Space in the Brain," 97.
90 Claire Bishop, "Outsourcing Authenticity?," 110.
91 Ibid., 113.

92 Harvey and Wong, *Landline*, 71.
93 Ibid., 72.
94 Ibid., 74.
95 Ibid.
96 Ibid.
97 Ibid., 72.
98 Ibid., 74.
99 Ibid., 71.
100 Ibid.
101 Ibid.
102 Edmund Husserl, *Cartesian Meditations*, §8.
103 Husserl, *Ideas: General Introduction to Pure Phenomenology*, §27.
104 Husserl, *Cartesian Meditations*, §15.
105 Harvey and Wong, *Landline*, 73–4.
106 Ibid., 74.
107 For each iteration of *Landline*, certain sections of the audio track were changed to align with the new location, including mentions of the cities' names, their populations, the percentage of the population of Canada represented by the combined cities, and the distance between the cities. In the first Field Recording, the narrator informs us that the background sound we are hearing is the sound of our "parallel location" (Harvey and Wong, *Landline*, 73).
108 Harvey and Wong, *Landline*, 74–5.
109 Ibid., 72.
110 Ibid.
111 Kwon, *One Place After Another*, 159.
112 Turner, "Finding a Vocabulary for Site-Specific Performance," 374.
113 Harvey and Wong, *Landline*, 73.
114 Ibid., 74.
115 Yi-Fu Tuan, *Space and Place*, 16.
116 Harvey and Wong, *Landline*, 73.
117 Ibid., 71.
118 Ibid.
119 Harvey and Wong, *Landline*, 74.
120 Ibid.
121 "rendezvous:" Canadian Oxford Dictionary.
122 Harvey and Wong, *Landline*, 71.
123 Ibid.
124 Tuan, *Space and Place*, 34–50.
125 Harvey and Wong, *Landline*, 71.

126 Ibid.

127 Ibid., 74.

128 Ibid.

129 Audience text conversations shared on condition of anonymity, 13 June 2016, Whitehorse–Ottawa.

130 Audience text conversations shared on condition of anonymity, 13–15 June 2016, Whitehorse–Ottawa.

131 Bennett et al., *Garden//Suburbia*, 9.

132 Ibid., 10.

133 Harvey and Wong, *Landline*, 73.

134 Ibid.

135 Ibid.

136 Ibid., 75.

137 Ibid., 76.

138 Ibid., 77.

139 Zaiontz, "Ambulatory Audiences and Animate Sites," 167.

140 Christopher Tilley, *A Phenomenology of Landscape, Places, Paths and Monuments*, 12.

141 Kwon, *One Place After Another*, 165.

Chapter 6

1 Bishop, "Outsourcing Authenticity," 4.

2 Adam Alston, "Audience Participation and Neoliberal Value," 129.

3 Janet Murray, *Hamlet on the Holodeck*, 98.

4 Keren Zaiontz, "Narcissistic Spectatorship;" White "On Immersive Theatre;" Fuchs, *The Death of Character*.

5 Jen Harvie, *Fair Play*; Jackson, *Social Works*; Claire Bishop, *Artificial Hells*.

6 Harvie, 41.

7 Ibid., 47.

8 Maurya Wickstrom, *Performing Consumers*, 4; Susan Bennett and Marlis Schweitzer, "In the Window at Disney."

9 Jacques Rancière, *The Emancipated Spectator*, 2.

10 Rancière, *Aesthetics and its Discontents*, 25.

11 Lavender, *Performance in the Twenty-First Century*, 139.

12 Rancière, *The Emancipated Spectator*, 49.

13 Ibid.

14 Adam Alston, *Beyond Immersive*, 7–9.

15 Ibid., 21–2.

16 Alston, *Beyond Immersive*, 23.

17 Slavoj Žižek, *The Parallax View*, 4.
18 Ibid., 6.
19 Boenisch, "Theatre of Encounter," 171–2.
20 Laura Levin, *Performing Ground*, 94.
21 Ibid.
22 Lavender, *Performance in the Twenty-First Century*, 81.
23 Ibid., 82.
24 Ibid., 87.
25 Stanton B Garner Jr, *Bodied Spaces*, 43.
26 Harley Hahn, *The Internet Complete Reference*, 553.
27 Murray, *Hamlet on the Holodeck*, 26.
28 Machon, *Immersive Theatres*, 63.
29 Ibid., 41. Machon cites Michael Coveney's review of *You Me Bum Bum Train* where he accuses the work of "triviality and low-level fascism."
30 Michael Billington, "E is for Experiment."
31 "Mark and Marichka," *Counting Sheep*.
32 Ibid.
33 Workshopped in February 2015 at St Vladimir's Institute in Toronto, *Counting Sheep* premiered in August of that year at SummerWorks. Subsequent productions have been mounted in Toronto (May/June 2016), at the Edinburgh Festival Fringe (August 2016), Recklinghausen, Germany (May 2017) and Kilkenny Ireland (August 2017). Counting Sheep was created by Lemon Bucket Orkestra. The members of Lemon Bucket Orkestra are: Mark Marczyk (violin, vocals), Marichka Marczyk (vocals, accordion) Os Kar (savage drum, vocals), Alex Nahirny (guitar), Jaash Singh (darbouka), Stephania Woloshyn (dance, vocals, tambourine), Ian Tulloch (sousaphone), Michael Louis Johnson (flugelhorn), Mike Romaniak (sopilka), Eli Camilo (trombone), and Nathan Dell-Vandenberg (trombone).
34 Written by Tim Carlson and directed by Jeremy Waller, *Foreign Radical* is performed by Milton Lim and Aryo Khakpour. Sound design by David Mesiha and lighting design by Kyla Gardiner, video design by Cande Andrade and dramaturgy by Kathleen Flaherty. *Foreign Radical* premiered at The Cultch Culture Lab in Vancouver in 2015. It was subsequently remounted in Vancouver in February 2017, after which it toured to Quebec City (June 2017) and the Edinburgh Festival Fringe (August 2017).
35 Ulrich Beck, "Living in the World Risk Society," 332.
36 Adam Alston, "Damocles," 347.
37 Beck, "Living in the World Risk Society," 322.

38 Ibid., 333–4.
39 Žižek, *Welcome to the Desert of the Real*, 19.
40 Hal Foster, *The Return of the Real*, 130.
41 Ibid., xiii.
42 Ibid., 132.
43 Roland Barthes, *Camera Lucida*, 26–7. "The second element will break (or punctuate) the *studium*. This time it is not I who seek it out (as I invest the field of the *studium* with my sovereign consciousness), it is this element which rises from the scene, shoots out of it like an arrow, and pierces me. A Latin word exists to designate this wound, this prick, this mark made by a pointed instrument: the word suits me all the better in that it also refers to the notion of punctuation, and because the photographs I am speaking of are in effect punctuated, sometimes even speckled with these sensitive points; precisely, these marks, these wounds are so many points. This second element which will disturb the *studium* I shall therefore call *punctum*; for *punctum* is also: sting, speck, cut, little hole – and also a cast of the dice. A photograph's *punctum* is that accident which pricks me (but also bruises me, is poignant to me)."
44 Foster, *The Return of the Real*, 136.
45 Ibid., 134.
46 Žižek, *The Parallax View*, 29.
47 Ibid.; Slavoj Žižek, "Grimaces of the Real," 59.
48 White, "On Immersive Theatre," 227
49 Erin Hurley, *Theatre & Feeling*, 33.
50 Gareth White, "On Immersive Theatre," 228.
51 Ibid., 232.
52 Ibid., 233.
53 Sophie Nield, "The Rise of the Character Named Spectator," 534.
54 Murray, *Hamlet on the Holodeck*, 101.
55 Ibid., 104.
56 Patrick Duggan, *Trauma-Tragedy*, 65.
57 Carlson, *Shattering Hamlet's Mirror*, 18.
58 Cathy Caruth, *Unclaimed Experience*, 4.
59 Duggan, *Trauma-Tragedy*, 58.
60 Ibid.
61 Michael Taussig, *Mimesis and Alterity*, 21.
62 Ibid., 61.
63 Duggan, *Trauma-Tragedy*, 64.
64 Ibid., 38.
65 Ibid., 39.

66 Ibid., 40.

67 Ibid., 53.

68 Scott Magelssen, *Simming*, 3.

69 Ibid.

70 Ibid.

71 Ibid., 13–18.

72 Drawing on case studies like *Follow the North Star* which casts audience members as African-American slaves seeking freedom from slavery by following the Underground Railroad, Magelssen directs critical attention to the problem of stepping into someone else's shoes and the ethical mismatch between threatened historical bodies (especially racialized bodies) and privileged (read secure) contemporary touristic bodies. (Magelssen, 189).

73 Žižek, *Welcome to the Desert of the Real*, 16.

74 Duggan, *Trauma-Tragedy*, 51.

75 Auslander, *Liveness*, 15.

76 Rebecca Schneider, *Performing Remains*, 112.

77 Ibid.

78 Duggan, *Trauma-Tragedy*, 67.

79 Ibid., 68.

80 Ibid., 69.

81 Gareth White, *Audience Participation*, 73.

82 Ibid., 124.

83 Evan Thompson, *Mind in Life*, 237.

84 Carrie Noland, *Agency and Embodiment*, 2–3.

85 Ibid., 3.

86 Duggan, *Trauma-Tragedy*, 57.

87 Sally Barnes and André Lepicki, *The Senses in Performance*, 1.

88 Allison Griffiths, *Shivers Down Your Spine*, 3, 285.

89 Alston, *Beyond Immersive*, 61.

90 Nield, "The Rise of the Character Named Spectator," 531.

91 Ibid., 534.

92 Ibid., 533.

93 It is my belief that this young man was indeed a member of the audience and not a "planted" member of the ensemble. I do not remember this happening when I saw the show live in June 2016 in Toronto. But I could be mistaken.

94 Magelssen, *Simming*, 16.

95 Ibid., 15–16.

96 Theatre Conspiracy, *Foreign Radical*, 61.

97 Gregory Bateson, *Steps to an Ecology of Mind*; Ivo Osolsobě, "Course de Théâtristique Générale."

98 Alston, "Audience Participation"; Zaiontz, "Narcissistic Spectatorship."

99 Fuchs, *The Death of Character*, 137.

100 Magelssen, *Simming*, 11.

101 Duggan, *Trauma-Tragedy*, 83.

102 Alston, *Beyond Immersive*, 168–9.

103 Theatre Conspiracy, *Foreign Radical*, 64.

104 Ibid.

105 Theatre Conspiracy, *Foreign Radical*, 66.

106 Alston, *Beyond Immersive*, 130.

107 Magelssen, *Simming*, 5.

108 Ibid., 6.

109 Richard Schechner, *Environmental Theatre*, 77.

110 White, "On Immersive Theatre," 222.

111 Theatre Conspiracy, *Foreign Radical*, 60.

112 Ibid., 62.

113 Ibid.

114 Hailing from Vancouver, the creators of *Foreign Radical* assumed an English-speaking audience. This linguistic frame had a significant effect on the show when I had the opportunity to see it during its run in Quebec City at the Carrefour International de Théâtre Festival in June 2017. Although the show proceeded in English, it was attended by a majority francophone audience at the two shows I saw. With varying levels of bilingual comprehension, audience members assisted others by whispering or quietly relating the translation of each question or instruction into French. In one performance, an audience member self-selected to translate aloud from English into French as the show proceeded. During the debate section, the conversation flowed in both French and English. This fluidity of cooperation runs counter to the ostensibly divisive effect of the Arabic and Farsi projections. I would be curious to see the show with speakers of those languages present in the audience. Having audience members repeat the Host's questions also changes the power dynamic of the play, insofar as instructions are no longer emitted from a single source of authority.

115 Theatre Conspiracy, *Foreign Radical*, 70.

116 Machon, *Immersive Theatres*, 23.

117 Ibid., 37.

118 Sima Sahar Zerehi, "Counting Sheep: A Play, a Dance Performance, a Concert?"

119 Kalyna Kardash, "Counting Sheep: A Story of the Maidan, Love and War."
120 Jessica Santone, The Economics of The Performative Audience," 30.
121 Rancière, *The Emancipated Spectator*, 56.
122 Tony Myers, *Slavoj Žižek*, 27.
123 Ibid., 28.

Chapter 7

1 Philip Lewin and J. Patrick Williams, "Ideology and Practice," 65.
2 Ibid.
3 Charles Taylor, *The Ethics of Authenticity*, 29.
4 David Boyle, *Authenticity*, 17.
5 Andrew Potter, *The Authenticity Hoax*, 3.
6 Ibid., 78.
7 Lionel Trilling, *Sincerity and Authenticity*, 93.
8 Gilmore and Pine, *Authenticity*.
9 Bernd H. Schmitt, *Experiential Marketing*, 13.
10 Ibid., 64–9.
11 http://www.rainforestcafe.com/.
12 http://www.firkinpubs.com/.
13 https://www.americangirl.com/create-your-own/.
14 Lavender, *Performance in the Twenty-First Century*, 165.
15 Fuchs, *The Death of Character*, 130.
16 I am using solo immersive as an umbrella term that included both one-to-one encounters between one audience member and one performance and also situations where there is only one audience member who encounters performers sometimes singly but also sometimes in groups. The key feature in solo immersive is that these works are constructed for an audience of one.
17 Alston, "Audience Participation and Neoliberal Value Risk," 130.
18 Zaiontz, "Narcissistic Spectatorship," 407.
19 Ibid., 408.
20 Ibid., 411.
21 Directed by Liam Karry. Produced by Danyal Martin. Performed by Alex Dault, Joanne Williams, Stephanie Vaillant, Adam Wray, Scott Dermody, Leslie Thorpe, Annie Briggs, Talia Acker, Ryan Graham, and Fernanda Fukamati. Stage management by Mary Fraser. Set design by Dan Rider. Lighting design by Conor Moore. Sound by Doug Brown. *Everyman* was presented by Single Thread Theatre Company in the basement of St James Anglican Church, Kingston.

22 Žižek, *The Parallax View*, 147.
23 Žižek, *Welcome to the Desert of the Real*, 10.
24 White, *Audience Participation*, 171.
25 Martin Welton, *Feeling Theatre*, 50.
26 Billington, "E is for Experiment."
27 Ibid.
28 Murray, *Hamlet on the Holodeck*, 135.
29 Laura Levin raises a similar concern in her discussion of her experience
    in Punchdrunk's *Sleep No More*, being acutely aware of being deliberately
    separated from her companions in an environment where fellow audience
    members also constituted part of the scenographic realm and being "bold"
    was specifically encouraged – an invitation bolstered by the consumption
    of alcohol in the theatre bar before the show. (*Performing Ground*, 84–5)
    Specifically, in the production of *Everyman* discussed here, I have a very
    clear recollection of my mental reaction when I found myself alone
    enclosed in a very small space, about the size of a closet, with a male
    performer who was also at the time my student. My dominant thought
    being "This is not good." Of course, all was well in the end, but in a
    critical analysis this train of thought is not to be dismissed as it colours the
    experience of that moment.
30 Murray, *Hamlet on the Holodeck*, 134–5.
31 Ridout, *Stage Fright*, 74.
32 Garner, *Bodied Spaces*, 50–1.
33 White, *Audience Participation*, 76, 82.
34 Erin Hurley, *Theatre & Feeling*, 58.
35 Ibid., 44.
36 Ibid., 48.
37 White, *Audience Participation*, 154.
38 *Everyman*, 379.
39 Ibid., 380.
40 Ibid., 381.
41 Ibid., 380.
42 Ibid.
43 Ibid., 385.
44 Ibid., 387.
45 Ibid., 390.
46 Fintan Walsh, *Theatre & Therapy*, 6.
47 Walsh, "Touching, Flirting, Whispering," 57.
48 Hurley, *Theatre & Feeling*; Michael Hardt and Antonio Negri, *Multitude*;
    Alston, *Beyond Immersive*.

49 Walsh, "Touching, Flirting, Whispering," 59.
50 Deirdre Heddon and Adrian Howells, "From Talking to Silence," 1.
51 Deirdre Heddon, Helen Iball, and Rachel Zerihan, "Come Closer," 123.
52 Ibid., 124.
53 Ibid., 127.
54 Ibid.
55 Alston, "Damocles," 352.
56 Ridout, *Stage Fright*, 80.
57 Alston, "Damocles," 344.
58 Ibid., 347–8.
59 Ibid., 348.
60 Ibid., 348–9.
61 Ibid., 353.
62 Ibid.
63 Ibid., 354.

Chapter 8

1 Edward Relph, "The Critical Description of Confused Geographies," 152.
2 Ibid., 155.
3 Diamond, "Mimesis, Mimicry, and the 'True-Real,'" 69.
4 Baz Kershaw, *The Radical in Performance*," 16–17.
5 William Davies, "The Age of Post-Truth Politics."
6 Jon Sharman, "What You're Seeing Isn't Happening."
7 "The Art of the Lie."
8 Peter Pomerantsev, "Russia and the Menace of New Reality."
9 Ibid.
10 Tomlin, *Acts and Apparitions*, 143–4.
11 Kwon, *One Place After Another*, 166.
12 Ibid., 165.
13 Ibid.
14 Jane Wagner, *The Search for Signs of Intelligent Life in the Universe*, 18.
15 Slavoj Žižek, *The Sublime Object of Ideology*, 35.
16 Žižek, *The Ticklish Subject*, 374.
17 Kwon, *One Place After Another*, 166.
18 Nigel Thrift, *Non-Representational Theory: Space, Politics, Affect*, 19.
19 Lehmann, *Postdramatic Theatre*, 186; original emphasis.

Bibliography

100% Vancouver. Performed 21–22 January 2011. Director Ami Gladstone. Casting director and dramaturge Tim Carlson. Casting assistants Donna Soares, Sara Bynes, Xanthe Faulkner. Produced by PuSh International Performing Arts Festival and Theatre Replacement.

300 TAPES. Performed 1 December 2010. Co-creators Ame Henderson and Bobby Theodore. Performers Joe Cobden, Frank Cox-O'Connell, and Brendan Gall. Sound designer Anna Friz. Scenographer Trevor Schwellnus. Costume designer Bojana Stancic. Dramaturge Vicki Stroich. Produced by Public Recordings.

Ahmed, Sara. *Strange Encounters: Embodied Others in Post-Coloniality*. London: Routledge, 2000.

– *The Cultural Politics of Emotion*. Edinburgh: Edinburgh UP, 2004.

Alston, Adam. "Damocles and the Plucked: Audience Participation and Risk in *Half Cut*." *Contemporary Theatre Review* 22.3 (2012): 344–54.

– "Audience Participation and Neoliberal Value: Risk, Agency and Responsibility in Immersive Theatre." *Performance Research* 18.2 (2013): 128–38.

– *Beyond Immersive Theatre: Aesthetics, Politics and Productive Participation*. New York and London: Palgrave Macmillan, 2016.

Auerbach, Erich. *Mimesis: The Representation of Reality in Western Literature*. Trans. Willard Trask. New York: Doubleday, 1953.

Auslander, Philip. *Liveness*. New York: Routledge, 1999.

Baggott, Jim. *A Beginner's Guide to Reality*. London: Penguin, 2005.

Bailes, Sara Jane. *Performance Theatre and the Poetics of Failure: Forced Entertainment, Goat Island, Elevator Repair Service*. London: Routledge, 2011.

Barber, John. "We Know Something the Fearmongers Don't." *The Globe and Mail*. 13 March 2004. M2.

Barnes, Sally, and André Lepicki. *The Senses in Performance*. London: Routledge, 2007.

Barthes, Roland. *Camera Lucida: Reflections on Photography*. Trans. Richard Howard. New York: Hill & Wang, 1980.

– "The Reality Effect." *French Literary Theory Today: A Reader*. Ed. Tzvetan Todorov. Cambridge: Cambridge UP, 1982. 11–17.

– *S/Z*. 1973. Trans. Richard Miller. Oxford: Blackwell, 1990.

Bateson, Gregory. *Steps to an Ecology of Mind*. New York: Ballantine, 1972.

Baudrillard, Jean. *Simulacra and Simulation*. Trans. Sheila Faria Glaser. Ann Arbor: U of Michigan P, 1994.

Bauman, Zygmunt. "The World Inhospitable to Levinas." *Philosophy Today* 43.2 (Summer 1999): 151–67.

– *Culture in a Liquid Modern World*. Trans. Lydia Bauman. Cambridge: Polity, 2011.

Beck, Ulrich. "Living in the World Risk Society." *Economy and Society* 35.3 (August 2006): 329–45.

Belsey, Catherine. *Culture and the Real*. London: Routledge, 2005.

Benjamin, Walter. "The Work of Art in the Age of Mechanical Reproduction (1936)." *Illuminations: Essays and Reflections*. Ed. Hannah Arendt. New York: Harcourt, Brace and World, 1968.

Bennett, Melanie, Hartley Jafine, and Aaron Collier. *Garden//Suburbia: Mapping the Non-Aristocratic in Lawrence Park*. 2010. Unpublished manuscript.

Bennett, Susan. "3-D A/B." *Theatre and AutoBiography: Writing and Performing Lives in Theory and Practice*. Ed. Sherrill Grace and Jerry Wasserman. Vancouver: Talonbooks, 2006. 33–48.

Bennett, Susan, and Marlis Schweitzer. "In the Window at Disney: A Lifetime of Brand Desire" *TDR: The Drama Review* 58.4 (2014): 23–31.

Billington, Michael. "E is for Experiment." *The Guardian*. 10 January 2012.

Bishop, Claire. "Outsourcing Authenticity: Delegated Performances in Contemporary Art." *Double Agent*, curated by Claire Bishop and Mark Sladen. Institute of Contemporary Arts, 2010.

– *Artificial Hells: Participatory Art and the Politics of Spectatorship*. London and New York: Verso, 2012.

Boenisch, Peter. "Towards a Theatre of Encounter and Experience: Reflexive Dramaturgies and Classic Texts." *Contemporary Theatre Review* 20.2 (2010): 162–72.

Bolter, Jay David, and Richard Grusin. *Remediation: Understanding New Media*. Cambridge, MA: MIT P, 2000.

Boyle, David. *Authenticity: Brands, Fakes, Spin and the Lust for Real Life*. London: Harper Perennial, 2003.

Brown, Ross. *Sound: A Reader in Theatre Practice.* New York and London: Palgrave Macmillan, 2010.

Bruzzi, Stella. *New Documentary: A Critical Introduction.* 2nd ed. London: Routledge, 2006.

Butler, Judith. *Gender Trouble.* New York: Routledge, 2006.

Carlson, Marvin. *Shattering Hamlet's Mirror: Theatre and Reality.* Ann Arbor: U of Michigan P, 2016.

Carlson, Tim. "Masters of Protokoll." *100% Vancouver* programme. 2011.

Caruth, Cathy. *Unclaimed Experience: Trauma, Narrative and History.* Baltimore: Johns Hopkins UP, 1996.

Chamberlain, Catherine E., and Robin M. Strode. *The Source for Down Syndrome.* East Moline, IL: LinguiSystems, 1999.

Chemers, Michael. *Staging Stigma: A Critical Examination of the American Freak Show.* New York: Palgrave Macmillan, 2008.

Choinière, Olivier. *Polyglotte.* 2015. Unpublished manuscript.

Christov-Bakargiev, Carolyn. *Janet Cardiff: A Survey of Works Including Collaborations with George Bures Miller and Carolyn Christov-Bakargiev.* New York: Distributed Arts Publishers, 2001.

Citizenship and Immigration Canada. *Discover Canada: The Rights and Responsibilities of Citizenship,* 2012.

Citoyennéte et Immigration Canada. *Decouvrir le Canada: Les droits et responsabilités lies à la citoyenneté,* 2012.

Citron, Paula. "*Winners and Losers*: Virtuoso Word Play Gives Way to Nasty Verbal Sparring in this Tour de Force." *The Globe and Mail,* 28 May 2013.

Colenbrander, Ariane. "100% Vancouver's Tim Carlson." *Vancouverscape.* 12 January 2011.

Coleridge, Samuel Taylor. "Biographia Literaria." *The Complete Works of Samuel Taylor Coleridge.* Ed. W.G.T. Shedd. Vol. 3: Biographia Literaria. New York: Harper, 1884.

– "Progress of the Drama." *The Complete Works of Samuel Taylor Coleridge.* Ed. W.G.T. Shedd. Vol. 4: Lectures Upon Shakespeare and Other Dramatists. New York: Harper, 1884.

Counting Sheep. Performed June 2016. Creators: Lemon Bucket Orkestra. Performers: Mark Marczyk, Marichka Marczyk, Os Kar, Alex Nahirny, Jaash Singh, Stephania Woloshyn, Ian Tulloch, Michael Louis Johnson, Mike Romaniak, Eli Camilo, and Nathan Dell-Vandenberg. Produced by Michael Rubenfeld.

Couser, G. Thomas. *Vulnerable Subjects: Ethics and Life Writing.* Ithaca: Cornell UP, 2004.

Coveney, Michael "Stage Directions: Immersive Theatre." *Prospect.* 19 August 2010.

Cushman, Robert. "Theatre Review: Judith Thompson's RARE Makes the Familiar Strange." *National Post*. 2 February 2013.

Davies, William. "The Age of Post-Truth Politics." *New York Times*. 24 August 2016.

Dawson, G.F. *Documentary Theatre in the United States: An Historical Survey and Analysis of Its Content, Form, and Stagecraft*. Westport, CT: Greenwood P, 1999.

Debord, Guy. *Society of the Spectacle*. Trans. Donald Nicholson-Smith. New York: Zone Books, 1994.

Derrida, Jacques. *Limited Inc*. Evanston: Northwestern UP, 1972.

– *Of Grammatology*. Baltimore: Johns Hopkins UP, 1976.

Diamond, Elin. "Mimesis, Mimicry, and the 'True-Real.'" *Modern Drama* 32.1 (1989): 59–73.

– *Unmaking Mimesis: Essays on Feminism and Theatre*. London: Routledge, 1997.

Dickens, Charles. *Sketches by Boz, illustrative of everyday life and everyday people*. Transcribed from 1903 London: Chapman and Hall edition by David Price. Project Gutenberg. 6 December 2009.

"Down Syndrome." Health Service Executive – Ireland (HSE).

Duff, Bryan. "Our Fledgling Theatre Company's Only Goal Is to Constantly Betray Our Audience's Trust." *McSweeney's Internet Tendency*. 3 May 2016.

Duggan, Patrick. *Trauma-Tragedy: Symptoms of Contemporary Performance*. Manchester: Manchester UP, 2012.

Eakin, Paul John. *Fictions in Autobiography: Studies in the Art of Self-Invention*. Princeton UP, 1985.

Egan, Susanna. *Burdens of Proof: Faith, Doubt, and Identity in Autobiography*. Waterloo: Wilfrid Laurier UP, 2011.

– *Mirror Talk: Genres of Crisis in Contemporary Autobiography*. Chapel Hill: U of North Carolina P, 1999.

Everyman. Performed 23 January–2 February 2007. Director Liam Karry. Performers Alex Dault, Joanne Williams, Stephanie Vaillant, Adam Wray, Scott Dermody, Leslie Thorpe, Annie Briggs, Talia Acker, Ryan Graham, and Fernanda Fukamati. Produced by Single Thread Theatre Company.

Everyman. *Broadview Anthology of Medieval Drama*. Ed. Christina M. Fitzgerald and John T. Sebastian. Peterborough: Broadview P, 2013. 379–91.

Féral, Josette. "Performance and Theatricality: The Subject Demystified." Trans. T. Lyons. *Modern Drama* 25.1 (1982): 170–81.

– "Theatricality: The Specificity of Theatrical Language." Trans. Ronald P. Bermingham. *SubStance* 31.2–3 (2002): 94–108.

Filewod, Alan. *Collective Encounters: Documentary Theatre in English Canada*. Toronto: U of Toronto P, 1987.

Fischer-Lichte, Erika. "Reality and Fiction in Contemporary Theatre." *Theatre Research International* 33.1 (2008): 84–96.

Foreign Radical. Performed 9–10 June 2017. Director Jeremy Waller. Performers Aryo Khakpour and Milton Lim. Produced by Theatre Conspiracy and Carrefour international de théâtre.

Forsyth, Alison, and Chris Megson., eds. *Get Real: Documentary Theatre Past and Present*. Houndmills: Palgrave Macmillan, 2009.

Foster, Hal. *The Return of the Real: The Avant-Garde at the End of the Century*. Cambridge, MA: MIT Press, 1996.

Fried, Michael. *Art and Objecthood: Essays and Reviews*. Chicago and London: U of Chicago P, 1998. 148–72.

Fuchs, Elinor. *The Death of Character: Perspectives on Theatre after Modernism*. Bloomington: Indiana UP, 1996.

Funk, Wolfgang, Florian Gross, and Irmtraud Huber, eds. *The Aesthetics of Authenticity: Medial Constructions of the Real*. Germany: Transcript Verlag, 2012.

Garde, Ulrike, and Meg Mumford. "Postdramatic Reality Theatre and Productive Insecurity: Destabilising Encounters with the Unfamiliar in Theatre from Sydney and Berlin." *Postdramatic Theatre and the Political*. Ed. Karen Jürs-Munby, Jerome Carroll, and Steve Giles. London: Bloomsbury, 2013. 147–64.

Garland-Thomson, Rosemarie. *Freakery: Cultural Spectacles of the Extraordinary Body*. New York: NYU P, 1996.

– *Extraordinary Bodies: Figuring Disability in American Culture and Literature*. New York: Columbia, 1997.

Garner, Stanton B. Jr. *Bodied Spaces: Phenomenology and Performance in Contemporary Drama*. Ithaca and London: Cornell UP, 1994.

– "Sensing Realism: Illusionism, Actuality, and the Theatrical Sensorium." *The Senses in Performance*. Ed. Sally Barnes and André Lepicki. 115–22.

Gilmore, James H., and B. Joseph Pine II. *Authenticity: What Consumers Want*. Boston: Harvard Business School, 2007.

– *The Experience Economy: Work Is Theatre and Every Business Is a Stage*. Boston: Harvard Business School, 1999.

Goffman, Erving. *The Presentation of Self in Everyday Life*. New York: Doubleday Anchor, 1959.

Goodwin, Andrew. *Dancing in the Distraction Factory: Music Television and Popular Culture*. Minneapolis, U of Minneapolis P, 1992.

Gorman, Sarah. "Richard Maxwell and the New York City Players – The End of Reality." *Making Contemporary Theatre: International Rehearsal Processes*. Ed. Jen Harvie and Andy Lavender. Manchester, Manchester UP, 2010. 180–201.

Grehan, Helena. *Performance, Ethics and Spectatorship in a Global Age.* Basingstoke and New York: Palgrave Macmillan, 2009.

Griffiths, Allison. *Shivers Down Your Spine: Cinema, Museums, and the Immersive View.* New York, Columbia UP, 2008.

Grossberg, Lawrence. "The Media Economy of Rock Culture: Cinema, Postmodernity and Authenticity." *Sound and Vision: The Music Video Reader.* Ed. Simon Frith, Andrew Goodwin, and Lawrence Grossberg. London, New York: Routledge, 1993. 159–79.

Gubrium, J.F., and J.A. Holstein *The Self We Live By: Narrative Identity in a Postmodern World.* New York: Oxford UP, 2000.

Hahn, Harley. *The Internet Complete Reference.* 2nd ed. Berkeley, Osborne-McGraw Hill, 1996.

Hahn, Harlan. "The Politics of Physical Differences: Disability and Discrimination." *Journal of Social Issues* 44.1 (1988): 39–47.

Hardt, Michael, and Antonio Negri. *Multitude: War and Democracy in the Age of Empire.* New York: Penguin, 2004.

Harvey, Dustin, and Adrienne Wong. *Landline*: Halifax-Vancouver. *Canadian Theatre Review* 159 (Summer 2014): 68–80.

Harvie, Jen. *Fair Play: Art, Performance and Neoliberalism.* London: Palgrave Macmillan, 2013.

Heddon, Deirdre. *Autobiography and Performance.* New York: Palgrave Macmillan, 2008.

Heddon, Deirdre, and Adrian Howells. "From Talking to Silence: A Confessional Journey." *PAJ: A Journal of Performance and Art* 33.1 (2011): 1–12.

Heddon, Deirdre, Helen Iball, and Rachel Zerihan. "Come Closer: Confessions of Intimate Spectators in One to One Performance." *Contemporary Theatre Review* 22.1 (2012): 120–33.

Historical Walking Tour of Lawrence Park. Toronto Public Library Board in partnership with Lawrence Park Ratepayers' Association and North Toronto Historical Society, 2007.

Horner, Mariah and Grahame Renyk. "Matter Matters: Performing a Stone in the Woods." *Canadian Theatre Review* 163 (Summer 2015): 59–63.

Hugo, Victor. "Preface to *Cromwell.*" The Dramas, Complete and Unabridged of Victor Hugo. Trans. I.G. Burnham. Philadelphia: George Barrie and Son, 1896.

Hurley, Erin. *Theatre & Feeling.* London: Palgrave Macmillan, 2010.

– ed., *Theatres of Affect.* New Essays on Canadian Theatre, volume 4. Toronto: Playwrights Canada, 2014.

Husserl, Edmund. *Cartesian Meditations: An Introduction to Phenomenology.* 1929. Trans. Dorian Cairns. The Hague: Martinus Nijhoff, 1960.

– *Ideas: General Introduction to Pure Phenomenology.* 1931. Trans. W.R. Boyce Gibson. London: G. Allen and Unwin, 1962.

Ihde, Don. "Parmenidean Meditations." *Sense and Significance.* Pittsburgh: Dusquesne UP, 1973. 69–81.

Ingarden, Roman. *The Literary Work of Art: An Investigation on the Borderlines of Ontology, Logic, and Theory of Literature.* Trans. George G. Grabowicz. Studies in Phenomenology and Existential Philosophy. Ed. James M. Edie. Evanston: Northwestern UP, 1973.

Isherwood, Charles. "Friendship Frays, a Topic at a Time." *New York Times* 7 January 2015.

Jackson, Shannon. *Social Works: Performing Art, Supporting Publics.* New York, Routledge, 2011.

Jacobson, Kelsey. "Through the Fictive to the Real(ish): Affective Time and the Representation of 'Real Newfoundland' in Rising Tide Theatre's Trinity Pageant." *Theatre Research in Canada* 39.1 (2018): 42–57.

Kaplan, Jon. "Mix Tape Mashup." *Now Magazine,* 25 November 2010.

Kardash, Kalyna. "Counting Sheep: A Story of the Maidan, Love and War." *Ukrainian Echo.* 17 January 2015.

Kaye, Nick. "Introduction: Site-Specifics." *Site-Specific Art: Performance, Place and Documentation.* Ed. Nick Kaye. London and New York: Routledge, 2000.

Keats, John. *The Complete Poetical Works and Letters of John Keats.* Boston and New York: Houghton Mifflin, 1899.

Kershaw, Baz. *The Radical in Performance: Between Brecht and Baudrillard.* London: Routledge, 1999.

Khonsary, Jeff, and Kristina Lee Podesva. "Vital Stats: (an afterword)" *100% Vancouver program.* 2011.

Kim-Cohen, Seth. *In the Blink of an Ear: Toward a Non-Cochlear Sonic Art.* New York and London: Continuum, 2009.

Kirby, Michael. "On Acting and Not-acting." *TDR: The Drama Review* 16.1 (March 1972): 3–15.

Knowles, Ric. "Documemory, Autobiology, and the Utopian Performative in Canadian Autobiographical Solo Performance." *Theatre and AutoBiography: Writing and Performing Lives in Theory and Practice.* Ed. Sherrill Grace and Jerry Wasserman. Vancouver: Talonbooks, 2006. 49–71.

– *Theatre & Interculturalism.* London: Palgrave Macmillan, 2010.

Kwon, Miwon. *One Place After Another: Site-Specific Art and Locational Identity.* Cambridge: MIT Press, 2002.

LaBelle, Brandon. *Background Noise: Perspectives on Sound Art.* New York and London: Continuum, 2007.

Lacan, Jacques. *Freud's Papers on Technique 1953–4 (Seminar 1)*. Trans. John Forrester. Ed. Jacques-Alain Miller. New York: WW Norton, 1988.

Lakoff, George, and Mark Johnson. *Metaphors We Live By*. Chicago and London: U of Chicago P, 1980.

Lavender, Andy. "The Moment of Realized Actuality." *Theatre in Crisis: Performance Manifestos for a New Century*. Ed. Maria M. Delgado and Caridad Svich. Manchester: Manchester UP, 2002. 183–90.

– "Viewing and Acting (and Points in Between): The Trouble with Spectating after Rancière." *Contemporary Theatre Review* 22.3 (2012): 307–26.

– *Performance in the Twenty-First Century: Theatres of Engagement*. London and New York: Routledge, 2016.

Lehmann, Hans-Thies. *Postdramatic Theatre*. Trans. Karen Jürs-Munby. New York: Routledge, 2006.

Lejeune, Philippe. "The Autobiographical Pact." *On Autobiography*. Ed. Paul John Eakin. Trans. Katherine Leary. Minneapolis: U of Minnesota P, 1989.

Levin, Laura. "Can the City Speak? Site-Specific Art After Poststructuralism." *Performance and the City*. Ed. D.J. Hopkins, Shelley Orr, and Kim Solga. New York: Palgrave Macmillan, 2009. 240–57.

– *Performing Ground: Space, Camouflage, and the Art of Blending In*. New York: Palgrave Macmillan, 2014.

Levitow, Roberta. "Some Words about the Theatre Today." *Theatre in Crisis: Performance Manifestos for a New Century*. Ed. Maria M. Delgado and Caridad Svich. Manchester: Manchester UP, 2002. 25–30.

Lewin, Phillip, and J. Patrick Williams. "The Ideology and Practice of Authenticity in Punk Subculture." *Authenticity in Culture, Self, and Society*. Ed. Phillip Vannini and J. Patrick Williams. Ashgate, 2009. 65–83.

Lippard, Lucy R. *The Lure of the Local: Senses of Place in Multicentred Society*. New York: The New Press, 1997.

Lo, Jacqueline, and Helen Gilbert. "Toward a Topography of Cross-Cultural Theatre Praxis." *TDR: The Drama Review* 46.3 (Fall 2002): 31–53.

Long, James, and Marcus Youssef. *Winners and Losers*. Vancouver: TalonBooks, 2015.

Lukács, Georg. *Studies in European Realism*. New York: Grosset & Dunlap, 1964.

Machon, Josephine. *Immersive Theatres: Intimacy and Immediacy in Contemporary Performance*. London: Palgrave Macmillan, 2013.

Magelssen, Scott. *Simming: Participatory Performance and the Making of Meaning*. Ann Arbor: U of Michigan P, 2014.

Malzacher, Florian. "Dramaturgies of Care and Insecurity: The Story of Rimini Protokoll." *Experts of the Everyday: The Theatre of Rimini Protokoll*. Ed. Miriam Dreysse and Florian Malzacher. Berlin: Alexander Verlag, 2008. 14–43.

Martin, Carol. "Living Simulations: The Use of Media in Documentary in the UK, Lebanon, and Israel." *Get Real: Documentary Theatre Past and Present*. Ed. Alison Forsyth and Chris Megson, London: Palgrave Macmillan, 2009. 74–90.

– *Theatre of the Real*. Houndsmills: Palgrave Macmillan, 2013.

Massumi, Brian. *The Everyday Politics of Fear*. Minneapolis: U of Minnesota P, 1993.

Meyers, Misha. "Situations for Living: Performing Emplacement." *Research in Drama Education: The Journal of Applied Theatre and Performance*. 13.2 (2008): 171–80.

Micallef, Shawn, and Marlena Zuber. *Stroll: Psychogeographic Walking Tours of Toronto*. Toronto: Coach House, 2010.

Miller, J. Hillis. "The Fiction of Realism: *Sketches by Boz, Oliver Twist*, and Cruikshank's Illustrations." *Victorian Subjects*. New York: Harvester Wheatsheaf, 1990. 119–77.

Morris, Joan K., and Evan Alberman. "Trends in Down's Syndrome Live Births and Antenatal Diagnoses in England and Wales from 1989 to 2008: Analysis of Data from the National Down Syndrome Cytogenetic Register" *BMJ – British Journal of Medicine* 13 July 2009 doi:10.1136/bmj.b3794.

Morris, Pam. *Realism*. London and New York: Routledge, 2003.

Mumford, Meg. "Rimini Protokoll's Reality Theatre and Intercultural Encounter: Towards an Ethical Art of Partial Proximity." *Contemporary Theatre Review* 23.2 (2013): 153–65.

Murray, Janet. *Hamlet on the Holodeck: The Future of Narrative in Cyberspace*. New York: The Free Press, 1997.

Myers, Tony. *Slavoj Žižek*. London and New York: Routledge, 2003.

Natoli, Jaime L., Deborah L. Ackerman, Suzanne McDermott, and Janice G. Edwards. "Prenatal Diagnosis of Down Syndrome: A Systematic Review of Termination Rates (1995–2011)" *Prenatal Diagnosis* 32 (2012): 142–53.

Nelson, Steve. "Redecorating the Fourth Wall: Environmental Theatre Today." *TDR: The Drama Review* 33.3 (Fall 1989): 72–94.

Nestruck, J. Kelly. "300 TAPES: Memories from Before Everything Became Digitized." *The Globe and Mail*. 2 December 2010.

– "The Year in Theatre: The Stage Tackled Topics to Drop Your Jaw." *The Globe and Mail*. 26 December 2013.

Nibbelink, Lisbeth Groot. "Radical Intimacy: Ontroerend Goed Meets *The Emancipated Spectator*." *Contemporary Theatre Review* 22.3 (August 2012): 412–20.

Nichols, Liz. "Citadel's *Winners and Losers* Insightful, Unsettling." *Edmonton Journal*. 10 April 2015.

Nield, Sophie. "The Rise of the Character named Spectator." *Contemporary Theatre Review* 18.4 (2008): 531–44.

Noland, Carrie. *Agency and Embodiment: Performing Gestures/Producing Culture.* Cambridge: Harvard UP, 2009.

Osolsobě, Ivo. "Course de Théâtristique Générale." *Études Littéraires.* 13.3 (1980): 413–35.

Paget, Derek. "The 'Broken' Tradition of Documentary Theatre." *Get Real: Documentary Theatre Past and Present.* Ed. Alison Forsyth and Chris Megson. London: Palgrave Macmillan, 2009. 224–38.

– "Verbatim Theatre: Oral History and Documentary Techniques." *New Theatre Quarterly* 12 (1987): 317–36.

Parker S.E., C.T. Mai, M.A. Canfield, R. Rickard, Y. Wang, R.E. Meyer, P. Anderson, C.A. Mason, J.S. Collins, R.S. Kirby, and A. Correa. "Updated National Birth Prevalence estimates for selected birth defects in the United States, 2004–2006." *Birth Defects Res A Clin Mol Teratol.* 88.12 (2010): 1008–16.

Patterson, David. "Molecular Genetic Analysis of Down Syndrome." *Human Genetics* 126 (2009): 195–214.

Pearson, Mike. "Site-Specificity and the Narratives of History" *Performing Site-Specific Theatre: Politics, Place, Practice.* Ed. Anna Birch and Joanne Tompkins. New York: Palgrave Macmillan, 2012.

Pearson, Mike, and Michael Shanks. *Theatre/Archaeology.* London and New York: Routledge, 2001.

Pendle, George. "Colour by Numbers." *100% Vancouver* Programme. 2011.

Petralia, Peter Salvatore. "Headspace: Architectural Space in the Brain." *Contemporary Theatre Review* 20.1 (2010): 96–108.

Phelan, Peggy. "Marina Abramović: Witnessing Shadows." *Theatre Journal* 56.4 (2004): 569–77.

Piatigorsky, Anton. *Eternal Hydra* (one-act version 2002). *Canadian Theatre Review* 115 (2003): 66–87.

Plato. "The Republic, Book II." *Dramatic Theory and Criticism: Greeks to Grotowski.* Ed. Bernard F. Dukore. Fort Worth: Harcourt Brace Jovanovich, 1974.

Polyglotte. Performed 31 May–4 June 2015. Directors Olivier Choinière and Alexia Bürger. Performers German Barragan, Tatiana Burtin, Mondiana François, Samira Ghorbani, Mahmoud Shawky Hamed Ali, Pamela Robertson, Somnath Shinde, Mireille Tawfik, Farlene Thelisdort, Edward Wong, and Jorge Suarez. Produced by Festival TransAmeriques.

Pomerantsev, Peter. "Russia and the Menace of New Reality." *The Atlantic.* 9 September 2014.

Potter, Andrew. *The Authenticity Hoax: How We Get Lost Finding Ourselves.* Toronto: McClelland & Stewart, 2010.

Power, Cormac. *Presence in Play: A Critique of Theories of Presence in the Theatre.* Amsterdam and New York: Rodopi, 2008.

Public Health Agency of Canada. *Canadian Perinatal Health Report, 2008 Edition*. Ottawa, 2008.

Pywell, Geoff. *Staging Real Things: The Performance of Ordinary Events*. London: Bucknell UP, 1994.

Rancière, Jacques. *Aesthetics and its Discontents*. Trans. Steve Corcoran. Cambridge: Polity P, 2009.

– *The Emancipated Spectator*. Trans. Gregory Elliot. London and New York: Verso, 2009.

RARE (Kingston). Performed 27 November–6 December 2014. Director Kathryn MacKay. Performers Jacob Ballantyne, Kevin Beauregard, Erin Bennett, Natasha Daw, Ashaya Garrett, Anna Gervais, and Nathan Sikkema. Produced by H'Art Centre.

Reid, Kevin. "MagNorth 2013 – Winners and Losers." *The Visitorium*. 12 June 2013.

Reid, Michelle. "100% Vancouver." *Sad Mag*. 22 January 2011.

Reinelt, Janelle. "The Promise of Documentary." *Get Real: Documentary Theatre Past and Present*. Ed. Alison Forsyth and Chris Megson. New York: Palgrave Macmillan, 2009. 6–23.

Relph, Edward. "The Critical Description of Confused Geographies." *Textures of Place: Exploring Human Geographies*. Ed. Paul C. Adams, Steven Hoelscher, and Karen E. Till. Minneapolis: U of Minnesota P, 2001.

Ridout, Nicholas. *Stage Fright, Animals, and Other Theatrical Problems*. Cambridge: Cambridge UP, 2006.

Roselt, Jens. "Making an Appearance: On the Performance Practice of Self-Presentation." *Experts of the Everyday: The Theatre of Rimini Protokoll*. Ed. Miriam Dreysse and Florian Malzacher. Berlin: Alexander Verlag, 2008. 46–63.

Sandahl, Carrie. "The Tyranny of the Neutral: Disability and Actor Training." *Bodies in Commotion: Disability and Performance*. Ed. Carrie Sandahl and Philip Auslander. Ann Arbor: U of Michigan P, 2005. 255–67.

Santone, Jessica. "The Economics of the Performative Audience." *Performance Research* 19.6 (2014): 30–36.

Sauter, Willmar. "Playing Is Not Pretending." *Themes in Theatre* 8.8 (2014): 63–82.

Schechner, Richard. *Environmental Theatre*. New York: Hawthorn Books, 1973.

Schmitt, Bernd H. *Experiential Marketing: How to Get Customers to Sense, Feel, Think, Act and Relate to Your Company and Brands*. New York: The Free Press, 1999.

Schneider, Rebecca. *Performing Remains: Theatricality, Civil War, Performance Art, Reenactment*. London: Routledge, 2009.

Schoenmakers, Henri. "'Being Oneself on Stage': Modalities of Stage Presence." *Themes in Theatre* 8.8 (2014): 225–42.

Shakespeare, William. *Hamlet. The Riverside Shakespeare*. 2nd ed. Ed. G. Blakemore Evans. Boston: Houghton Mifflin, 1997.

Sharman, Jon. "'What You're Seeing Isn't Happening,' Trump Tells Veterans' Convention in Meandering Rant against 'Fake News.'" *The Independent*. 25 July 2018.

Shields, David. *Reality Hunger: A Manifesto*. New York: Alfred A. Knopf, 2010.

Siebers, Tobin. *Disability Aesthetics*. Ann Arbor: U of Michigan P, 2010.

Simons, JoAnn. *The Down Syndrome Transition Handbook: Charting Your Child's Course to Adulthood*. Bethesda MD: Woodbine House, 2010.

Smith, Keiron. *The Politics of Down Syndrome*. Alresford, Hants, UK: Zero Books/John Hunt, 2011.

Soans, Robin. "Robin Soans." *Verbatim: Contemporary Documentary Theatre*. Ed. Will Hammond and Dan Steward. London: Oberon, 2008. 15–44.

Soutar, Annabel. *Seeds*. Vancouver: TalonBooks, 2012.

States, Bert O., *Great Reckonings in Little Rooms: On the Phenomenology of Theatre*. Berkeley: U of California P, 1985.

Stephenson, Jenn. "Meta-enunciative Properties of Dramatic Dialogue: A New View of Metatheatre and the Work of Sławomir Świontek." *Journal of Dramatic Theory and Criticism* 21.1 (Fall 2006): 115–28.

– "Singular Impressions: Metatheatre on Renaissance Celebrities and Corpses." *Studies in Theatre and Performance* 27.2 (Summer 2007): 137–53.

– "Portrait of the Artist as Artist: The Celebration of Autobiography." *Canadian Theatre Review* 141 (Winter 2010): 49–53.

– *Performing Autobiography: Contemporary Canadian Drama*. Toronto: U of Toronto P, 2013.

– Foreword. "Uncertainty: A User's Guide." *Winners and Losers*. James Long and Marcus Youssef. Talonbooks: Vancouver, 2015.

Strindberg, August. "Preface to *Miss Julie*." *Dramatic Theory and Criticism: Greeks to Grotowski*. Ed. Bernard F. Dukore. Fort Worth: Harcourt Brace Jovanovich, 1974. 572–73.

Świontek, Sławomir. "Le dialogue dramatique et le metathéâtre." *Zagadnienia Rodzajów Literackich* 36.1–2 (1993): 7–44.

– "Excerpts from *Le Dialogue Dramatique et le Metathéâtre* by Sławomir Świontek." Trans. Jenn Stephenson. *Journal of Dramatic Theory and Criticism* 21.1 (Fall 2006) 129–44.

Taussig, Michael. *Mimesis and Alterity: A Particular History of the Senses*. New York: Routledge, 1993.

Taylor, Charles. *The Ethics of Authenticity*. Boston: Harvard UP, 1992.

"The Art of the Lie." *The Economist*. 10 September 2016.

Theatre Conspiracy: Tim Carlson, Jeremy Waller, David Mesiha, Kathleen Flaherty, Milton Lim, Aryo Khakpour, Florence Barrett, and Cande Andrade. *Foreign Radical. Canadian Theatre Review* 175 (Summer 2018): 58–70.

Thompson, Evan. *Mind in Life: Biology, Phenomenology, and the Science of Mind.* Harvard UP, 2010.

Thompson, Judith. "Interview with RH Thomson: Judith Thompson on *Rare,* Collective Creation, and Authenticity." Theatre Museum Canada. 13 March 2014.

Thompson, Judith, and ensemble. *RARE* (Toronto). 2013. Unpublished manuscript.

Thompson, Judith, and ensemble. *RARE* (Kingston). Adapted by Kathryn MacKay and ensemble. 2014. Unpublished manuscript.

Thrift, Nigel. *Non-Representational Theory: Space, Politics, Affect.* London: Routledge, 2008.

Tilley, Christopher. *A Phenomenology of Landscape: Places, Paths, and Monuments.* Oxford: Berg, 1994.

Timson, Judith. "The Actors in This Judith Thompson Play Are Rare." *The Globe and Mail.* 5 July 2012.

Tomlin, Liz. *Acts and Apparitions: Discourses on the Real in Performance Practice and Theory, 1990–2010.* Manchester: Manchester UP, 2013.

Trilling, Lionel. *Sincerity and Authenticity.* Cambridge: Harvard UP, 1972.

Tuan, Yi-Fu. *Space and Place: The Perspective of Experience.* London: Edward Arnold, 1977.

Turner, Cathy. "Palimpsest or Potential Space? Finding a Vocabulary for Site-Specific Performance." *New Theatre Quarterly* 20.4 (November 2004): 373–90.

Vincentelli, Elizabeth. "A Parlour Game has Serious Consequences in Soho Rep's Winners and Losers." *New York Post.* 7 January 2015.

Voegelin, Salomé. *Listening to Noise and Silence: Towards a Philosophy of Sound Art.* New York: Continuum, 2010.

Walsh, Fintan. *Theatre & Therapy.* New York: Palgrave Macmillan, 2013.

– "Touching, Flirting, Whispering: Performing Intimacy in Public." *TDR: The Drama Review* 58.4 (2014): 56–67.

Wagner, Jane. *The Search for Signs of Intelligent Life in the Universe.* New York: Harper & Row, 1986.

Watt, Ian. *The Rise of the Novel: Studies in Defoe, Richardson and Fielding.* London: Chatto & Windus, 1960.

"Welcome to H'art Centre" H'art Centre. hartschool.ca.

Welton, Martin. *Feeling Theatre.* London: Palgrave Macmillan, 2012.

White, Gareth. "On Immersive Theatre." *Theatre Research International* 37.3 (2012): 221–35.

– *Audience Participation in Theatre: Aesthetics of the Invitation*. London: Palgrave Macmillan, 2013.

Wickstrom, Maurya. *Performing Consumers: Global Capital and its Theatrical Seductions*. New York, Routledge, 2006.

Williams, Kirk. "Anti-Theatricality and the Limits of Naturalism." *Against Theatre: Creative Destructions on the Modernist Stage*. Ed. Alan Ackerman and Martin Puchner. New York: Palgrave Macmillan, 2006. 95–111.

Winners and Losers. Performed 22 November–1 December 2012. Director Chris Abraham. Performers James Long and Marcus Youssef. Produced by Theatre Replacement and Neworld Theatre in association with Crow's Theatre.

Wurtzler, Steve. "'She Sang Live, But The Microphone Was Turned Off:' The Live, the Recorded and the Subject of Representation." *Sound Theory Sound Practice*. Ed. Rick Altman. New York: Routledge, 1992. 87–103.

Zaiontz, Keren. "Ambulatory Audiences and Animate Sites: Staging the Spectator in Site-Specific Performance." *Performing Site-Specific Theatre: Politics, Place, Practice*. Ed. Anna Birch and Joanne Tompkins. New York and London, Palgrave Macmillan, 2012. 167–81.

– "Narcissistic Spectatorship in Immersive and One-on-One Performance" *Theatre Journal* 66.3 (October 2014): 405–25.

– "Performing Visions of Governmentality: Care and Capital in 100% Vancouver." *Theatre Research International* 39.2 (2014): 101–19.

Zerehi, Sima Sahar. "Counting Sheep: A Play, a Dance Performance, a Concert?" *Living Toronto*. 4 February 2015.

Žižek, Slavoj. *The Sublime Object of Ideology*. London and New York: Verso, 1989.

– "Grimaces of the Real, or When the Phallus Appears." *October* 58 (Fall 1991): 44–68.

– *The Ticklish Subject: The Absent Centre of Political Ontology*. London and New York: Verso, 1999.

– *Welcome to the Desert of the Real*. London and New York: Verso, 2002.

– *The Parallax View*. Cambridge and London: MIT P, 2006.

Zola, Émile. "Naturalism on the Stage." 1880. *Dramatic Theory and Criticism: Greeks to Grotowski*. Ed. Bernard F. Dukore. Fort Worth: Harcourt Brace Jovanovich, 1974. 692–718.

Index